HUMANI

JOHN CARROLL, born in Eng...
Australia. Educated at the universities of Melbourne and
Cambridge, his doctoral studies in sociology were super-
vised by George Steiner, and also Anthony Giddens. He
taught at Cambridge from 1968 to 1971 before moving to
La Trobe University in Melbourne, where he has been,
since 1978, Reader in Sociology. Among his other publica-
tions are an edition of Max Stirner's *The Ego and His Own*
(1971), *Puritan, Paranoid, Remissive, a Sociology of Modern*
Culture (1977), *Sceptical Sociology* (1980), *Guilt, The Grey*
Eminence Behind Character, History and Culture (1985) and
edited books on both Australia, *Intruders in the Bush* (1982,
1992), and its economy, *Shutdown* (1992).

Fontana Movements and Ideas
Series Editor: Justin Wintle

titles available:

JOHN CARROLL

HUMANISM

The Wreck of
Western Culture

FontanaPress
An Imprint of HarperCollins*Publishers*

Fontana Press
An Imprint of HarperCollins*Publishers*
77–85 Fulham Palace Road
Hammersmith, London W6 8JB

A Fontana Press Original
First published 1993

2 4 6 8 9 7 5 3

Copyright © John Carroll, 1993

John Carroll has asserted the moral right to be
identified as the author of this work.

ISBN 0-586-09233-1

Set in Linotron Baskerville

Printed and bound in Great Britain by
HarperCollinsManufacturing Glasgow

'If it doesn't show the glory of man, don't do it.'
Jean Renoir

'It is a fearful thing to fall into the hands of the living God.'
Hebrews 10.31

For Philip Rieff, teacher

CONTENTS

ILLUSTRATIONS

1

PROLOGUE

We live amidst the ruins of the great, five-hundred-year epoch of Humanism. Around us is that 'colossal wreck'. Our culture is a flat expanse of rubble. It hardly offers shelter from a mild cosmic breeze, never mind one of those icy gales that regularly return to rip men out of the cosy intimacy of their daily lives and confront them with oblivion. Is it surprising that we are run down? We are desperate, yet we don't care much any more. We are timid, yet we cannot be shocked. We are inert underneath our busyness. We are destitute in our plenty. We are homeless in our own homes.

What should be there to hold our hands, is not. Our culture is gone. It has left us terribly alone. In its devastation it cannot even mock us any more, sneer at the lost child whimpering for its mother. That stage too is over. Our culture is past cruelty. It is wrecked. It is dead.

What are we to do? Is it a time to lament, to complain, to laugh? Is it a time to seize hold of some fine marble fragment and dream it whole? Is it a time to close our eyes and try to lose ourselves in our own little back-gardens? Or is it a time to embrace one of the lingering ghosts, squeeze it for its warmth, and pretend we are alive? No! It is the time for a new beginning, but not quite yet. First, the old must be buried, and with due rites. A requiem must be sung, one that gets the story right, in its magnificence and in its meanness. Less to honour Caesar than to bury him, that there be no mistaking that he is dead, that we understand him so as not to choose him again. The occasion is grave, our own sorry state makes that plain. Therefore there shall be honour too.

We are gathered here to bury a myth, a myth that failed. This myth, through its long and struggling foundation, then its middle period when it systematically demolished all of its competitors, and finally its autumn when it turned against itself and in its insatiable hunger devoured its own heart, through all of this, has held us Westerners in thrall. It drove our ancestors relentlessly on as it worked through its inexorable logic. In the process it created a huge and brilliantly lit metropolis of a culture, next to which all that had gone before seemed but a handful of small towns. It put everything in question in the most revolutionary and categorical either-or in human history. It set its converts so much on edge that they were for a half-millennium driven into the most sustained bout of philosophical, literary, artistic and musical wrestling known to man. What was at stake was the future of the Western soul.

Humanism sought to turn the treasure-laden galleon of Western culture around. It attempted to replace God by man, to put man at the centre of the universe, to deify him. Its ambition was to found a human order on earth, in which freedom and happiness prevailed, without any transcendental or supernatural supports – an entirely human order. The challenge facing it, and with it modernity, had been put graphically by Archimedes in a quite different time: 'Give me somewhere to stand and I shall move the earth.' To place man at the centre meant that he had to become the Archimedean point around which everything revolved. A world without such a point is relativity and chaos, without direction, bearings or sense – a world in which men cannot live and stay sane. But if the human individual were to become the still-point in the universe he had to have somewhere to stand that would not move under his feet. Humanism had to build a rock. It had to create out of nothing something as strong as the faith of the New Testament that could move mountains. Luther, whose instinct about these matters was sure, whose life-long battle was really against Humanism and not the Catholic Church, could assert at his decisive moment: 'Here I stand, I can do no other.' In the choice of words Luther was taunting his time, and above all the humanists like Erasmus, challenging them to see if *they* could find a place to stand. We can imagine him, under his breath, giving the answer to his own rhetorical question: 'That'll be the day!'

The axiom on which the humanist rock was to be forged was put as well by Pico della Mirandola in 1486 as by anyone: 'We can become what we will.' It is more complete than Alberti's earlier and more celebrated formulation: 'Men can do all things if they will.' So the humanist fathers put their founding axiom: man is all-powerful, if his will is strong enough. He can create himself. He can choose to be courageous, honourable, just, rich, influential, or not. He is creator and creature in one. Out of his own individual will he can move the earth. The great individual stands alone; under his feet the earth does not move.

Here is not only a radical inflation of the power of the human will, but a new conception of being, of what it is to exist, of what it is that exists. All religions predicate being in the way the Lord God of the Old Testament did to Moses: 'I am that I am.' The divinity, whether single or multiple, is primal and all-encompassing Being. It is first cause and source of all life and spirit. There are no questions to be asked about primal being: it simply is. Moreover, in that everything derives from it, the rallying cry 'We can become what we will' is highly problematic, if not impossible. In fact Humanism had to undermine the 'I am that I am' if it was going to establish its rock. It had to replace it with 'I am', where the 'I' is the individual man. This was the central task of the Renaissance. It attempted it in the only way possible: by example. Its examples were formidable, a procession of great men, men of awesome character, who by their deeds and their creations – works of statecraft, of art, of science – demonstrated that it is possible to *be*. Their implicit boast was 'I have made myself what I am, and that is good, even more, it is great. I am!' The world of ordinary mortals looking at the Renaissance man, astride his destiny, composed, knowledgeable, secure, an authority unto himself, could cry out in spontaneous wonder: 'He is!' That, at least, was the idea, and for a time it seems to have worked. After all, the West has chosen to live for five hundred years under the humanist credo. We *can* become what we will.

The early men of the Renaissance were not aware that they would have to choose. They were Christians. The most instructive example was Erasmus himself, who in his moderate Christian humanism tried to adapt his religion to the methods of the new secularism. It took Luther to smell a rat, and in his rejection of free-will to establish the metaphysical either-or which was, from behind the scenes, to dominate the humanist epoch. When Luther said to Erasmus with uncharacteristic politeness: 'You are not devout!' he had, philosophically speaking, hit the nail on the head. He had prophesied the inevitable path of humanism once it had chained itself, as it must, to a belief in free-will. This simple and direct, uncouth German peasant had told the most refined, best educated, wittiest and most eloquent man of his time, a man he admired: 'You stand on nothing.'

Three hundred and fifty years later, the last great humanist philosopher, Nietzsche, staked his entire work on defending the pre-eminence of the human will. By this time, however, the battle had been lost, as he knew, and his twilight struggle is consequently feverish, full of wild gesticulation and despair, by the end demented. Nietzsche too was a German, and shared Luther's directness and sureness of instinct. He repeatedly ranted against his great predecessor as 'that German barbarian'. He knew that it was Luther or him. The last line of Nietzsche's last work reads, 'Dionysus versus the Crucified,' by which he meant, Myself or Christ, one or the other, either-or. When he typed these words in 1888 he was already far down the slide into catatonic madness. His words were mad. They are the dying cry of humanist philosophy.

What is so admirable about Nietzsche is that he saw clearly what was at stake, and refused to give up the hopeless struggle. Man had to be able to move the earth, by his own will, or he would be paralysed. The philosopher's job was to remove all mental impediments to the will, especially the moral ones. The

Renaissance was for Nietzsche the last era of wilful men. Since then man had progressively lost his still-point. He had become more and more at the mercy of any fickle breath of wind, at the mercy of what the ancients called Necessity. The material forces of birth and death, of disease and war, of this fate or that, could once again play with a man's life as if it were a bit of flotsam in the cosmic void. Will meant the conquest of Necessity, of fate. A man must be able to make his fortune, get hold of the fates by the scruff of the neck and force them to bow to his will. When Goya in the humanist waning was to paint the fates hovering over human life, remorseless, dark, directing by whim, he was painting against the bright confidence of Pico and the founding fathers.

Necessity reduces ultimately to one thing, death. When necessity rules mankind finds that it has subjected itself to the most severe of all metaphysics, that life is under the command of death, that mortality rules. Christianity had focused itself in all its formative intensity on the crucifixion, on one tragic image of death and its transcendence. Humanism had to find a credible alternative to the Christ crucified preached by St Paul. Otherwise it would leave its own pilgrims helplessly vulnerable, gone the moment they relaxed their control, one careless instant would do it and they would be staring into the eyes of their Medusa. The weakening of Christian faith would lead the West back into the arms of the other parent of its culture, the ancient Greek father. The Greek tragedians had known all about the eyes that would freeze any man in his tracks, turn him to stone. They had found their own means of countering them, one that humanism would have to recapture if it were to survive. Archimedes too knew the Medusa: 'Give me somewhere to stand and I shall move the earth' has as its implicit corollary, 'If I don't find a place to stand I shall not be able to move even myself.' Thus from the outset humanism was confronted with the metaphysical challenge of neutralizing the fear of death. It had to give a man enough support, a reliable enough hand to hold, so that when he caught the whiff of a corpse he would not go weak at the knees and collapse in pale terror. It had to give him enough gravity in himself, enough 'I', to be able to withstand the gale of mortality.

Kierkegaard had already seen the cracks in 1846. He told the anecdote of the wager. Two English lords were riding along when a man whose horse had bolted galloped past shouting for help. One lord said to the other: 'A hundred pounds he falls off!' 'Taken,' was the immediate reply, at which they wheeled their horses, spurred them on, and galloped past the runaway horse to open the gates and prevent anything getting in its way. Kierkegaard concludes scornfully that his own age lacked even the stylish sporting zest of the aristocracy. The dismal message in the story is that the humanist will has atrophied to nothing, now it has lost its higher conscience, the 'I am' has degenerated into that of a chronic invalid watching life from the window of the hospital. The advice to the few active ones is, don't go riding lest your horse bolt and you need help.

The cracks in the humanist edifice were to be seen from the beginning. The mortar was still damp between the foundation stones when the hairline fissures appeared. Luther saw them, with his conscious eye, and wrote his *Enslaved Will*. Holbein and Shakespeare saw them, in their cases unconsciously and therefore with a special force. It will be one of the main theses of the work to follow that Humanism was doomed from the start, that it carried within its own seed the elements of its destruction.

There is another side to the story. For the humanists the age that had come before, what we know as the Middle Ages, had been an age of darkness. They were right. The darkness had been both mental and physical. Medieval thinking had been steeped in superstition, a phantasmagoria of devils and sorcerers, of saints and relics, of the threat of a ghastly hell inhabited by demonic hybrids, part-human and part-monster. For most people most of the time, everyday life had been a miserable struggle to survive. It was an unremitting cheerless toil, further cursed by endemic warfare, famine, disease, and from the fourteenth century plague of such virulence that almost entire cities were wiped out. The Hobbesean epithet of the life of man being solitary, poor, nasty, brutish, and short was a realistic description of the European Middle Ages. The humanist response to this nightmare was necessary and correct, to use everything in man's power to change his infernal condition. The medieval slum was to be replaced by a new city, planned and built by confident rational men of fine character. The clarity and light of Reason, of precise classical forms, would drive out the darkness of superstition and squalor.

This image was to prove so persuasive that to counter it Luther had to preach a new darkness, that of faith, that of the dark night of faith.

Humanism succeeded in building its city of light. Today, it is culture's metropolis that is in ruins, not the metropolis itself. The wreck of humanist culture is in stark contrast to the physical edifice that its drive to know, channelled into science and technology and applied in factories, has produced. Humanism's lasting achievement has been industrial civilization and its brilliant triumph over most of the trials inflicted on man by age-old Necessity – poverty, starvation, disease and brute labour. The material comfort enjoyed by Western societies in the twentieth century represents a giant advance in human experience, and we are duty-bound to acknowledge the fact. Who in their right mind would choose to live in the filth and stench of medieval Europe?

The subject matter of this work is in essence the spiritual history of the post-Christian West. The task is to find the beacons lighting that history, and to distinguish what they represent at each key stage. During the humanist half-millennium the spirit's finest projection has been High Culture. High Culture has its own hierarchy, with a few supreme masterpieces at the top. This study concentrates on those masterpieces. They are worked for all their worth. In other words this is not a cultural history in the sense of looking comprehensively at all the major theorists and artists of a period. It seeks the best, and neglects the rest.

Such an unorthodox method rests on the assumption that the rare masterpieces of culture have as the root of their greatness that they have tapped the deepest truth of their time. They are illuminated by what they have touched, and they gain a timeless surety and clarity thereby. As such they stand as the signposts of our cultural history. If we manage to read them we shall know the path along which we have come, and what we have alternatively lost and gained along the way.

There is such a difference in quality between the exceptional works and the rest that more is to be learned from sitting day after day with them, than in taking a broad sweep of the whole field. The story those few works tell is deceptively simple, and yet they never reveal all. There are many veils. Even the most concentrated devotion leaves the penitent with the feeling that he has found the only path that matters, yet he is not permitted to see it clearly.

Within the great works there is a division. This is an elite with two factions. Some works are in touch with the eternal laws, and they are oriented to their own time according to them, in obedience to them, striving above all to represent them. They judge their contemporary world by the light of those universal laws. The other works do not have this special virtue, and they are, as a consequence, unsettling. They rattle their times, imposing on them a commanding turmoil. This distinction will gain major significance as our story unfolds.

PART I

Foundation

2

THE GLORY OF THE
RENAISSANCE

For over five hundred years now the small square in front of the
Cathedral of St Anthony in Padua has worshipped a different
God than the one who rules once one enters the church doors
and plunges into the dark. There is awe in that square, open to
the heavens. Once one comes in sight of it, and it is best to do
so at noon, in the full light of day, and one lifts ones eyes and
looks, from that moment on one is in the thrall of humanism.
True, it is possible to sidle up to the cathedral with one's eyes
lowered, the first signs the stalls for tourists and pilgrims selling
plastic knick-knacks, garish red charms and crudely painted vir-
gins, all the paraphernalia of modern Italian Catholicism. They
can crowd out the square.

What does command here, set on a high and massive stone
pedestal, is the Gattamelata. He is the Venetian general, Erasmo
de Narni, on horseback, immortalized in bronze a few years after
his death in 1443, by Donatello. His form is that of the medieval
condottiere, the warrior who by means of his own singular brute
strength and courage could win any war. The condottiere was
the hero of the earlier epoch, one embodying sub-human fantasies
of the monstrous force of animal nature, at times sublimated into
the chivalrous ideal of the Christian knight. The most brilliant
representation of the medieval condottiere stands less than thirty
miles from Padua, in the Campo of Saints Giovanni and Paolo
in Venice – that is Verrocchio's equestrian statue of Il Colleoni.
This is a mountain of a man, rearing up erect in his stirrups, his
huge armour-clad left shoulder thrust up and forward, shielding
his massive torso and neck, his thick and crude features glowering

Donatello, *Gattamelata*, Padua

like those of an enraged beast from under his steel helmet. He is an invincible hulk of power. The Gattamelata is quite different. Already in the late 1440s Donatello could anticipate the Renaissance ideal, the 'We can become what we will', and project it into its three-dimensional visual form. The genius of Donatello presents a new measure of human power.

The Gattamelata's mount is a strong square war horse, formidably serviceable, with stocky legs, the neck and chest of a bull, and a fierce head. It is neighing and chafing at the bit, as it strides forward. This charger has the attributes that Verrocchio was to give to his warrior. The Gattamelata himself is quite different, the epitome of balance, and a confidence the source of which is inward. He sits lightly in the saddle, his posture straight and relaxed. He looks ahead, without helmet. In his right hand, which is forward over the horse's mane, he delicately holds a baton. Whereas his charger strives, he is composed. Donatello underscores the point by making the rider proportionately small in relation to the bulk of his horse. Man is master of powerful forces surging beneath him, they champ, they pull, they are vastly stronger than he is, yet through his own will, his own force of character, nothing to do with physical strength only to do with balance, and a clear and concentrated mind, he is master. The baton is also suggestive of a scroll, symbol of knowledge, of the rational human mind conquering the volcanic chaos of nature. The Gattamelata is the Renaissance man.

He has nothing to obey but himself, he needs nothing beyond the 'I am'. He is the value-creating individual, and he is on the move. There is such an intensity between the brows, an inviolable purpose buried in the eyes, that the head itself, bare to the heavens, becomes the sacred site. Concentrated mind may move the earth.

Humanism, however, needed an ethic, a central moral axiom, to secure its foundation. The clarity represented in the Gattamelata is not enough, the steady vision with which he looks straight ahead, taking in the world. His commanding will is also not enough. He is so superbly in form because he embodies the humanist ethos, its moral. There is one external that he does obey. He is a gentleman, or in the Italian characterization of Castiglione, a courtier. As gentleman, he is under the thrall of honour.

The humanist ethos was founded on honour. If humanism was going to find its place to stand it had to enshrine the value of honour, and without any higher transcendental backing. For the preceding epoch, the Middle Ages, it had been easier: its ideal, the *saint*, including the warrior-saint (for example, St Joan of Arc or Sir Galahad), was the direct human representative of the divinity. For humanism, honour had to stand alone, by itself. Then everything else would follow. The principal role of the humanist hero was therefore to become so awesomely noble that the rest would believe. The ease and the grace of the Gattamelata in his command is because he knows he is right, doing what he has to do. Machiavelli was keenly aware of the challenge, placing "virtu" at the core of his ideal politics. However, to learn of the significance of the struggle to enshrine honour, of just what was at stake, and of the enormity of the task, we need to move on to the last period of Renaissance humanism, and to Shakespeare. It is fitting that humanism's quintessential genius should have provided the key text, *Julius Caesar*.

As the most perceptive character in the play puts it at the start, 'honour is the subject of my story.' In particular, the aim of *Julius Caesar* is to honour the name of Brutus. Brutus is cast as the highest example of man, and Shakespeare sets out to examine what it means to be Brutus. The 'hallowed be Thy name' of the Lord's Prayer is almost explicitly transposed here onto the humanist hero. What is really at stake is the replacing of Christ crucified by Brutus. The structure of the play works in simple obedience to this plan, with the defeat and death of Brutus constituting the climax, and their significance stipulated in the funeral oration by Mark Antony, his enemy:

> This was the noblest Roman of them all;
> All the conspirators save only he
> Did that they did in envy of great Caesar;

He only, in a general honest thought
And common good to all, made one of them.
His life was gentle, and elements
So mix'd in him that Nature might stand up
And say to all the world, 'This was a man!'

Even Mark Antony's earlier funeral oration, in Act III for Caesar, the best known speech in the play, opening with 'Friends, Romans, countrymen . . .', relates to the climax. It has the surface function of turning the people against Brutus, and starting the chain of events that will lead to his defeat. It has the deeper function of anticipating the second oration as the significant one. It is only in the second speech that Mark Antony is sincere. The main aim of the stirring rhetoric of 'Friends, Romans, countrymen' is less grief for Caesar than a crafty eloquence to move the mob for Antony's own political ends, to avenge Caesar's murder.

The argument of the first Antony oration hinges on Brutus' character. It will succeed if the repeated and increasingly bitter and satirical 'And Brutus is an honourable man' can get through. It does. Brutus is destroyed because the master orator succeeds in impugning his honour. Without honour he is nothing. He is worse than nothing, he is a betrayer and a murderer.

Henry V and *Julius Caesar* are Shakespeare's most idealistic plays. *Henry V* projects the strongest representation in literature of the "good king". It is a simple and telling drama. In *Julius Caesar* nothing is simple. It is a true late Renaissance work. The drama opens with peppery zest, with the cobbler, the mender of bad soles, and his string of puns. But he is merely the bright foreground, setting off the reality of grave politics. The day is the feast of Lupercal, a Roman festival of expiation; however, what is being celebrated is the greatness of Caesar, whose pride and ambition, many fear, are about to break all limits.

Enter Brutus. Who is he? What ideal does Shakespeare paint? Brutus loves principle, and always seeks to act by it. He is a poor politician, lacking the capacity for expedient action. He is contrasted with Cassius, who has good political and military judgment, who has few qualms about employing evil means for a necessary end, but who is a malicious and envious man. Brutus rejects Cassius' advice to kill Mark Antony while they can; later he rejects his military advice. In both cases he is disastrously wrong, in terms of the practical consequences, in terms of politics. In terms of honour, certainly on the first occasion, he was right. Brutus is also rational and prudent, at least early in the drama. On another front, he says of himself that he lacks Antony's quick spirit. He loves his wife, and she he. In fact, almost everybody in the play loves Brutus. He is a good man.

Brutus is the man of just action, in the tradition of Antigone. He is no Hamlet to dither around while the State falls apart. His cogitations lead him to the conclusion, after many sleepless nights, that Caesar is abusing his high office. Power has gone to his head. It has lost its necessary tie to compassion. Liberty is under threat. Brutus decides to kill Caesar, who is his friend, a reasonable man and great, for the good of the State. His mind is now clear, his character firm. When the conspirators next meet Cassius urges them to swear to their resolution. Brutus opposes him, arguing that an oath is unnecessary. It is men with a bad or doubtful cause who need to swear. They are above this. Their promise is enough, their word. They are gentlemen. Brutus later uses the same noble argument to oppose the killing of Mark Antony:

> Let's be sacrificers, not butchers, Cassius
> ... purgers, not murderers.

Brutus justifies his having killed Caesar, to Antony, by saying:

> ... so pity, pity —
> hath done this deed on Caesar.

In other words he has acted not only to save Rome from tyranny, but also for Caesar, to save him from himself, to save *his* honour. Brutus has acted out of friendship, tragic friendship. Here is the

burden carried by the man of honour. As Brutus puts it to the
people in his oration over the corpse of Caesar:

> As Caesar loved me, I weep for him; as he was fortunate, I rejoice at it; as he
> was valiant, I honour him; but, as he was ambitious, I slew him. There is tears for his
> love: joy for his fortune: honour for his valour: and death for his ambition.

The words "honour" and "noble" litter the text of *Julius Caesar*
from beginning to end. Apart from those already noted a number
are remarkable. After Caesar's judicious concern about Cassius,
'Yond Cassius has a lean and hungry look ... such men are
dangerous.' Antony's consoling reply is 'He is a noble Roman'.
Decius talks Caesar into going to the Capitol by playing on his
honour:

> If Caesar hide himself, shall they not whisper
> 'Lo, Caesar is afraid'?

The crowd's response to the orations is 'There's not a nobler man
in Rome than Antony.' Brutus' greatest insult to Cassius is to
contrast him with "noble men". Once they are reconciled it is
'Noble, noble Cassius.' And hearing of Cassius' death:

> It is impossible that ever Rome
> Should breed thy fellow.

If the first question in *Julius Caesar* is what is it to be noble, the
second focuses on Reason. Reason is the second and independent
value, in the service of honour. After the assassination Brutus
promises to give Antony the grounds on which they acted. Antony
stakes his allegiance to the plotters on his getting these reasons,
and on their being plausible. Furthermore, the speeches of Brutus
and Antony to the people present the opposing arguments. In
effect the people listen to a debate, which they then judge. The
first plebeian response to Antony is: 'Methinks there is much

reason in his sayings.' Justice requires reasons, a convincing case. Both Brutus and Antony speak cogently, but Antony's argument is the stronger. Again Shakespeare is positing an ideal, of political life founded on honour and justice, served by reason.

Much of this is rhetoric, and brilliant and effective rhetoric. This play is the English language at its peak, a sustained and intoxicating eloquence of precise meanings and beautiful cadences. What is not rhetoric is that Brutus kills Caesar. Here is the bite of 'We can become what we will.' The value-creating individual, the great I, can with a good conscience break the moral code, or so the theory goes. What Brutus does is extreme. He could hardly have chosen any greater violation of what any normal morality regards as good. He kills. Not only does he coolly and deliberately take human life, his victim is the king, and a good king, a great leader who has done prodigious service for the State. Worse, this king is Brutus' friend, and he trusts him. Caesar's last words 'Et tu Brute' are intimate and tragic. Mark Antony insinuates that Caesar really died from a broken heart, at being betrayed by the ungrateful Brutus:

> For Brutus, as you know, was Caesar's angel.
> Judge, O you gods, how dearly Caesar loved him!
> This was the most unkindest cut of all.

Brutus as honourable man of action attempts by his own will to impose virtue on law and tradition. He breaks the civic law in a manner that makes Antigone's disobedience look like a childish prank. His is the definitive act of regicide in Western culture, all done in the name of his own self-decreed higher law. Brutus is a noble reworking of Macbeth. More interestingly, he is the forefather of Dostoevsky's Raskolnikov, who sets out in the nineteenth century to prove he is a superior man, a superman, by taking the power over life and death into his own hands – *he* kills merely an old skinflint. What is at issue here is Luther's free-will. Raskolnikov is out to prove that he is free by breaking the central moral injunction against murder. If he can do it with a clean conscience he is free; he has become who he will. He fails: guilt destroys his freedom. Brutus is the same. He attempts the supreme act of free-will: out of calm, rational choice to kill the most glorious and powerful man in the world, to do it with reason, honourably. Brutus' metaphysical cry to his humanist god is: 'I am free to kill Caesar.' In other words what 'I am free to make values' comes down to, reduced to its essence, is 'I am free to kill Caesar.'

It goes without saying that if a man is not free to make his own values, he cannot be free to make himself.

The making of values is the choosing of how and when to apply them. Brutus does not invent honour. Firstly, he chooses it as his god, then he chooses the acts through which to give it form. He gives easily comprehensible, concrete shape to an abstraction. In this he is not an immoralist like Raskolnikov, who obeys no value apart from himself. Brutus obeys a higher principle, that of honour, indeed his whole purpose is to enshrine it as the central principle determining human behaviour, in terms of which it is possible to Will. The 'I am' does not stand completely on its own.

'I am free to kill Caesar' has as its complementary ethical formulation, 'I am free to judge,' or more bluntly 'I judge.' The simpler axiom of the early Renaissance now gains more flesh, in the figure of Brutus. The new philosophy has it that I, the great individual, am rational and thereby both know the moral law and may apply it to the affairs of men, reaching judgment about what men do. Having reason, judgment and will, it is my duty to kill Caesar. I shall do it.

More is at stake though than the metaphysical status of the individual. *Julius Caesar* is a political play. Without Brutus, politics would be reduced to an endless series of ruthless and bloody power struggles. Cassius and Mark Antony are the political men, perceptive, calculating, shrewd, practical, and capable of swift and brutal action – Antony has a hundred senators killed. The core of Cassius' great love for Brutus is respect, that he is the better man, a good and honest man, a man of honour. Similarly Mark Antony's 'he was the noblest Roman of them all' at the end is the quite genuine homage of politics to virtue. Shakespeare rams the point home by painting both Cassius and Mark Antony as the politician at his best, and showing the man they look up to as having weak military judgment and a lamentable sense of political realities. The point is that there can be no political authority without honour. Machiavelli gave it the broader notion of *virtu*. Without honour, there will be cynicism, deals, corruption – in short a nihilistic, Hobbesean public life. The gentleman was to become, in the descent from Brutus, the linchpin of humanist politics. The ethic of public duty, of selfless service to the community and the State, derives from the code of honour. For Brutus, self-preservation and personal happiness are of no account in his political life: they are entirely subordinate to the preservation of his name.

So far we have considered only the first half of the story of Brutus. Whilst Shakespeare's aim was to glorify the name of Brutus, the realist in him rebelled. He cast a clear, cool and urbane eye on what he had made. Brutus was not to escape as an ideal. By the time he commits suicide the man of principle has become a rather tarnished hero.

Like Macbeth and Raskolnikov, Brutus is destroyed by his own guilt. He cannot kill with a clean conscience. He is unhinged by his free act. In an explicit parallel with Macbeth, his wife, after the assassination, goes mad and commits suicide. Unlike Lady Macbeth, she herself is quite innocent. As a result, Brutus is left with not only the grief over her loss, but the guilt for it. The most direct manifestation of his rampaging conscience is that it twice conjures up the ghost of dead Caesar. The ghost carries dire warnings; it is a messenger of impending retribution.

The starkest symptoms of Brutus' deterioration are not, however, the visitations by ghosts. They appear in the way he mistreats his devoted friend and fellow general, Cassius. The evidence in the play is unambiguous about the fact that the strongest passion in Cassius is his love for Brutus. The most moving thing in the whole drama is the way Brutus tramples on

this love in Act IV, and the despair into which Cassius sinks.
Here is the emotional centre of the play. The episode starts with
an indirect report to Brutus that Cassius has cooled towards him.
Brutus starts talking about "hollow men" and "deceitful jades".
Cassius, upon their meeting, explains his coolness as due to
Brutus having slighted off his letters on behalf of a man taking
bribes from the local population in order to pay their joint army.
There is a battle to be fought, everything hangs on victory, but
first of all the army must be paid. Cassius is obeying political
necessity. Virtue's reply is that Cassius has "an itching palm"
for gold. Cassius is rightly outraged at this demeaning and unjust
language. After further exchange during which Cassius retains
his self-control, Brutus loses all composure and shouts 'Away,
slight man!' He then accuses Cassius of rash anger and testy
humour, in fact a pure projection of his own state of mind, and
produces the extravagant insult that from now on Cassius will
merely be an object of Brutus' mirth. Cassius' reply is the pained
'Is it come to this?', which the irrepressible Brutus shrugs off
with a reference to "noblemen", in whose company Cassius does
not belong. Cassius is conciliatory, but after further taunting he
asserts:

> Do not presume too much upon my love.
> I may do that I should be sorry for.

At this, the man of principle boasts in his self-righteous anger
that 'I am arm'd so strong in honesty', and continues with a
pompous speech about his own virtue. Brutus has become an
unhinged caricature of himself, his honour a charade.

Cassius is flattened by this unconscionable behaviour from his
friend. His final response is that now he is 'hated by one he loves'
he is weary of life. He asks Brutus to kill him. He reflects that
Brutus loved Caesar more than him. At this Brutus softens, and
they are reconciled. But even after the reconciliation it is Cassius
who blames his own rash humour for the dispute. The truth is
that throughout Cassius has been the constant and devoted

friend, and his temper has been remarkably restrained. Yet even now Brutus acknowledges that the whole episode has been the result of Cassius' faulty self-control.

The retribution follows. The two generals discuss strategy. Cassius' plan is wise, Brutus' foolish. Cassius defers to Brutus out of love. Mark Antony cannot believe the stupidity of their strategy when the opposing armies meet at Philippi. What has really happened is that Cassius, the great soldier, loses his balance when Brutus turns against him. He never fully regains it. In the final battle Cassius acts quite out of character, impetuously killing himself because he wrongly believes that Brutus has been defeated. The greatness in his character has been irreparably fractured, by the violence with which his untrusting friend has turned against him. The guilt-hounded Brutus has destroyed them both.

Through all of this Shakespeare remains a humanist. An instructive contrast is with Dostoevsky. For the Christian fatalist, Dostoevsky, murder is a cardinal sin, and that is the end of the matter. Unless the murderer is a monster he will suffer from an annihilating conscience. Shakespeare's picture is more rational. There is a logic to events. Brutus is unhinged by his guilt not simply because he has killed, but because his reasons were not good enough. Mark Antony wins the debate before the people because he is right. There is not enough evidence that Julius Caesar will become a tyrant. Brutus himself gives away his cause in Act II, Scene 1, referring to Caesar:

> He would be crown'd:
> How that might change his nature, there's the question.

It is not sure that Caesar will accept the supreme power that being crowned implies. Even if he is crowned, Brutus can do no better than that power *might* go to his head. True, there is some evidence later in the play of Caesar's growing arrogance. On the other hand, Mark Antony can remind the people how generous Caesar has been to them with his spoils of war. The play stresses reasons, and the bald fact is that Brutus' are not nearly good enough for the extremity of the action he takes. Therefore he is overwhelmed with guilt in the aftermath. There is nothing obscure about this guilt. There is a plain logic to its source, and to its self-destroying workings, starting with Brutus' demented treatment of Cassius.

Shakespeare is not a fatalist. Brutus is not an Oedipus, crushed by an inviolable and harsh fate, a dark and incomprehensible force from the beyond that determines human events. Brutus is punished for what he has done: it is the free act of the rational man that starts the chain of events that lead to his defeat and death.

What remains of 'We can become what we will'? The play has attempted to unify virtue and happiness, the ambition of much of Western ethics, by finding a way of life governed by honour which will produce a just and peaceful politics. It fails, and for a number of reasons. Brutus loses his happiness, destroying his cause and his own life, because he is too narrowly a man of principle, without enough practical sense to see that he is being manipulated by crafty men and that his reasons for killing Caesar are weak. As an honourable man his conscience is severe: it undermines him. Cassius suffers from failure of will, and because of the most admirable thing in his character, that he loves the man who is better than he is. It is the nobility in this not very noble man that funds the passion that cripples his strength. We may conclude that the complexity of the human condition – of character, passion, conscience, not to mention the pattern of external events – makes any simple humanist utopia impossible.

In *Julius Caesar* the final twist is consummate. Act IV has undermined the principle of honour, by showing the man who embodies it as a narrow-minded and pompous idealist with little sense of reality. It gives weight to Antony's ironical 'And Brutus is an honourable man.' In Act V Brutus is punished, comprehensively so, and in keeping with the psychological laws of guilt he regains his composure and his dignity. He is again himself. The enduring goodness of his character is echoed at the end in the devotion and love his soldiers show him. He claims just as he is about to run on his sword:

> I shall have glory by this losing day
> More than Octavius and Mark Antony
> In this vile conquest shall attain to.

The man who will benefit in every material sense is the young Octavius, who in the play has done nothing, and stands for nothing. But Brutus is right, and Mark Antony knows it, himself sealing the judgment with the finale, 'he was the noblest Roman of them all', and even more, 'This was a man!' By the end both Octavius and Antony are in awe of Brutus. The moral logic has it that once Brutus has suffered enough in retribution – in this case unto the death – then he is again free to be what he is. Brutus has to lose his happiness in order to regain his virtue. What he is, is the man of honour, now enshrined as humanism's formative ideal.

Honour, will, reason and no illusion were the foundation stones of the Renaissance. In the highest formulation, that of Shakespeare, reason and realism are integrated. Reason does not find its greatest authority in the mathematical genius of Newton, or the later philosophical rationalism of Descartes or Kant; it does so in the expansive intelligence of Shakespeare. In *Julius Caesar* Reason's role is in part the logic of justice as already discussed. It is equally, and more enduringly, in the breadth and depth of perception in the play. A simple story of plot, assassination and military retribution is turned into an entire philosophy of life, morals and politics. Shakespeare knew too much for him to be capable of any straightforward lesson. He follows Alberti's injunction to live without illusion, which in his case means to describe what he sees. His intelligence is not abstract; it is concrete and literal. It is sceptical. No one understood as much about what Nietzsche called the human-all-too-human. Indeed, the very term Humanism has no more powerful association than with the shrewd and humane intelligence of Shakespeare. In humanism's search for exemplary individuals, Shakespeare himself becomes a hero – a man who could create the very world.

Shakespeare leaves no lucid, readily decipherable code of behaviour. What remains is something like: be an honourable man, and all that implies, especially being honest and true to friends, be as gentle as is possible given the manifold turbulence and constraint of reality, a reality which includes your own character, that of those you encounter, and the good and bad fortune of events into which you are cast. You have some influence over that fortune, as a free, rational and wilful individual. Life calls for action, doing the right thing, as opposed to some form of contemplative or religious withdrawal. If you act wrongly, as does Brutus, then you will be punished, but in spite of that, what remains of higher significance is your character, and if it is honourable you will leave your mark as an example, both commanding and engaging, of what it is to be a man. Shakespeare follows much of classical antiquity in advocating virtue over happiness – he finds that the two are usually at odds. There is wisdom here, of a tender, sceptical, urbane, all-encompassing sort. It is a humanist wisdom, quite different from that of Homer or of the Fourth Gospel.

Yet humanism had another mode, oblique to the melancholy Stoic realism of Shakespeare. It was earlier and simpler, naive in the way Brutus is naive, but not the less enduring for its narrower path. It was Pico della Mirandola's man is the great miracle, set at the world's centre, maker and moulder of himself, constrained by no limits. This is the Gattamelata. Shakespeare had found the limits, but he thereby lost the purity and the force of the vision. Brutus is a great miracle, he sets himself at the centre of the world by killing Caesar, he does make himself. But he is transformed by the limits. His call is no longer the clear peal of honour. It is muted. Donatello was unencumbered by these complexities, although not because he was naive – his other work makes that plain. His vision was different. He saw the concentrated, essential value, and stripped away the rest. What remains is the grace of pure form. The Gattamelata on a bright noon is an exhilarating tribute to man. Its message is: 'I like him!'

3

HOLBEIN AND HAMLET

Humanism did not need Luther to point out that its condition was precarious. There were premonitions from within, and from very early on. If a place to stand were not found then what would follow? The conscious mind went blank at this question. But there were signs. Indeed a dismal foreboding pervades major work of two of the humanist masters, both Northerners, the work itself created in England. When Hamlet stands skull in hand, oppressed by mortality, his entire metaphysical universe crushed, and he cries out 'Alas, poor Yorick', he is at his wits' end. 'Alas, poor Yorick' is humanism's 'My God, my God, why hast thou forsaken me?'

Eighty years earlier Holbein had had the same vision, and then he painted his *Christ Entombed*, the work hanging in Basel that would, centuries on, obsess Dostoevsky, who described it as the most horrible thing he had ever seen. Holbein's vision took another eleven years to mature, when in 1533 he painted his huge masterpiece, *The Ambassadors*, which now hangs in the National Gallery in London.

The Ambassadors is a double portrait, of Jean de Dinteville and his friend, Georges de Selve. De Dinteville, the twenty-nine year-old Sieur de Polisy, was the French envoy in London. De Selve, Bishop of Lavour, was visiting his friend, but also on an official yet secret mission on behalf of the French king. De Selve was a learned scholar, and de Dinteville a patron of scholarship, especially in relation to translations of the Bible into French. Holbein paints the two men as massive, their physical bulk taking up almost entirely the left third and the right third, respectively, of

Hans Holbein the Younger, *Christ Entombed*, Öffentliche Kunstsammlung, Basel

the painting. The remaining section of the work, between the ambassadors, is occupied by a two-level table, on which is placed an array of instruments and books. On the bottom level or shelf there is a terrestrial globe, a book of arithmetic, an open hymn-book and two musical instruments, one of which is a lute. On the upper shelf there is a celestial globe, two sundials, two quadrants, an instrument for determining the position of the stars, and a book. There are assorted other tools of geometry.

In fact, what we have is two exemplars of the Renaissance. They are men of great eminence in the secular and clerical worlds. They have wealth, power and high office, both by birth and appointment. They have the trust of their king, François I. They are also men of learning, with all the symbols of humanist culture at their command. Their dress, their relaxed stance, their sober gaze straight out of the painting, tell of their authority. They are masters of their world. They are more than ambassadors of France, they are emissaries of Humanism. They are the worthy heirs of the Gattamelata, the noble gentleman on whose shoulders the success of the new culture rests.

All is not well, however. Holbein has magnified the two figures so they are cramped within the seven foot square frame less to show their size, than that they are trapped. The painting has no background, no third dimension behind the ambassadors. They are closed off to the rear by a comprehensive green curtain. Furthermore, there is little space between de Dinteville and the left border, and de Selve and the right one. There is no exit to either side and no depth at all. Beneath their feet is an ornate tiled floor, leading forward. The painting has an eerie two-dimensionality, with the exception of the one permitted movement out of the static vertical plane of the figures, forward from them and down.

The claustrophobia is intensified by the bolt immobility of the two men. It is as if they are frozen in their pose. The faces are expressionless, dead-pan, pale and without emotion, the lips straight and closed, the gaze straight out of the work, but blank. Holbein confirms the mood in the block symmetry of his design, which is only fractionally offset by the larger bulk of de Dinteville, and the displacement of the table slightly right of centre, both neutralized by the diagonal form of the object in the foreground, echoed in the lute. Even the arrangement of objects on the table has minimal perspective; it is a clutter, and one which has no relationship to the two men.

The one way out is forward and down, a tipping motion from the line of the eyes to the front lower border, as if the vertical plane containing de Dinteville and de Selve were a cardboard sheet rotating forward on an axis through their feet. They would then meet head on the distorted spherical object that hovers above the floor alone in the foreground of the painting, the object that commands the work, the focal point of *The Ambassadors*. The eyes of the two gentlemen may look straight ahead, avoiding the forward incline, but those eyes are dead, without inward depth or outward penetration, and they relinquish their direction of the scene to the stance of the two men, which is oriented inwards towards the front centre, and to the positioning of their hands, which in both cases creates a line of force from the centre of mass of the bodies moving out and down through the midpoint between the hands and intersecting at the object in the foreground. The effect is strengthened by the cramping of the bodies within the frame of the painting, which serves to place the figures higher than they would be normally, putting the viewer lower down, beneath the heads, concentrating at a point somewhere in the midriff – again reducing the importance of the eyes.

The distorted spherical object which dominates the work is, of course, a skull. Using an established technique Holbein painted the skull so that its true form can only be made out from standing to one side of the painting. From front on, viewed as the ambassadors themselves do, it is a confusing blur. The men are under its power, pale in their unconscious fear, unable to make out what it is that has taken them over. They know they have been turned to stone, they know that their cultural toys are powerless to help them – unable even to distract any more – they can sense from where the debilitating force is streaming at them, and yet they cannot make out its form. They do not want to: their eyes are averted, staring blankly straight ahead, over the skull.

Death is master, and there is no other. The ambassadors have failed to find a place to stand. Their inner eye stares into the face of their Medusa, into nothingness, and they are stricken blind, rooted to the spot. There are other signs in the painting. De Dinteville has a miniature silver skull set on a gold badge on his cap. The lute has a broken string:

> or ever the silver cord be loosened, or the golden bowl be broken,
> then shall the dust
> return to the earth as it was.

But death in *The Ambassadors* has none of the succouring gravity of Ecclesiastes. It is rather pale terror.

Like Hamlet, these men are high courtiers, learned, perceptive, adept in all the arts and sciences. Perhaps they are even wise. Yet for them life has lost all sense. Without God, without a transcendental law, there is only death. Culture is what stops a man in his tracks, the No's that limit his desires. For the ambassadors the single No that remains is death, the limit of limits. It is the one thing that may check them, that may limit their freedom. The problem is that when it is all there is, when culture is reduced to the skull, then it takes over. It becomes all. So Holbein who had the foolishness to ask the decisive metaphysical question, will humanism have enough gravity to stay on its feet, answered in the negative. No, there is little gravity. No, a place to stand does not exist. Holbein is thus the first truly modern theorist, having got himself to the brink of the nihilist cliff. He paints life as either horrible or absurd. For his ambassadors it is both.

Holbein's dour mockery of the bright humanist dawn does not stop here. His gentleman heroes, his masters of civilization, are standing stock still. They have their place to stand, and cannot move. But their fixed position is not out of security, but terror. Moreover, the skull hovers; it is mobile; it is free. That which roots them to the spot may move at will. Worse, that skull is the one thing in the entire painting with strength, with vitality. Life and death, under the humanist constellation, have exchanged places. The humanist aspirant must through an immense act of concentrated will forge his 'I am'. When he opens his eyes again he finds that he has turned into Jean de Dinteville and Georges de Selve. Such is Holbein's reading.

Further elaborations are pretty mechanical. The pursuit of knowledge is futile. What is its point if it provides no defence against the skull. Plotting the motion of the stars will not help a man find direction in his own life. Playing the lute will not soothe his raw nerves once the whiff of a corpse has penetrated his nostrils, not unless the music intimates of a greater frame, one within which he can stand. The greatest of all humanist institutions, the university, is a mausoleum of dead ideas, a rattling of dry bones. Its teaching is incapable of reaching out to hold the hand through the dark night of the soul. Holbein has put it with brutal simplicity: there is no humanist solution, the most learned men have no answer to death. Once faith is gone then fate is reduced to necessity, and the ultimate necessity is Death.

The ambassadors are not only learned, they are free. They enjoy free-will. They move about the civilized world using their power to organize the possibilities of men; the fate of kingdoms is in their hands. They carry, in a strictly hierarchical age, the responsibilities for the aristocracy and the Church, for the elite. Through their science they know the time accurately, they can chart the seas and cross them safely, they can map the heavens, in short they have access to the secrets of Nature. This is not little. They are the forefathers of the steam engine and of penicillin. Reason and free-will, they are powerful tools, and mankind has benefited prodigiously from their exercise by these ambassadors and their progeny. As long as de Dinteville and de Selve are absorbed in their science, as long as they keep on the move in their diplomacy, all is well. These are two fine-looking young men in their prime. No one was more eligible. But we have been shown that there is nothing behind them, beneath them or above them. There is no past or future. There is no anchor below nor light from on high. There is no way out. Holbein, callous and pitiless German that he was, has caught them in a moment when they have stopped, and looked up from their work. He has caught them exposed. He has shown them and us that it is precisely because they have free-will that they are rooted to the spot.

Holbein had been a mere twenty-five years old when in 1522 he painted his *Christ Entombed*. On that occasion he had stood himself in humanist shoes and with a brilliant intuition had seen the new culture's necessary first step, if it were to establish itself. It had to kill Christ. What an unerring sense of the first principles! Holbein has not left much work behind him, most of it portraits, but in the masterpieces of 1522 and 1533 his assault on the old, Christian culture is done from so close to the bone that it ends up as a challenge to humanism itself.

Holbein kills Christ by demolishing the crucifixion. His Christ is no more than a dead body. It lies, life-size, inside the grave. We look in from the side. Around the wounds in the visible foot, hand and side the flesh is black-green with decay. The dried-out hair and beard is a jutting brittle black. The skeletal right hand, the hand of authority, is stiff with *rigor mortis*, the middle finger elongated and pressing down on the stone slab like a dead twig. The light is even along the whole body, without highlight or direction. The expression on the face is one of horror, the mouth open, the white of the visible eye enlarged. This man died a gruelling death and in his last moments there was no peace or radiance, just the sheer terror of the pain and nothing beyond. There is no serene smile of redemption. What we see is rot and shrinkage, no different from a dead fish washed up on the beach. This man did not rise from the grave. There was no resurrection. Flesh is flesh, which means festering wounds, stiffening joints and the stench of decomposition. Death is death.

The *Christ Corpse* has uncanny force. This is difficult to understand for Holbein has merely painted a dead man and titled it 'Jesus of Nazareth, King of the Jews'. Surely, there is mockery in the title, but most people have seen a dead body, so why is this one – not even real, just a painted image – so shocking?

Dostoevsky was not alone in reeling away from it and exclaiming that it was enough to make one lose one's faith. Nor is the challenge restricted to Christians like Dostoevsky. Holbein hit the central nerve of humanist thought, and with it every member of modernity. No one can escape the elongated, bony middle finger of Holbein's Christ, as it collapses downwards onto the stone slab – the new world is empty of authority. Mortality rules. Man is no more than a dead fish stranded on the beach. That he is endowed with consciousness just brings suffering: the fish that lives by instinct does not foresee its own end. Man, by virtue of his consciousness, sees the hideous death of Christ, and is trapped already years ahead of his time.

In 1522 Holbein plotted humanism's first step, to destroy the authority of Christianity, to clear the cultural decks. Over the next three hundred years the destruction would work its fill. In 1533 he asked the second question: with what shall we replace Christ crucified? There was no problem for him about the answer: free-will and reason. However, Holbein was not a utopian. His dark vision of 1522 had taught him the singular importance of the Archimedean challenge. The answer he painted is that once there is free-will then reason becomes an indifferent plaything, and Will collapses. He lost faith in the humanist solution. And yet Erasmus had been a friend of his. He painted the portrait of the great humanist many times – indeed it is the one repeating theme in the surviving work of Holbein. Holbein is best known in most quarters for his portraits of Erasmus; reciprocally, Erasmus is best known as painted by Holbein, the calm, gentle-faced scholar at his desk, putting his thoughts on paper, the exemplar of the intellectual life. It was in the year or two following the *Christ Corpse* that most of these portraits were done. Is there not here some unconscious identification of Reason with Death? The philosophy of Erasmus is founded on nothing, the metaphysics of a dead fish endowed with consciousness.

In all of this there remains one untied knot. Holbein did not consider Brutus, the possibility of an ethic based on honour. Brutus had no fear of death: he was contented to die, and the

end was no great agony. If Holbein is right then it means that
free-will excludes honour. Alternatively, if the Shakespeare of
Julius Caesar is right then it has to be agreed that while the pursuit
of knowledge will not save humanist man, the code of honour of
the gentleman may.

The Ambassadors has one last curse. The eyes of de Dinteville
and de Selve may be blank eyes, yet the viewer as he walks
around the room looking at the painting, as he moves from left
to centre to right, as he moves from up close to far back, will find
that the eyes follow him. Once inside the room in the National
Gallery in London, the wall opposite the entrance taken up exclu-
sively by this work, it is impossible to escape the dead stare of
the two ambassadors. The next thing one realizes is that through
this stare I, the viewer, am locked into the skull, which because
of its distortion I cannot see. The indirection of the skull is that
it commands through the hands and then the eyes of the ambassadors, who also do not make it out. The deeper representation of
these two humanists is therefore not on behalf of François I to
Henry VIII, but from the skull to us. They are the emissaries of
death. The highest representatives of Humanism deliver their
message to whom they look at, you and I. We thereby come
under the thrall of the skull. In other words, more than a century
before Velázquez was more explicitly to bring the viewer into the
picture, in his *Las Meninas*, Holbein had done the same, but with
a singular propensity to menace his audience.

Once the blood began to slow in the humanist veins, as it did
precipitately from the early nineteenth century, and the darker
imagery emerged from the shadows, it would not be Holbein
who would be instated as principal teacher. That role went to
Shakespeare's Hamlet. The fascination that this late Renaissance
"tragedy" has held for modernity is easy to document. Apart
from the Bible it is the most written about work of Western
culture. It is the most performed play. Indeed in English it has
been, from its first appearance, the most regularly performed
work in the literature. Modern critical consensus holds that
Hamlet is the hub of Shakespeare's whole work, the centre from

which the other plays reach out as spokes. Up until 1770 Hamlet himself had been taken as a brave heroic man, a sentimental hero. After 1770 the focus on his character began, stressing his madness, his weakness, his intellectuality. The "Hamlet problem" commenced. For the next century "Hamlet fever" took hold in Germany. After 1820, throughout northern Europe, Hamlet scholarship turned into a deluge. As one instance, A.A. Raven's bibliography of Hamlet literature published between 1877 and 1935 lists over two thousand items.

There are a number of reasons why *Hamlet* has touched the nerve of modern culture in a way no other work has. Hamlet is a typical modern man of the hyper-sensitive, introspective and lonely type, suffering from a paralysing inner torment which has no obvious source. He is exceptionally gifted in intelligence, perceptivity and articulacy. As Freud pointed out, the play brings to the surface deeply buried family tensions, universal ones. The play discourses at length on the problem of the meaning of life in a non-religious world. It contrasts simple and gregarious men of action with their modern opposite.

Hamlet himself in many ways fits the model of the humanist hero. He is a gentleman, gracious and honourable, the Prince of Denmark beloved by his people. He is a man of reason, educated in a German university. He is a realist, under no illusions about the ways of the world: one of his strengths is that he sees into the motives of others instantly.

Free-will is again a pivot. In the case of Hamlet, however, it is a negative freedom. Hamlet is free *not* to kill Claudius – it is a brilliant inversion by Shakespeare of the metaphysics of Brutus. Freedom is freedom not to do what you have to do, freedom from morality. Hamlet is the individual as hero, the modern individualist unconstrained by the laws of kin or State – which all point in one direction, vengeance. The conflict is not between two different ethics. There is no suggestion in the text that Thou Shalt Not Kill is an overriding ethic: Hamlet is not inhibited by this injunction, he is not in the least concerned about the blood-guilt that might arise from his murdering Claudius. Morality is simply focused on his duty, to avenge his father's murder by killing his uncle. He is free not to do his duty. It is this freedom that destroys him, and in the process all the main characters in the play. The consequence of Hamlet's dithering is that in the ensuing chaos everyone gets killed.

Free to choose against duty leaves Hamlet bogged down in his own depression. This is a man sunk in profound melancholy. His first oration opens with the lament:

> How weary, stale, flat, and unprofitable
> Seem to me all the uses of this world.

He refers to the earth as a "sterile promontory" and man as "this quintessence of dust". The examples may be multiplied. His thoughts return again and again to suicide, an alternative preferable to having to 'grunt and sweat under a weary life'. From beginning to end Hamlet is lethargic, bitter, morose, introverted, restless yet tired, and at times dementedly rash. The substance of the play is in fact his own long monologue of complaint about life, interrupted here and there by a bit of drama.

The problem of Hamlet, as countless thousands of critics have noted, is simple: why cannot he do what he knows, and what everybody knows, he should do, avenge his father by killing Claudius? There are three reasons in ascending order of significance. There is the psychological inhibition in Hamlet, as interpreted by Freud and elaborated by Ernest Jones in his book, *Hamlet and Oedipus* (1950). Hamlet's incestuous attachment to his mother is pathologically strong, and the thought of killing his uncle arouses parricidal guilts that paralyse his ability to act. Secondly, Hamlet undergoes a moral crisis. The person to whom he is closest in the world is his mother, whom he loves and admires. A month after the death of her husband, a fine man, she marries his brother, a low character whom Hamlet rightly despises. This act of his mother's is incomprehensible to him. His first response to the account of Claudius' infamy is 'O most pernicious woman' and from then on there is a litany of abuse of women. Hamlet's sense of a moral order has been destroyed by his mother. The person whom he trusted above all others has proved unreliable, has destroyed trust in the most gross fashion. If there is no trust, how can there be any law. If the most intimate ethical bonds are fickle, how can anything be relied upon? At this level Hamlet is flattened by his mother's behaviour, and loses interest in everything else.

The third and predominant reason for Hamlet's inability to act is that he has met Death. Death opens the play. It is midnight and the sentinels discuss the ghost. It appears. By the end of Act I Hamlet himself is talking to the ghost of his murdered father, conversing with death, whose parting words are: 'Adieu, adieu Hamlet: remember me.' How can Hamlet forget? Indeed as he staggers away from this scene his entire speech apart from his outburst against his mother, 'O most pernicious woman', and his uncle, 'Oh villain, villain, smiling damned villain!' is that from now on his life is under the command of his father's ghost. He identifies with the parting words of Death, and swears allegiance to him. He will never again manage to return to the land of the living. The critic, Wilson Knight, went so far as to title a fine essay on *Hamlet*, 'The Embassy of Death' (*The Wheel of Fire*, 1930).

Hamlet's talk has two recurring themes. The first is why he cannot do what everything commands him to do. He compares himself with men of action like Alexander and Caesar, with the young Fortinbras going to war for a useless piece of ground, and with the actors who can work up a great passion over an imaginary cause – he has a great cause but no passion. He calls himself a coward; he likens himself to a whore, whose heart is hollow. In short he is appalled by his own paralysis, ashamed of it. In part he blames consciousness: he thinks too much. Here is the link with the other recurring theme, that of death. When Hamlet utters his famous phrase that action is 'sicklied o'er with the pale cast of thought' he has specific thought in mind, that of death and its aftermath. The line comes at the end of the most famous speech in the play, the 'To be or not to be' speech, which is a meditation on suicide. All the sentiment is on the side of death, that 'consummation Devoutly to be wished.' The speech catalogues the 'slings and arrows' that are life, a list of reasons against it. The one argument for life is negative, fear of the unknown, the 'dread of something after death'.

In Hamlet's early mad speech to Polonius his raving is drawn to thoughts of the grave and how willingly he would give up his life. Later, after killing Polonius, instead of showing remorse for his unwarranted murder, Hamlet jokes about mortality. When asked where he has hidden the corpse he replies that it is at supper, being eaten by maggots. In Act V when he comes upon Ophelia's funeral he jumps into her open grave and asks to be buried with her. At the end, his dying words pleading with Horatio not to kill himself include the telling phrase: 'Absent thee from felicity awhile.' The play itself ends with a funeral procession, the body of Hamlet borne off with martial rites.

These are, however, merely flashes as the light touches the silver thread through the work, the spirit of *Hamlet*. That thread has its source in the first meeting with death, Hamlet and the ghost in Act I, in which the thirty-year-old Prince takes his oath of loyalty, the oath he will not break. It terminates in the third and last meeting with death, early in Act V as the now pale and enervated prince holds the skull in his hand, and addresses it 'Alas, poor Yorick.' This, the gravediggers' scene, is the climax to the play. As much as the shattering of Hamlet's character is determined by the first meeting with the ghost, that formative early scene has its completion, the end-point of its logic, in 'Alas, poor Yorick', the meditation on death stimulated by memories of his father's court jester. Any audience having sat through the gruelling first four acts of long-winded discourse, unrelieved by much action or change of tone, immediately lifts as Act V opens and the earthy gravediggers clown through their scene together. The play comes alive, the morose fog lifts for a moment, there is lightness as the two yokels crack skulls with their shovels and pun through their philosophy of life. Hamlet too, for a moment, is a different man. The words he speaks to Yorick's skull are the only ones of real attachment and affection he utters in the entire play:

> Alas! poor Yorick. I knew him, Horatio; a fellow of infinite jest, of most excellent
> fancy; he hath borne me on his back a thousand times; and now, how abhorred in my
> imagination it is! my gorge rises at it. Here hung those lips, that I have kiss'd I know
> not how oft . . .

Hamlet switches from this quiet moving reminiscence into further musings on death, on the noble dust of Alexander now a bung stopping a beer-barrel. He is then confronted by Ophelia's funeral. His response is to jump into her grave with her brother, having announced himself with pathetic bombast, 'This is I, Hamlet the Dane,' and then boasting beyond all sense that he loved Ophelia more than forty thousand brothers could. Innocence is dead, driven out of her mind by the events and words for which Hamlet is largely responsible, and this is his response. Rather be Yorick. Hamlet has again lost his poise. From this point on the play works mechanically through predictable routines until trumpets or bugle bring down the curtain.

Yes, the gravediggers are the only cheerfulness in the long dirge that is *Hamlet*. The last of the gods is Death, the one abiding and true love is Yorick, twenty-three years dead, his skull stinking. Metaphysics, in the form of the great ontological question to be or not to be, what is the essence of being, is reduced to the profane issue of suicide. Hamlet is as indifferent to whether he kills himself or not as Beckett's tramps in *Waiting for Godot*, although by comparison their nihilism is full of zest. Productions of the play have usually sensed all this, in that Hamlet is almost always dressed in black, with a wan complexion, long bohemian hair, and he is shown as obliteratingly alone. Hamlet in black, emissary of Death, takes us back to Holbein's ambassadors. He is paralysed, as were they, by the skull. The difference is that Shakespeare elaborates the consequences. Were he properly alive, Hamlet would kill Claudius, order would be restored in Denmark and the kingdom would prosper. As it is his stone-like being, his free choice of not to do what he has to do, his individualist refusal to obey the laws of his tribe, results in everyone being killed, guilty and innocent alike. After 'Alas poor Yorick' he fills the stage with corpses. Free-will means no place to stand, means frozen to the spot, means havoc. That everything is rotten in the state of Denmark is the legacy of humanism.

Hamlet has been classified as tragedy. It is rather melodrama. There can be no humanist tragedy. Shakespeare demonstrates that. For tragedy, as Homer, Aeschylus and Sophocles sang it, there has to be a greater order of things, which is violated by the supra-human forces of destiny, with or without human help. In the chaos resulting from the violation, men do what they can to restore order. *Hamlet* belongs to a different cultural universe. There are no higher laws. Hamlet himself is it: the well-being of the world depends on his 'I am'. His failure is the single reason for the moral and political chaos. Hamlet in failing to restore order is the major contributor to greater disorder – Claudius was in fact a highly competent king. Tragedy, by contrast, ends in the triumph over death, Achilles carrying out funeral rites as his reparation before he is killed, Oedipus accepting what he understands, blinding and banishing himself to meditate alone on his cursed fate. For Hamlet, for humanism, there is nothing above or beyond death.

Hamlet is the finish of Western tragedy, for as long as the humanist epoch was to last. It is a futile attempt at the genre. Where is the cleansing metaphysical exhilaration at the end, the exhausted audience rising out of the ashes with the inspired feeling that in spite of all life is fresh and good, that it is out of the suffering, the humiliation, yes even the death, that the life-force triumphs, that out of the tragic wreck the annihilated individual transcends the bounds of his own self and is united with the grander order of things? It is not there, not a hint of it. The tragic experience teaches that Death is not the ultimate No, the limit of limits. In *Hamlet* it is, and the audience is left stranded on a melancholy beach.

This is the humanist negative, to *Julius Caesar* as positive, written a mere two or three years later. The dramatic forms tell the story. *Julius Caesar* had a strict classical structure, beautifully orchestrated, precise and without superfluous elements. It was Roman itself, as if the ethic of honour in place secured the dramatic limits. In *Hamlet* the erratic ebb and flow of the moods of the central character takes over the form, and hitches it to its own self-centred anarchy. There are many sudden digressions in the plot, a number of doubtful relevance. It is as if all limit has gone. Apart from the two anchoring points, the first meeting with death and the gravediggers, the play meanders, all over the place.

It is, however, a little glib to separate the humanist positive and negative so readily. Hamlet is close to Brutus. Shakespeare is explicit on this. Polonius remarks that in his youth he played Julius Caesar: 'Brutus killed me.' In reality it is Hamlet who kills him. Hamlet is a bleak reworking of Brutus, the change of circumstances being that the skull has appeared. Honour is not enough to neutralize it, or so is Shakespeare's later reading. In the light of how seriously we must take this change of vision by the greatest humanist we should also note that, viewed up close, the Gattamelata has an awfully melancholy expression on his face.

By 'Remember me!' the ghost had meant 'Avenge me!', a call to honour. But Hamlet is incapable of the active side. In his case the decline of honour is proportional to the rise of reason. As honour predominates in Brutus, so reason predominates in Hamlet. That reason is a curse, no more than the endless chattering rationalization of why he cannot do what he should. It is excusing reason, and under its influence Hamlet becomes the feeblest of men. He has the eloquence and wit of a god, but what is that worth if its practical consequence is to reinforce what in him is ignoble, meriting only scorn, making him a millstone around the neck of the human spirit. In the phrase echoing through Western culture in which he finds the cause of his immobility, 'the pale cast of thought', we are told much. Reason, that pale and therefore spectral force, is deadly. It is not just that the divine eloquence of Hamlet cannot talk itself out of the arms of the Medusa; that talk is itself an engine of mortality. Talk cannot create a rock on which to stand; worse, talk is very bad for sureness of step. The Prince of Reason is at one and the same time the Prince of Death.

Hamlet has come to love the last of the gods. He is not just under the authority of Death, he has embraced it. 'Absent thee from felicity awhile' speaks his deep longing, the pitiable last dream of a man tormented to his wits' end, uttered with a heart-rending sigh, the dream of peace and happiness, which he sees only in death. Thus at the end of the road the question about *Hamlet*, the play that late humanism was to take to as the work of works, the one that held the secret truth, the central creation of Europe's greatest literary figure, the question of what it is essentially about, produces a most strange answer – death worship.

Humanism was stopped in its tracks in its prime by Holbein and Shakespeare. It was to recover in its own sort of fashion, and flourish for another couple of centuries before its irreversible decline set in. Its recovery was largely due, as we shall see, to its connecting itself to another source of strength, one tapped by Luther and Calvin. However, it also found some inspiration from within, from a figure born out of the late Renaissance crisis of humanism. As much as Hamlet is Brutus a few years on, he has a brother, his opposite in character but clearly of the same genealogical stock. That is Don Quixote. Cervantes died in the same month of the same year, 1616, as Shakespeare. The first part of his masterpiece appeared two or three years after *Hamlet*. His heroic knight is an explicit attempt to find a principle of action, a man who can move in the humanist universe.

In 1860 the Russian writer, Ivan Turgenev, wrote an essay on 'Hamlet and Don Quixote'. Turgenev took Don Quixote as the perfect gentleman, a man who with no thought of self dedicates himself to chivalrous causes. He has faith in his ideal and therefore can act. The introspective, self-obsessed, sceptical Hamlet is his opposite. This reading fails to get to the heart of the matter. Don Quixote is not an ordinary knight errant, nor a simple parody of one. He has a capacity for action, for noble action, that all others lack. It is based on his chaste, single-minded devotion to his ideal of the knight – the man of honour. Don Quixote is Brutus as man of honour, without any other traits or complexities, he is Brutus stripped to the bare bones. His ideal is so strong that he is blind to reality: governed by the ideal he does not see the real, except through the radically distorting lens of his vision. He sees thirty windmills as thirty monstrous giants, attacks, gets tangled in one of the sails, and is flattened. Such are his adventures, leaving him battered and bruised, and the world no better. Usually he gets no thanks: the convicts whom he frees beat him half to death.

Cervantes too was taking up the Archimedean challenge. He saw that in order to live a man must act. To be able to act he must have a place to stand. Where is such a place in a godless universe? The only possibility is Don Quixote, faith in honour. Indeed he is the one thing that moves in the thousand-page epic. Sancho Panza loves his master and sacrifices all comfort to follow him, the down-to-earth Sancho who puts wine, food and sleep before everything else. Half the time he believes in his master, for the rest he suspects he is a deluded madman. In the second part of the story we follow courts across Spain as they lionize the now famous knight, and set up adventures for him for their own entertainment. They trick and deceive him and in his simplicity he usually makes a fool of himself. But the joke turns back on the audience, partly because the naive honesty of his mission leaves him untouched by humiliation, but more because the courtiers need him, are dependent on him. He brings life to the aimless and half-hearted pastimes of the court. Without Don Quixote before them these courtiers would turn into Jean de Dinteville and Georges de Selve. Sancho himself learns from his master. When he is made governor of an island, another court jest, he applies himself to his job with utter seriousness, makes wise decisions, and transcends the tricks and deceits practised upon him. In short he too has a period in which, as a convert to his master's faith, he can stand, in which he moves the earth – in the form of a town which he rules well, if briefly. That town was never so justly governed, by a man with Will.

The message is extreme: to be able to act you must be under an illusion, to the point of madness. This is what Nietzsche, a great admirer of Don Quixote, was to call "redemptive illusion", the consoling dream that keeps our eyes off the truth about modern existence, that it is horrible or absurd. Cervantes goes further. There is no difference between fantasy and reality, nor between asleep and awake. In the incident of the wineskins it is the sleep-walking Don Quixote who slashes them to pieces, believing them to be giants. He would act no differently were he awake. In Montesinos Cave he falls asleep after entry and dreams his adventure. It is exactly the same as if he had actually had it, and only the witnesses from ordinary life are concerned about whether it physically happened – the irrelevant concern of those who themselves cannot move, the equivalent to the futile thinking of Hamlet. But wait a minute, the alternative to Hamlet is now a conception of action in which the heroism of the warrior is identical with the hallucinations of a certifiable lunatic.

Don Quixote pits his 'I believe, therefore I am' against Hamlet's 'I think, therefore I am turned to stone.' The 'I am' can act even in his sleep, whereas the ultra-conscious Hamlet might as well be sleep-walking. Cervantes had recognized Shakespeare's Brutus-Hamlet problem, and that everything depended upon its solution. His answer was to produce his knight errant, and a story that remains a pure joy to read, so full of life is it. The vitality is the sign of Cervantes' success. However, this is honour's last stand, for it has become ridiculous. The courageous knight's acts of chivalry are all dedicated to his lady, the fantasized Dulcinea del Toboso. The fantasy is based at best on an unreliable memory of a peasant girl, who when met in the flesh turns out to be gross and vulgar, an unpalatable fact that is explained away by the knight of faith as a cruel enchantment. Moreover, at the end of the long tale the illusion–reality inversions suddenly stop, and a now sober and worldly Don Quixote repents "my former madness", and he dies. Reality has returned, a bleak and profane order ruled by Necessity.

There is an urbane humanist reading of *Don Quixote*, what we might call a Shakespearean reading. This story is a parable of all life. The good life depends upon a sizeable dose of unreal fantasy to keep it going, ideally mixed with some of Sancho's peasant earthiness. The shape of its events is pretty absurd when looked at dispassionately, not so different from tilting at windmills. The fortunate man sees profane windmills as sacred giants and acts accordingly, and with a bit of luck is not too bruised in the event. While existence is horrible or absurd, the heroic absurd if achieved may neutralize the horror. It is only the dying Don Quixote who recants, knowing the illusion is over.

Well, maybe! Even grant this sceptical line and the question remains, in this universe is there a firm enough place to stand? I think Cervantes followed Holbein in saying No, although he fought tooth and nail to prove the opposite, and out of the struggle produced the most extravagant and likeable of humanist heroes. What of Shakespeare? Well, for him the story has not progressed beyond the enormous question mark that is Brutus. Shakespeare took a look into the hollow sockets of the skull and wrote *Hamlet*. Finding himself in the shoes of de Dinteville he saw what Holbein had seen, and his anguish was to reverberate through the next four hundred years of humanist culture, shaking it to the foundations. Hamlet, Hamlet and Hamlet again – the West would come to know it by heart. Shakespeare himself stumbled on, and could still manage the closest he would get to a true tragedy, in *King Lear*, a partial and inferior reworking of the Brutus theme in *Coriolanus*, and his beautiful, late, escapist fantasy, *The Tempest*.

4

THE GREAT
COUNTER-RENAISSANCE OF
LUTHER AND CALVIN

The story of the rise and fall of humanism is woven from three threads. They run right through it. We have located two of them already, the generative ideal cast by the Renaissance, and the sceptical counter from within, humanism's own self-doubt. It is to the third that we now turn. That is the Protestant counter, launched explicitly against Catholicism and Rome, but at its philosophical heart being a life-or-death attack on Humanism. Luther's most important work, *On the Enslaved Will*, the theological cornerstone of the Reformation, was written not against the Pope but against Erasmus. At the end of the day what Luther and Calvin had established was a counter-ideal to that of the Renaissance, the alternative metaphysics. To know just how different it was we need only consider one formulation of Luther's: 'the darkness of faith where neither law nor reason shines.'

The decisive battle was fought in 1524 and 1525, between Erasmus and Luther. Erasmus was a reluctant combatant, but urged on by authorities as diverse as Henry VIII and the Pope he wrote his *Discourse on Free-Will*, as he put it himself, pitched against Luther's assertion that free-will is an "empty word". It appeared on 1 September, 1524, printed in Basel, where he was living at the time. Luther replied a year later with his *On the Enslaved Will* (*De Servo Arbitrio*). It was triple the length of Erasmus' *Discourse*. The angry and intimidated humanist called it "a huge book". Luther himself was later to refer to it as his best book – certainly it was his most important.

Erasmus was a reasonable man. He was comfortable in the world, moderate, conciliatory, gentle and eloquent. He was more

47

Hans Holbein the Younger, *Erasmus Writing*, Louvre, Paris

concerned that the Church be at peace than with doctrinal controversy. Christianity for him was the goodness of men in everyday life, and if it worked in practice fierce examinations of faith were a bit beside the point. As a result his *Discourse* is somewhat half-hearted. Nevertheless its aim was true, as Luther acknowledged in his reply:

You alone, in contrast with all the others, have attacked the real thing, that is, the essential issue. You have not wearied me with all those extraneous issues about the Papacy, purgatory, indulgences and such like – trifles, rather than issues – in respect of which almost all to date have sought my blood (though without success); you, and you alone, have seen the hinge on which all turns, and aimed for the vital spot.

That vital spot was free-will.

Erasmus' argument is that of a reasonable man. He accepts that God determines most things, but leaves man some freedom. 'God indeed preserves the ship, but the sailor steers it into harbour.' He argues for a little bit of free-will. His reason was offended by Luther's doctrine of *sola fide*, for he quite logically saw that its implication was that man was a slave with no incentive for moral behaviour. If faith alone can save a man, and he has no free-will, why should the wicked try to reform? Necessity, even when it is God's necessity, eliminates moral responsibility. There is no point in me trying to be a better person if I have no will of my own: whether I behave badly or well is determined by God, outside of my control, so my only rational response is to resign myself to what is given. 'Faith alone' is incompatible with morality. As Erasmus put it there is no point exhorting those who have no power of their own. 'It is like saying to someone in chains: "Move over here!"' Furthermore, justice becomes an absurd notion: 'How is condemnation just, when it is the judge who compels evil doing?'

The argument is persuasive. It is Reason's reply to the contradictions inherent in 'faith alone'. It is an appeal in effect for a moderate version, allowing man some freedom. This would allow works some place. If a man has free-will then it is partly his own choice when he does good works. Thus he merits reward. We are back with the Catholic doctrine of works: that living a good life is taken into account by God, and increases the individual's chance of salvation. Again, this is the reasonable view, for any common-sense notion of justice has virtue being rewarded. If the gods are just then surely one of their tasks is to judge man, which means punishing vice and rewarding virtue. Erasmus is articulating a standard theology, common to most human religions.

Luther understood the argument. Indeed he pulled out its strongest parts and quoted them in his *Enslaved Will*. This was his 'you alone have aimed for the vital spot.' Erasmus showed him the full picture of what he was up against. He showed him that reason and faith were incompatible. Once man starts to reason, as does Erasmus, then he has to have free-will. What starts out with a bit of free-will ends with the death of God. The picture Erasmus painted showed him more, that morality too has nothing to do with faith. Faith belongs in the dark, with the night demons, out of the securing light of the human order, down where the torch of human reason cannot penetrate. It is the darkness of faith, or nothing. *Sola fide* had been the easy half of Luther's Reformation: he now moved into the harsh terrain where, against all reason, will is nothing. Everything hinged on this. If Erasmus won here then Christ was done for. History was to prove Luther right.

No free-will is the crux of the Reformation. Luther's entire work centres on proving it. He is not just against Erasmus and humanism here, but against the mainstream of Christian theology. Etienne Gilson wrote in his *The Spirit of Medieval Philosophy* (1940) that 'all Christian ethics of the Middle Ages, like those of the Fathers that inspired them, have their necessary basis in the doctrine of an indestructible free will.'

Luther's first argument is that God's own will is 'immutable, eternal and infallible'. By that will he foresees and directs all things. Luther's own faith, explicated through the Scriptures, tells him this. Given the foundation of God's infallibility there is no place for human freedom. Man is small, ignorant and powerless. The immediate consequence of this argument is *sola fide*, by faith alone, granted by God alone. God chooses whom he saves. Man has no role in this choice. It happens or it does not happen. Man cannot buy salvation with good works: what a presumption! It is the free act of the all-powerful divinity that grants grace. Moreover, ignorant man can have no idea of what is God's will.

The second argument is the demolition of Reason. 'If you regard and follow the judgment of human reason, you are forced to say, either that there is no God, or that God is unjust.' On earth, the wicked prosper and the good suffer – reason shows this to us all. God's earth is not a just place. Once reason becomes an active force then it applies its logic to human experience and comes to the conclusion that all is not well with the divine plan. Reason gains airs 'in her knowing and talkative way'. In her presumption she seeks to measure God, thus reducing his authority. She turns God into a passive actor, entrusting more and more to man. She seeks to make excuses for God, 'not reverencing the secrets of His majesty, but peering and probing into them'.

Once reason is given the authority to investigate the ways of God the battle is lost. Its authority is already equal to that of God. But there can only be one ultimate authority. In this progression God will lose. In the end Reason proudly condemns God. The Renaissance 'I am' has forced Luther on to the other peak of the metaphysical either-or, 'I am nothing.' Once there is a bit of reason there is a bit of questioning, and there is no means of stopping the progression. This is why Luther calls Mistress Reason the "Devil's whore". She is seductive, deceiving, offering a moment of pleasure in order to seize the whole soul. It is the same with the bit of free-will: grant that and you have the universe upside down, with man on top.

Luther's third argument concerns guilt. 'No free-will' has two sides to it. One is that God chooses whom he chooses. The other is that man is enchained in sin. All men are damned in the sight of God. Original sin is the premise of the human condition. 'The whole world is guilty before God.' As a result how good men are is essentially irrelevant. Here is the reason the law does not shine in the darkness where faith dwells. As Paul put it: 'By the deeds of the law shall no flesh be justified in his sight.' Luther amplifies Paul: the best of men, obeying the law, using their highest faculties – will and reason – are all condemned as sinners. This is the fact. It follows that there is no free-will. What also follows is the even harsher Protestant doctrine that morality has no relationship to faith.

Luther clarifies his view of the law by distinguishing between two worlds, that of heaven and that of earth. The fuller exposition is in his *Commentary on the Epistle to the Galatians* (1531). On earth there is law, and works are significant. The Ten Commandments apply. The law bridles the wicked and makes them conscious of sin – those are its functions. However, in revealing sin it does not reveal God. It has no relationship to grace. The most it does is to lead to what Luther calls an active righteousness, a worldly righteousness. It is the Bible which is the source of the knowledge that makes possible the consciousness of sin. The goal of philosophy is the knowledge of sin.

Heaven is an entirely separate world. It is ruled by God, not the law. It is the domain of grace. It has a different righteousness, a passive sort, whose source is in Christ. As Moses delivered the law, Christ is the path to grace. In other words good works do not make a good man, but a good man does good works. It is necessary to follow the law, but that will not bring grace.

We are now squarely in the Protestant contradiction, which Erasmus had seen, and which Calvin will intensify, making it the crux of his theology. Man has no freedom yet he is responsible. At this point Luther changes direction. Unlike Calvin, he selects Reason as his direct target. Reason in its presumption instates its own law, contrary to the law of God: that is the law of non-contradiction. Those who worship at the temple of Reason will not stomach contradictions. Erasmus is the living example. In the darkness of faith where the light of reason does not shine there are bewildering contradictions.

Luther, the master combatant, chooses the contradiction with

which to flay Reason. In his *Commentary on Galatians* he goes
beyond the 'No free-will but obey the law' of *On the Enslaved Will*.
He was to hit precisely the nerve that was to stop Holbein and
Hamlet in their humanist tracks: 'Death killeth death: but this
killing death is life itself.' Thus he breaks out of humanist nihilism
and at the same time strikes Reason.

'These are marvellous words, and unknown kinds of speech,
which man's reason can no wise understand.' Reason teaches
that if you will live unto God you must keep the law. Paul says
the opposite, that we cannot live with God unless we be dead to
the law. Dead to the law means it has no power over us. Moses
or Christ. If the law of Moses accuses and condemns me, I have
another law, which is grace and liberty. 'This law accuseth the
accusing law and condemneth the condemning law.' Luther then
moves directly into his 'death killeth death'. He does not make his
argument any more concrete. He lets the paradox stand. Indeed it
will not be until Rembrandt and later Kierkegaard that the full
ramifications of this paradox at the heart of the Reformation will
be pursued, and then with the anxiety of men who fear that it is
on the edge of tearing their lives apart. For them the first death
has become problematical: they are in danger of turning into the
ambassadors, left with death alone. In Luther's paradox too is
the seed of the argument put by Dostoevsky's Kirilov, that the
only proof of free-will is to kill yourself – Kirilov is the mad,
nineteenth-century heir of Erasmus.

The death that killeth death must be the crucifixion. Luther
does not say so. He does not need to. 'This killing death is life
itself.' The death of Christ, which means the transcendence of
death, enshrines the authority through which faith is possible.
This overrides the authority of the law. On earth we still have
to obey that authority, which is no authority. There can be only
one altar, and that altar is the crucifixion. Our own will, which
is no will, being determined, may drive us to obey the law. That
does not help our relationship to the crucifixion, before which
the best we can do is know our sin, that we are guilty before
God, and hope for passive righteousness, which means being open

to grace. The vivid Gospel image of this is the Annunciation, in which the passively meditative Mary is in her whole concentrated being receptive to the news brought by the angel.

The deeper purpose of Luther's *Enslaved Will* is not to debate with Erasmus. It is to create the authority with which to counter humanism, to annihilate it in its infancy. Luther too has to find his place to stand. With his 'faith alone' and 'no free-will' he sets about forming the new Christian and subjecting him to fate. His message is that I shall so bury you under your own guilt, your own pitiable weakness, your total dependency on the Lord God that I shall have you living on your knees in prayer. You are nothing. You are nobody. I shall fling you back into the spiritual dungeon where your thinking faculty has no chance of creating the illusion in you that you have some control over your own destiny. It is down there in the dark, where the light of neither reason nor law shines, where only God can help you, that you may find grace. It is all determined. Your fate is set. Subjected as you are to this overbearing condition I shall give you gravity and depth. Without them you will not be able to stick it. I shall give you the openness to faith, to becoming a rock.

Let us not forget Holbein. Luther and Erasmus fought it out in 1524 and 1525. Erasmus, a friend of Holbein, had written his *Discourse* in Basel, a year after most of the portraits, two years after the *Christ Corpse*. Luther writes his *Galatians* in 1531. Holbein paints *The Ambassadors* in 1533. The open hymn-book on the bottom shelf of the table displays Luther's renderings – of the first verse of his version of the *Veni Creator Spiritus* on the left page, and on the right the beginning of his *Ten Commandments*. At the top left-hand corner of the painting the green curtain is slightly open, partly revealing a crucifix. What can this mean? The ambassadors themselves have no relationship to the crucifix, and the table and its objects are dead to them. Theirs is the darkness where faith does not dwell. Might this not be Holbein's way of saying that he was with Christ and Luther, the Christ of Luther's Reformation, and not with his own ambassadors?

Holbein was not the only one to make something prodigious

from what he took from Luther. The greatest work in the English language, the King James' Authorized Bible, was largely derived from the translation by William Tyndale, a fanatical Lutheran. Tyndale's New Testament appeared in 1526. He had met Luther personally in 1524 in Wittenberg – incidentally where Hamlet had been at university. So in the very years of the Luther– Erasmus controversy on free-will the translation was being made that would exert a formative influence over English Elizabethan culture, by a man whom history would most unjustly neglect. All is attributed to the humanist hero, Shakespeare, whereas he who was first is forgotten.

As Luther was the cheerful, companionable, earthy half of the Reformation, Calvin was its sternly thoughtful and inwardly tormented half. To compare their portraits shows the latter as the Protestant of Protestants, the archetypal Puritan. Calvin's *Institutes of the Christian Religion* in its massive two volumes is clear, tense, systematic and comprehensive. Its first edition was printed in Basel in 1536; five times longer, its final edition was published in Geneva in 1559. Calvin is the father of inwardness. Against Brutus and the ideal of the gentleman he establishes the psychological and metaphysical basis for the self-rigorous, spiritually concentrated yet this-worldly pilgrim.

Calvin takes up the Protestant contradiction and makes it the centre of his theology. It is the irritant in the soul which gives Calvinism its generative energy. Man's fall was ordained but he is guilty. It is as if man's very weakness makes him the more damned, the more removed from God. The fact that his state is wretched makes him the more guilty. In Calvin, the contradiction is capitalized. It is stressed that man's state is preordained; for that reason he is the more responsible. Calvin could already have asserted Kierkegaard's view that faith is rooted in paradox. Paradox and contradiction are now active forces.

There are three principal areas of difference with Luther that give Calvinism its distinctive character. The first is that Calvin heavily underlines the notion of predestination. The question of election becomes central, whether I am among those chosen by

God in advance for salvation. 'No free-will' is shifted back into the divine plane, with God choosing whom he chooses in the beginning. All is set, fixed, immutable – determined. Man is merely acting out predetermined routines. That is no ground for concern. What is important is salvation: am I among the elect? Thus *sola fide* is more focused, slanting in on the lonely individual who scrutinizes his everyday life in a vigilant search for signs that he is chosen.

For Calvin it is as if the argument over free-will has finished. Luther has won. The issue no longer concerns him. Likewise he is less concerned about Reason. He does criticize Plato for the view that it is ignorance that produces sin; he does stress 'through a glass darkly' and that human intelligence is far too miserable to comprehend the ways of God. However, none of this is problematic for him. He is a generation on, as he knows, and he inherits Luther's successes, as he does the responsibility for the continuance of the Reformation. The sites of battle have moved, and the style of fighting has changed. He calls Erasmus an atheist then passes on, leaving the sharp aside to the rationalist complaint about how can it be just when the judge compels the evil-doing, that when a corpse stinks who blames the sun.

Having focused on predestination and election Calvin then tightens the contradiction, and thereby the spiritual pressure on the individual, by giving man a greater eminence than Luther had. There are two dimensions to this. The first is conscience. Man may be fallen, damned, a wretched sinner, but he contains within himself a fragment of divinity. It is inborn. It is the divine intermediary, the inner voice given to him to speak God's instruction. Man's highest duty is to learn to hear the voice of his conscience. Calvin's definition of conscience is the truest in our culture, and it has the vital role in his work that 'faith alone' and 'no free-will' had in Luther's. Conscience is 'that which does not allow man to suppress within himself what he knows'.

In other words true knowledge is given to man, a knowledge that has nothing to do with Reason. It is conscience not intellect which has access to this knowledge. It is not knowledge of the law

– here Calvin takes Paul and Luther further. That is conscience in
a superficial sense, what is taught by parents, teachers and elders.
The Thou Shalt Nots are embedded only in the plane of conscience under social construction. 'The human law does not bind
conscience.' The important conscience is deeper, and is inborn,
planted by God. What it knows is eternal. Calvin also puts it
that the knowledge of God is more of the disposition than the
understanding. Milton was to call this conscience God's representative in man, Jane Austen was to refer to 'the better guide in
ourselves than any other person can be' – Milton and Austen
two of Calvin's greatest heirs.

The second dimension of the greater eminence Calvin bestows
on man is through "vocation". Luther's notion of the calling is
more traditional, being a religious calling. It is Calvin who starts
the Protestant transformation of everyday activity in the world,
the individual's work, into the central form of religious devotion.
It is through Calvinism, and in particular English neo-Calvinism,
as Max Weber pointed out, that work becomes holy. The true
Protestant form of prayer is the individual at his work, head
bowed, concentrating, hour after hour, day after day, year after
year, to produce something of quality, done to the best of his
ability. Vermeer would, a century later, catch this meditative
work beautifully in his studies of Lacemaker, Geographer and
Astronomer. Every man and woman has a predetermined
vocation, a type of systematic activity that it is their task to
discover, and then execute. The contradiction, however, remains:
dutifully and faithfully carrying out one's chosen vocation will
not bring grace. At the most it may be a sign that one is among
the elect. It is more certain that those idlers without a vocation
are not among the chosen.

The reasons given for vocation are that it is a means of learning
God's will, and a discipline that helps tame the passions and
reduce restlessness. A vocation is a "sentry post", a fixed point
– we are back with Archimedes – a man's vocation helps secure
him. Thus Calvinism provides an outlet for the controlled release
of some of the enormous psychic pressure built up by the punitive

theology of faith alone, no free-will, predestination and total responsibility. This theology had eliminated the traditional forms of release – confession, good works, veneration of the saints, and most of the other consolations of Catholic community. The vitality of Calvinism, its extraordinary capacity to seize the psychic-spiritual jugular, was in large part due to the manner in which it built up its intolerable theological contradiction and then exploited it. In the founder's own words:

when a man has been taught that no good thing remains in his power, and that he is hedged in on all sides by the most miserable necessity, in spite of this he should nevertheless be instructed to aspire to a good of which he is empty, to a freedom of which he has been deprived.

The third significant way in which Calvin diverged from Luther was in his religious doubt. Calvinism is pervaded by doubt – am I among the elect, will I be saved, can I be sure? Such qualms are inherent in the theology. Man in his ignorance can never really know. Calvin is himself throughout his *Institutes* nagged by these doubts, and he twists and turns in an attempt to find a reliable answer. On the one hand doubt is Satan's most dangerous temptation, the elect know in their heart of hearts that they are saved, and the damned that they are damned – what after all conscience is for. There is assurance, and those who truly believe cannot fall away. On the other hand you can never really be sure, confidence may be a sign of pride – the chief vice. Faith is never perfect: at best 'through a glass darkly'. 'Let him who stands well, take heed lest he fall, for God can cut you off again.'

Calvin himself must have been plagued by doubt. There is no other explanation for this endless to-ing and fro-ing. There is severe anxiety here. There can never be full assurance. You can never relax – if you are relaxed, beware, for you are at your most vulnerable. Even Calvin's discussion of the Church centres on doubt, his principal distinction being between the visible and invisible churches. The former is those who attend, who can be seen and counted, the earthly Church. The latter is the only one that matters, the Church of the elect, and only God knows who belongs to it.

The everpresent brooding atmosphere of doubt is darkened further by what Calvin calls "right fear". The right relationship to God is one of fear. It is fear of provoking divine wrath, having seen all around the disasters that strike the ungodly. Believers fear offending God; unbelievers fear punishment. There is also fear in the recognition of the paltry humility of man, his total dependence on God. 'I will worship in fear', quotes Calvin. Faith and "fear and trembling" go hand in hand. It is another matter when fear is too strong and disheartens conscience. False fear is anxiety, and it undermines faith.

In short the man is blessed who is always afraid in his own heart. What an extraordinary basis for religion! The Old Testament certainly has its fill of 'Fear the Lord', but that is one part of a much larger picture. In Calvinism it is total. All is fear. All is trembling. All is doubt. The one antidote to the intolerable, constant psychic anguish that results is work, work with such intensity and rigour and wholehearted concentration that it is as if it were the work of the Lord. It is not. There is no comfort there either.

The leading sign of the success of Calvinism was the Protestant work ethic, and how rapidly it took hold in the West. It is a mark of how receptive were Northern European middle-class dispositions to the Protestant contradiction. Calvin touched the dispositional core with his perplexing cycle of faith alone, no free-will, predestination, yet total human guilt and responsibility, and therefore the necessity of vocation. Reason cannot understand why anyone should believe this, but they did, and in doing so changed the direction of the West. Furthermore, Calvin's version of the darkness of faith – doubt – articulated a real human experience, that the religious path is obscure and overgrown, its end invisible.

Calvin had extended Luther's assault on the Renaissance – 'the darkness of faith where neither law nor reason shines'. Luther had staked out the environment. Calvin then turned more insistently to the man in the environment, to the inner. He preached severity over self, a colossal self-discipline. There is the littleness of man and the harsh magnificence of God, against the humanist projection of the potential grandeur of man. But that little power-less man of Calvin has a formidable inner strength, once he comes to hear the still small voice of his conscience. He asserts this strength through his vocation. The new hero is not the gentleman, Brutus, but the Puritan warrior, Cromwell – remorseless, ungentle, unlikeable, mercilessly severe. Calvinism could only establish itself through the Cromwells, and all those Puritan fathers, the patriarchs who wielded the rod over their children, who demanded unwavering obedience. It was harsh, but neces-sary. Without it we could already be back in the squalor of the Middle Ages. It is correct that in the nineteenth-century twilight the two most insightful late heirs of Protestantism, Kierkegaard and Nietzsche, should both have singled out "comfort" as the decadent heart of their time, the last god that is no god. Luther and Calvin had taught darkness and suffering against the reason-able and the comfortable.

The Puritan in politics failed. The messianic Protestantism of Cromwell was unsuited to running the State. However, in the ordinary everyday life of society, of men and women at work and forming their families, its influence was profound, way beyond what any of its pioneers could have imagined. There is no better summary of the reason for this than Milton's tribute to Cromwell, which might equally apply to any of the descendants who have managed to find their vocations:

. . . he was a soldier well-versed in self-knowledge and whatever enemy lay within—vain hopes, fears, desires—he had either previously de-stroyed or long since reduced to subjection. A commander first over himself, the conqueror of himself, it was over himself he had learnt most to triumph. Hence he went to encounter the external enemy as a veteran accomplished in all military duties.

Milton portrays a man who has found his place to stand, on the Puritan rock.

From Machiavelli to Shakespeare, the Renaissance had taken

over the plausible Roman notions of Virtue and Fortune. What man has no control over is his fortune, which he is given, good and bad. This is fate, and it is female. Brutus suffered from some bad fortune. At the same time a man can make something of his fortune, influence it, through his own power or will – his "virtue". Luther and Calvin tore these notions apart and refashioned them. Fortune becomes divine will, and as predestination it is total. Virtue becomes conscience, which has no influence over fate, as it cannot will. But it is responsible and has the channel of vocation through which to act. Fate and faith are fused together in the anti-humanist crucible. The fate that counts is whether a man is chosen; all else is smoke. What comes out of the crucible is not the virtuous man, the gentleman, but the Puritan.

After the Renaissance, as the dynamic centre of European culture shifted to the North, it became clear that Calvin had won, and Brutus lost. The reason for this was guilt. There appeared in Northern Europe from the period of the late Middle Ages a rapid development within the dispositions of individuals from expanding strata of the societies of new levels of inner control – of what later came to be called "repression". Renaissance culture had no affinity with the new type of self-disciplined, guilt-hounded individual. It had nothing to say to him, just as, for even more obvious reasons, the imagery of medieval Catholicism had become culturally obsolete. It was precisely here, at the dispositional turning point of the modern West, that Luther, and even more, Calvin, took the pulse of the time. It was Northerners, especially Germans, Dutch, Scots and English, who, experiencing the "fear and trembling" erupting without reason from within, took to the Reformation because it gave form and therefore sense to what they were feeling. The Protestant contradiction, as irrational as it was, gave expression to some fundamental psychic knot. It is not my task here to follow the story of how this happened. Let it suffice that the decisive historical force behind the Reformation was the rise of guilt.

Calvinism may have won in the short term, but it would not endure. Guilt and doubt were an explosive combination that

would in the end kill God far more effectively than the rational
gentleman ever could. Protestantism's problem was aggravated
by the demise of community. The Puritan's constitutional inability to relax in the world combined with his reliance on his
own conscience to undermine the role of both priest and church.
Protestantism is in essence, under Calvin's huge shadow, a conglomerate of one-man sects loosely held together by a common
metaphysics. Its achievement was to create another powerful
individualism with which to counter the new humanist individualism. The cost was the decline of community. Once there is faith
alone and Calvin's conscience, the vital unifying role of family,
village and town has been eclipsed. The Reformation threw out
the incense and holy water, the chanting, the bleeding madonnas
and most of the sacraments. It burnt the relics and smashed the
statues; it banned the dancing. It found, however, that the
Church it occupied had cold floors and bare walls. The communal
warmth had gone.

Luther and Calvin against humanism was in its first principles
a replay of the cultural battle at the down-turn of the high period
in classical Greece. In the Greek case the sequence had been in
reverse. The humanist position, championing will and reason,
had been staked out by Socrates, and later Aristotle, against the
quite different metaphysics of Homer, Aeschylus and Sophocles.
Socrates too was a man of honour, deciding to die for his beliefs
rather than escape into exile. Against Will and Reason, the
Reformation restored the earlier Greek view of the world, the
tragic view. It restored the metaphysics of Greek tragedy.

For the early Greeks everything was predetermined, by the
gods. There was no free-will. Oedipus is the clearest case, a
Calvinist hero, a good man cursed to break the law, although he
does his best not to do so, breaking it because he does not understand what he is doing, breaking it simply because it is fated.
Oedipus is innocent before the human law – what he did was
unwitting – but he is damned by the only law that matters, the
eternal one that abides in the darkness. Oedipus was the man of
knowledge who could shine the light of reason where other men

could not see. That knowledge was useless, worse than useless for it gave him a false sense of power, of 'I am'. In Aeschylus' great work, the *Agamemnon*, however hard reason tries to plumb the meaning of things, it fails, remaining perplexed by the course of events, and especially by the logic of why humans must suffer so. All that is left is to pray and to wonder, and if you cannot help it, to curse. In *The Iliad* too, the greatest tragedy of them all, predetermined fate rules, and all that remains for men is to play their allotted parts, getting carried away by their all-too-human passions, and then expiation, expiation, expiation, before the necessary death. By the last chapter of Homer's masterpiece we are very close to the death of death, which is life, very close to the Fourth Gospel and to Luther. The "darkness of faith" means the return to Greek tragedy. When Luther calls Aristotle the "stinking philosopher" he does so with a precise historical sense.

The Reformation was founded on first principles. Both Luther and Calvin had the philosophic virtue of going to the central issue and stating it simply, often overstating it to ram the point home. By contrast the strength of Renaissance culture was in its literature and art; its philosophers were of the second rank. We shall return in the next chapter to Donatello when we consider the reply from the South, the Counter-Reformation. His Gattamelata was only an opening gambit. Shakespeare, as a Northern humanist, was profoundly divided, arriving at Death, but unable to follow Luther in his revival of Greek metaphysics. Shakespeare's own answer to 'Alas, poor Yorick' was the escapist fantasy of *The Tempest*, a delightful pastime but not very helpful with the central issue. The darkness of faith was not for him. Holbein, another profoundly divided Northern humanist, also arrived at Death, and stopped with his ambassadors, perhaps sensing that the only answer was Luther's, but unable himself to do more than gesture, to a half-concealed crucifix and the open text.

PART II
Development

5

THE BATTLE OF THE
ARTISTS: 1630–1670

Our scene is now set, with the two great opposing forces of
Renaissance and Reformation in place. Humanism's own self-
doubt is also there. We can now move into the middle acts of the
story. Between 1600 and the terminal decline in the nineteenth
century humanism passed through an unfolding drama with a
number of major stages. There was the attempt to integrate
Renaissance and Reformation by forming a composite character
ideal of gentleman and Puritan. This bourgeois fusion, with its
own theory of family, education and politics, and its own ultimate
metaphysics, was to prove the most stable and enduring of the
humanist offspring. We shall examine it in the next chapter. As
the bourgeois fusion itself began to disintegrate there was one
last attempt to revive humanism, by two polarized schools, one
the Enlightenment, which reverted to a narrow hard-core humanism stipulated on a deified Reason, the other and opposed,
Romanticism, which staked its individualism on trying to invest
passion with sacred status. We shall consider Reason and
Romance in Chapter 7.

The aftermath of the head-on clash between Luther, Calvin
and humanism was high cultural volatility. Once the dust had
settled notable movements in three quite different directions
became visible. First, there was a momentous act of cultural
subversion, which because it had digested the Protestant–
humanist debate was far more broad-ranging in its nihilism than
Holbein's *Ambassadors*. It set the scene for what was to come as
a flood two hundred years later. Second, there was the first crisis
of Protestantism, in which tensions from within began to erode
the fortitude necessary to maintain a theology centred on contradiction. Third, there was the Counter-Reformation, the move to

take up the best in Luther and Calvin and refashion it in a Catholic manner.

Strangely enough it was one generation of painters, in a short forty-year period in the middle of the seventeenth century, that got closest to the heart of these new directions. Three very different men from three different cultures, Velázquez, Rembrandt and Poussin, from their distant locations in Madrid, Amsterdam and Rome, gave the right form to the immediate post-Reformation trials of humanism. Indeed, in the history of Western art there is only one other generation – that of Donatello and van der Weyden – that both coincides with one of the seminal crises in belief and gives that crisis its most profound expression. Moreover, in considering the period 1630–70 there are other major figures in art, notably de la Tour and Vermeer, both of whom appear in minor roles in our story, de la Tour as an independent contributor to Poussin's French Counter-Reformation, and Vermeer in the next chapter on the bourgeois fusion.

Las Meninas

Still, today, *Las Meninas* is regarded as the most important work of art in Spain. It dominates the Prado, with a room to itself in the heart of the collection. The title is the Portuguese for Maids of Honour, and was first used in the Museum's 1843 catalogue. One of the traditional titles had been *The Family of Philip IV*. Velázquez painted it in 1656. It is a humanist masterpiece. It is also the most subversive work of art in Europe.

There are five figures and a dog in the foreground of the painting. The central one is the Infanta Margarita, the five-year-old princess. On either side of her are Maids of Honour. To the right are two court dwarfs, the second with his left foot resting on the sitting mastiff's back. In the middle ground to the right are a female servant and a butler. To the left is Velázquez himself standing at a huge canvas (we see its back), holding palette and brush. All these figures are in a hall-like room with a high ceiling,

Diego Velázquez, *Las Meninas*, Prado, Madrid

walls covered with paintings, and an open door in the back wall. Through that door we see, on stairs leading into the room, the Queen's chamberlain. Next to the open door is a mirror reflecting the figures of the King and Queen.

Velázquez is painting the King and Queen – that is the canvas within the canvas. They are not, however, posing for him. The Infanta's expression shows a sudden alertness, looking straight out of the painting. She has just seen her mother and father, who must have only now entered the room. The standing maid, Isabel de Velasco, in the middle of her curtsy, is half turned towards the front, as if the mark of deference to her mistress, the Infanta, is now reoriented towards her ultimate superiors.

The great power of *Las Meninas* is founded on the covert but pervasive authority of King Philip IV, which structures the whole work. His presence is indirect, seen in the mirror, and through his command over the alerted figures in the frame. The Infanta in her splendid robes, bathed in light, is an image of delicate innocent obedience to the authority that has just entered. At the same time she herself has a queenly poise. The kneeling maid, side-on, serves the princess, gazing at her with complete dedication, bowed forward. In her reverent devotion she illustrates the inexorable royal hierarchy. So too does the curtsying maid. Her reason for being is to show proper obedience. Her service is to the royal chain of authority. The dog also, the princess's protector and the most forward figure in the canvas, has head bowed and eyes closed. He is at ease, for all is in order. The mastiff is himself a leonine symbol of authority. Finally, the female dwarf is at attention, acknowledging her master. The front five figures and the dog form a semi-circle welcoming the King and Queen. They are the inner circle, led by the Infanta, of the true court.

The large room with its dark walls and high tenebrous ceiling is oriented forwards. Its gloomy spaces are suggestive of a closed world bounded by a strict order. The light shines where it should. The darkness is finite, under control. It is resonant with the authority of the King. The mirror on the back wall, framed in black, glistens with a blue aura, its figures blurred as if seen through a glass darkly. It is the sacred icon, commanding the room, its inhabitants, and the viewer.

The authority of the King is compromised by two features of the painting. The open door at the rear breaks the closed chamber of royal command. There is a clear light through the door and it is brighter than the mirror next to it. Moreover, the chamberlain is outside the door, half down the stairs, half up them, casual and independent. It is unclear whether he is coming or going, or merely observing. Whatever, he is a free agent outside the chamber of authority, his nonchalant mien showing no sign of deference. He has free-will. Above all, the door is open. There is a way out. The authority is circumscribed.

The second compromising feature is the painter himself. At a first view it fits that he is in the painting, a member of the second circle of the court. He is at work. That, however, is as far as it goes. His stance shows him recoiling slightly. This might be in response to the King. It is not. It is pride and self-assertion. He looks straight at the monarch, his head cocked to one side and slightly backwards, aloof, the opposite of a bow. There is a sinister aspect to the closed thick sensual lips. This is a relaxed defiance, in marked contrast to the sensitive recognition by the Infanta. The painter's right hand holds the brush, the left the palette, with a similar ease – indeed the tools of his trade are suggestive of sword and shield, in keeping with the large red cross on his jet-black doublet. Velázquez is the modern Crusader. The artist stands to one side, his canvas larger than the actual canvas; he is outside the hierarchy. His head is higher than that of anyone else in the painting.

Here is the first direct representation in Western culture of the artist as the great man, the free individual. It is a development of Pico's 'I can become what I will.' The humanist crusader here has one further devastating trick, to complement his aggrandisement of himself at the expense of the King. The King and Queen stand in the same spot as the viewer. The Infanta and her circle look straight at you and I; so does the painter. You and I have equal status to the King and Queen of Spain. Here is the ultimate disrespect, and it is a simple and logical extension of the humanist credo, 'I am.' Velázquez is a democrat. We are all equal. The authority that orders *Las Meninas* doubles as the authority of each individual. Every passing tourist with his thirty second gawk at the great work is equal to Philip IV. No wonder the work is so popular, making everyman the royal source of order and meaning in the world. The first to catch your eye, with her intense quizzical stare, straight at you, respectful and welcoming, is the Infanta. The last is Velázquez himself, perusing you from head to foot, inviting you into his magic circle. Now you are an intimate part of the painting. But you do not know in whose shoes you stand.

None of this was necessary. Velázquez could have still kept the King and Queen out of the frame, standing them to one side, skewing the room to face them, and then reflecting them in the mirror. Poussin would have done it that way, but then he would not have dared to include himself in the painting. He had no humanist ambitions for personal grandeur.

That mockery was the motive of *Las Meninas* was clear to Spain's other great painter, Goya. In 1800 he reworked it as *The Family of Charles IV*. Here the entire family including the King and Queen are in the light in the foreground. Following Velázquez, the painter and his huge easel are on the left, receded into the shadows behind the group. Superficially this is a standard royal portrait. However, the family is staged as an assembly of stiff cardboard figures. The painter is painting them from behind, seeing behind the mannered front their true empty selves. He shows them up mercilessly. The difference from *Las Meninas* is that by 1800 the King has no authority at all, and the triumphant painter is restricted to a grim psychological analysis of failed monarchy.

Las Meninas is on the cultural brink. Here is the secret to its power. The old order retains its immense authority and this is shown magnificently, from the delicate responsiveness of the pretty, innocent girl princess to the reverence of her two maids, the dwarf at attention, the slumbering solidity of the mastiff, to the glistening mirror image of their majesties. The King rules.

The artist, although by himself on the left, still serves. In fact Philip IV valued the painting highly – legend has it that the King himself painted the red cross on Velázquez' doublet, to represent the Order of Santiago, which he bestowed on the painter in 1659. Indeed as a private portrait, viewed only by the King and Queen themselves, *Las Meninas* is possible. The royal presence, doubling in the mirror, keeps the chamberlain and artist in check. However, once a courtier stands in front of it, not to mention a commoner, the sedition begins. There are two immensely powerful figures confronting each other. The man of the future, the scornful crusading artist, has the measure of his King. The King and Queen are half-way to becoming models, at the mercy of the image the creative individual will make of them.

Culture must serve right authority, and unequivocally. The moment it wavers, as here, it becomes subversive. Velázquez had the genius to be honest and at the same time deceive his monarch, who admired the work – mind, the painting is of such technical mastery it is easy to be carried away. Once the 'I am' is on stage there is no God. Without God there is also no King. Velázquez has taken this next inevitable humanist step. Each 'I am' becomes God and King in one. Each individual becomes dependent on his own charisma – here Velázquez himself decked in his glorious crusader tunic is the exemplar. He makes his universe as he will. He is the most powerful man in the world. He is, as Nietzsche will call him, a value-creator. The Reformation freed man from the law, now High humanism frees him from faith, leaving nothing but the **I** that, believing in itself, creates its own law.

I, the viewer, take in the painting not only from the front. I am also represented by the chamberlain, the observer from the rear, who drops in to see what is happening. The actual chamberlain's name was Velázquez, perhaps a relative, certainly a fortunate link between the two subversive figures. The chamberlain has the free choice of joining or leaving. But does he? Once there is that free choice – call it free-will – then there is no choice, for once one lounges on the back stairs one is outside, and cannot get back in, one is stranded in a cultural no-man's land. The magic circle of faith is broken, and free-will cannot restore it. The viewer has become a tourist.

Without God there is no above and beyond. The only beyond in *Las Meninas* is through the open door. All that is there, however, is a profane staircase, going nowhere, and the viewer, you and I. The deception is that next to the door is the mirror, leading forward out of the painting. It should be the beyond, and it is at a first viewing. It loses that power once the subversive forces exert their sway.

Today, *Las Meninas* is revered as one of the marvels of the Western world. And it is. It has its own room, dark like a crypt focused on its priceless relic. It is lit by a single spotlight from the right side, much to the disgust of art historians and the man who directed its modern restoration, on the grounds that much of the subtlety of the paintwork and its multiple planes is lost. This may be, but the lighting suits the moral tone of the work. It is the lighting of the bordello, seductively exaggerating the subtle features of this degenerate beauty.

Finally, Velázquez introduces a new element that will come to plague humanism as it develops – rancour. *Las Meninas* is so grand that the rancour against royal authority is highly diffused, the needling away at the King heavily concealed. The more common face of rancour appears in the painter's many studies of dwarfs, buffoons and cripples. They are painted with sympathy, suggestive of a genuinely compassionate egalitarianism. But there is a perversity too, a fascination with the deformed as such. That Velázquez is not sound is most clear in his portrait of revellers, who have glistening sinister eyes. But his self-portrait in *Las Meninas* is enough to warn us. Shakespeare, who was sound, felt driven to compromise his own humanist hero, Brutus, as did Holbein his ambassadors. Velázquez is of the new breed. They do not blush. He is the man of the future, the pioneer of the rancorous glorification of self.

Rembrandt and the First Crisis of Protestantism

Rembrandt was not rancorous. His problem was rather that of the Protestant who had great difficulty carrying the burden of his tribe, the honest Puritan who following his vocation saw too much, and was paralysed. This is a long story, one of a tireless life-long wrestling with the angel, one of the Reformation's illustrious chapters. In the ways that matter, however, Rembrandt was a failure. Let us examine why. The message is that humanism's one viable alternative, the place that Luther and Calvin had found to stand, had as its own greatest threat not the external enemy, but its own internal ordeal.

The key work is *The Sacrifice of Isaac*. The first version, painted in 1635, is in the Hermitage. The second version, from a year later, now in Munich, is the more complete vision. Rembrandt chooses the climax of the story. Abraham is under instruction from God to prove his faith by sacrificing his only legitimate son, Isaac. Abraham has faith – Kierkegaard will call him the father of faith because of this same trial – so he agrees to journey with his son to Mt. Moriah, without telling his wife Sarah his reason. They travel for three days with an ass and two servants. Isaac is himself a miracle given to Abraham and Sarah in old age. We can assume that mother and father dote on their only child – he is their future. Now Abraham is asked to kill him.

Rembrandt rightly sees that this story is the most demanding test of 'faith alone'. He paints the moment of the sacrifice. Isaac lies on the wood for the fire, naked apart from a loincloth, his arms bound behind his back. Abraham has his huge left hand clamped down brutally over the boy's face, forcing his head back. He kneels in the shadows over what in a few seconds will be his son's corpse. His right hand holds the dagger. It is poised to swing down and cut the boy's throat. The angel has just hurtled down from the sky – not like the Genesis version in which he merely calls out from heaven. Rembrandt has him violently seizing Abraham's right wrist, the knife falling from the old man's grasp. The angel's left hand is raised. It is about to strike Abra-

Rembrandt, *The Sacrifice of Isaac*, Altepinakothek, Munich

ham. His look, too, is angry. Beyond the bare bones of the story this version has little to do with the Old Testament. It is all to do with the Reformation.

Rembrandt's concern here is not over faith itself. His Abraham has unquestioned faith: he does not hesitate to obey God's command. Calvin's doubt is not the issue. The painting's focus is rather on the demands faith puts upon a man. It is Luther's 'the darkness of faith where neither law nor reason shine' that is under examination. It is the incompatibility of faith and law that troubles Rembrandt. Why is the angel enraged? It is a most unusual angel, no ethereal delicacy but tough and powerful, a harsh Protestant divinity. Why is he about to strike the father of faith? Because he is furious with him. Rembrandt's Abraham is a failure. The old man's eyes are mad. He has had so to steel himself to carry out this terrible act that he has become a machine, hostile even to the angel's interruption of its motion. In the 1636 version Abraham's mouth is open, agog, not just at the violent angel, but at the horror of it all. He has seen his own Medusa. The act demanded of Abraham has driven him mad.

This is all very human. God has required Abraham to ruin his life. The boy is the father's pride and joy. He has to kill him. How will he live on, day after day, night after night, haunted by one nightmare image, of his own right hand slitting his son's throat. How will he live on with Sarah, who will not understand – how could anybody? She will look at him with uncomprehending hatred whenever he enters the room. Abraham is not only asked to destroy his happiness but to break almost every important law. Thou shalt not kill. Thou shalt protect the innocent, especially your own children – the trusting Isaac calls out 'Papa, what are you doing?' Abraham further is breaking his duty as head of family and tribe to continue the blood line. God has not set Abraham any old test, he demands what is most difficult, what may be humanly impossible. He demands that his chosen representative on earth break the human law and destroy his own happiness, in effect ruin his life. That is what faith alone requires.

The faith holds, but the human character does not. Abraham loses his mind, which means the death of the soul.

The angel is very angry. Man has failed his divine mission. He is not up to it. You cannot separate faith and law and expect the human animal to survive. Faith is too demanding. Man must obey the law in order to keep his sanity. It is false that the death of death is life, it is insanity. There is not just anger in the 1636 angel's face. There is also tenderness and grief. He is sorry for Abraham. Here is the sorrowful recognition that the fragment of divinity in man is only a fragment: he is not godlike, at best he glimpses. Not too much should be asked, in fact not very much at all. Angels are powerful; men are weak.

There are parallels with Brutus. Rembrandt reworks Shakespeare's theme, in relation to faith rather than honour. Just as Shakespeare had a rigidity of character that was almost demented in the archetypal man of honour, so Rembrandt imagines the same in the man of faith. However, Brutus recovers whereas Abraham does not – he is merely a broken old man. Any hope is concentrated in the lithe young body of Isaac.

There are two possible conclusions. Either Protestantism is impossible: it asks too much of lowly man. Luther's darkness of faith is too intimidating. Even the greatest of men, the father of faith, could not bear up. The alternative conclusion is that Rembrandt himself cracked. Born into the Protestant fold, in his genius seeing more clearly than anyone else between Calvin and Kierkegaard what was required, he could not carry it. I want to examine this second possibility. It is of great moment for our story.

Rembrandt was keen on powerful angels. They reappear again and again. The finest of all dominates his version of the *Resurrection*, also in Munich, painted a few years after the second *Isaac*. It is a dark work, all in deep shadow except the brilliant burst of light in the centre, which is a huge angel, wings open with a vast eagle span. It is wrenching the lid off the coffin, sending the soldiers guarding it flying. The human world is a murky tumble of confusion and fear, weapons and armour useless against the messenger of the Lord. It is a richly Protestant rendition of faith alone, no free-will, guilt, responsibility, and above all right fear. Yet Rembrandt destroys the grave Calvinist mood by including a comic Christ on the right, also in light, sitting up dazed in the open coffin, a sort of night-cap on his head, if anything wondering why he has been disturbed. So the great Dutch painter in again achieving a compelling image of sacred force, close to the Protestant heart, undercut it, leaving the human world without direction. Faith is too demanding; the Resurrection is a joke. Somewhere Rembrandt did not believe, he could not take it all quite seriously, he was unconsciously driven to wreck his greatest potential achievements, both very close to a death of death. The Protestant nerve was failing. Rembrandt ruined both paintings.

Recognizing that his attempt at assault has failed, Rembrandt tries to turn retreat into a sort of compromise victory. There is a favourite solution that recurs from his early to his late work. That is soulful resignation. The individual withdraws into introspection, giving up the pilgrim ideal as super-human. Rembrandt settles down with his characteristic portrait of the individual soul gazing out helplessly from under the burden of its failure, its inability to make anything of the world. The more dynamic side of this is the quixotic Puritan, images like the *Polish Rider* (1655) in which the external world is a detached stage, with all its pomp, costumes, finery, swords and sturdy horses as a charade. Only the inner is real. Here is Calvinist inwardness in visual form. The Gattamelata is rejected as worldly show, as sham. The outcome, however, is passive, as exemplified in the numerous self-portraits, the consummation of the Rembrandt solution. The artist throughout his adult life returns endlessly to look into his own eyes for signs of the fragment of divinity, for signs of grace. Again this is vintage Calvinism, the only question being, Am I saved?, the only journey that of self-discovery, for signs of election in one's own soul, communicated by conscience. No one before or after Rembrandt has asked the question so intently of his own face.

Yet all the self-portraits are a further sign of failure. They give away a disconnected inwardness. Calvin knew that vocation is essential: action in the world is the only way for man. Conscience needs the **I** to act if it is to set up its bearings. It is in what a man does that signs may be seen. There is both an impudence and a hopelessness in an obsession with self. On the one hand Rembrandt overrates his own importance; on the other he finds the world contracted to no more than himself. Also, there is something adolescent about a fixation on one's own mirror image. Protestantism in decline becomes detached from the world and bogged down in a lonely subjectivity.

Certainly the soul stays vividly alive in Rembrandt's world. It is only in his Abraham that we see the dead eyes of the ambassadors, and for a different reason. But it is a soul trapped in the body, bewildered and melancholy, unable to make anything out of its earthly mission. His old philosopher meditating, in the Louvre, has no way out. The window is closed, he has lost contact with the outside light; the door down into the cellar is locked; and the lovely spiral staircase upwards is not for him. The only life is in the fire tended by his simple wife, and she is apart, also alone by herself.

Rembrandt left a vast body of work. It was in his late years that we see a number of attempted ways out of the metaphysical paralysis into which he had found himself cast. In 1666, at the age of sixty, with only three years to live, he paints his *Jewish Bride*. It is a tender idealization of marriage. The inwardness of both husband and wife has an external focus, the other person. It is not disconnected inwardness. The painting presents a poignant image of companionship, in which each is devoted to the other, trusts and is trusted, and shares an intimacy with the whole fidelity of their being. It is marriage as a type of vocation, with the Puritan inwardness of each (there is no evidence that they were Jewish) giving a peculiar intensity to the union. It is the visual representation of the greater emphasis both Dutch and English Protestants placed on the conjugal bond.

This is one way out for Rembrandt, but the solution is only partial. The problem is not with choosing the institution of marriage as the earthly domain for the experience of reverence – such was central to the bourgeois achievement. It is rather that the bridal couple, with their companionate friendship, can be no more than one element in either the social or the metaphysical hierarchy. They are not the whole world. To ask too much of them will crush them, in the end.

A second resolution attempted by Rembrandt is to portray a Christianity of compassion and forgiveness. Twenty years after *The Sacrifice of Isaac* he reworked the same theme in an etching. This time Abraham is distraught, and very old, but he is not mad. A compliant Isaac kneels, bending over his father's knee – there is no tension in his body, which this time is clothed. The greatest difference is in the angel, who is close up behind Abraham in the middle of the etching. His huge wings are open, spanning the work. The angel is tender, virtually embracing the old man, whispering to him over his right shoulder, his own right hand merging with Abraham's, covering the boy's eyes. This angel does not command or judge. It has come to succour and forgive. Its huge wings are protective, of humiliated man. It expects little. Rembrandt was never tempted by humanism. There is not a hint of the value-creating individual in his work. His focus is not the active man deciding events but the helpless soul hurt by a harsh fate. His wholeheartedly Protestant interest is in fallen man, in his impotence and his guilt. It is significant that the great theorist of the Renaissance, Jacob Burckhardt, should have dismissed Rembrandt's forms as ugly. In the later work the need of fallen man for a blessing becomes more pronounced, leading to the second attempted solution. The problem is whether there is left any room for action, for movement – that is, outside the companionate marriage. The 1655 etching is titled *Abraham's Sacrifice*. The reversed title is suggestive of the new metaphysics. Abraham has given up his heroic mission as the father of faith, in abject failure. As failure he is worthy of compassion. It is the worthless, incompetent human individual, Abraham, who is sacrificed, in order to be embraced by the angel. Isaac is incidental. But what comes after the weeping? This is another old and broken man. When there is only the weeping can man survive it, for what else is there? Is this right fear or false fear? Rembrandt's penitential imagery is problematic because it does not follow a day in the field of battle: it is not Achilles with gore on his hands carrying out acts of penance for the outrageous impiety of his murdering without limit. There is no normal story here of temptation, transgression, remorse and punishment. There is just inwardness and more inwardness: the Protestant pearl may be cursed.

Rembrandt's third and last way is to be predicted, given the logic of the other two. It is tragedy. The date is around 1665, and the work, *David and Uriah*, hangs now in the Hermitage. The story is from II Samuel 11 and 12. King David sees Bathsheba bathing and is taken by her beauty. He orders her to his bed. Her husband, Uriah, is away fighting for him. Bathsheba becomes pregnant, Uriah returns but refuses to sleep in his own house. David sends him back to war, with a letter to the general commanding him to put Uriah in the front line of the hottest battle, and let the other soldiers withdraw so he is killed. This occurs. The Lord God is angry and sends Nathan the Prophet to accuse David through a parable. Rembrandt paints the moment of David ordering Uriah back to the fighting. Uriah is the central figure, dressed in a deep crimson robe. Under a bejewelled turban his head is bowed, his eyes lowered. His right hand is across his breast, a gesture of submissive resignation to the heart-stopping shock. His left hand is clasped in the sash which binds his robe, not a gesture of strength or command, but of tension, of bracing himself for disaster. He knows. The King has taken his beautiful wife, and now he sends him to his death. He must obey the King. The King is all-powerful and his lord. Such is his fate. It is terrible. All he can do is bow to it. Rembrandt paints tragic recognition.

Behind Uriah, on the right, is King David, golden crown sitting on top of his own bejewelled turban. He wears a heavy gold chain around his neck. His beard is luxuriant, his lips are thick and red. His head is turned away from Uriah. He too is meditative, seeing the awfulness of what he does. He retains, however, the complacency of the king. He will not change his mind. Pleasure wins out over law. The die is cast. To the left, lower down and further to the rear than David, is an old man. He, presumably, is Nathan, yet to arrive on the scene. His face is sadly inward-looking. When the time comes he will speak his judgment.

Rembrandt has returned to a more traditional mode, a story of the strongest human passions, power and lust, combining to drive a man to excess. It is a return to universals, of the law checking temptation, the punishment of transgression. The central theme however is Uriah's tragic fate, and the mood is Protestant, of fate being predestined. David is merely acting out what is in his character, more the agent of what is given than the free, wilful King. Uriah suffers the consequences, without curse or protest – that is how things are. The change from other Rembrandt works is that his inwardness is focused, not on an intangible resignation, but on his own quite explicit fate. He has been honourable, a Brutus, serving his King faithfully, risking his life. In return his wife, who loves him and whom he loves, is stolen, and he, the victim, is sent to his death because his innocence shows up the King's shame, and his presence stands in the way of the King's lust. Fidelity is repaid with betrayal. The companion work is the *Jewish Bride*, which expounds trust as the highest human value. *David and Uriah* accepts that prescription then moves on to a higher plane, more explicitly Protestant: its focus is conscience dwelling on fate, the attempt to move through a state of inner dejection, of tragic recognition, into an openness to grace. Rembrandt has followed his mentors Luther and Calvin back to the ancient Greeks. This work is almost Homeric.

There is a problem too with *David and Uriah*. Tragic works either have it or not, that ineffable sacred force which stops the viewer in his tracks, scarring the imagination for life. This work does not quite survive the savage test; so very few do. Rembrandt's genius, in the end, is one of almost, and therefore of failure. But what a failure!

There is one masterpiece. It is perhaps the last work Rembrandt painted, the gigantic *Return of the Prodigal Son* in the

Hermitage. Rembrandt retreats from tragedy back to the main thread in his life's work, redemption through failure and suffering, in soulful resignation. The son has been broken by life. He had left his father's house young, naive, optimistic and rich, eager for the world. He has returned a vagabond, in rags, filthy, alone, his head shaven, the soles of his sandals worn away. Now he kneels abjectly nestling into his father. That father is old and weary. He too has had enough of life, the final burden the grief at the loss of the son who has now returned. He welcomes him home, in forgiveness and joy. His huge right hand is on the middle of his son's back, drawing him closer in embrace. The left hand is on the son's right shoulder, steadying, forgiving, and blessing. These hands are the centre of the work. The old man looks down, weeping dry tears of gratitude, almost collapsing with happiness. This is reconciliation.

The son has come home, and is redeemed by his father's forgiveness. However, he is not the subject of the work, the father is. Here is the last act in his life. Now he can die. Rembrandt has managed to project a sacred intensity into this old man that is lacking in his other work. The father, broken with life and with grief, is given a last illumination. He is so frail it is almost as if the shock of joyful solace will kill him. This is not tragic suffering, not the world of Homer or Aeschylus, of King Lear, or even of Uriah. There is neither the valour nor the fortitude. There is no heroism, no grandeur. This is not the father of faith, nor the noblest Roman of them all. Here is misery, failure and humiliation. It is through the annihilation of all worldly hope, and with it the **I**, that a muted type of redemption becomes possible. We are back to the early Christianity of the meek and humble, the human condition accepted with a passive resignation rather than the staunch fighting resolve of a Luther or Calvin.

The Prodigal Son is young, but now he has crawled home in defeat he has nowhere else to go. His life is over. On the crumbling rock the old man is showered with divine pity. It is not clear that this is a state of grace. It is not clear that Luther's monster has been killed.

None of this bodes well for Protestantism. One of its greatest sons, with a prodigious vocation and talent for painting, dedicates his life to the cause. He has brilliant theoretical instincts, he sees clearly, he is sane, and he has an indomitable will. A life-time of struggling with 'the monster without whose killing man cannot live' produced more than six hundred paintings and two thousand drawings and etchings. He never gave up. In his last years he tried his most interesting new tactics for killing the monster. On the way he had found that the faith which transcends both happiness and the law, annihilating them, cannot be lived. He retreated into himself, into a soulful inwardness disconnected from the world. He tried to break out. There is the sacred intimacy of husband and wife, there is the compassionate Christ blessing the broken man, but neither are enough. There is the tragic suffering of Uriah, but it is just not intense enough to forge a place to stand – not enough steeped in what Henry James was to call "sacred rage". Finally there is the Prodigal Son. Rembrandt cannot manage a death of death. If a man of his instinct and talent cannot, then who can? Moreover, Luther and Calvin were abstract men, theologians. Rembrandt stuck to depicting life here and now, in visual images that cannot lie, where fantasy is checked in its comforting distortions. Here was a major empirical test of Reformation doctrine, and it failed to kill the monster. In Rembrandt, Protestantism suffered its first great crisis.

Poussin and the Counter-Reformation

There was another way. It makes sense that the serious intellectual reaction against the Reformation, in defence of Catholicism, should not have come from the south of Europe but from the middle, from France. I exclude the reactionary dogmatism of the Inquisitorial Spanish Counter-Reformation, which offered no way forward. Luther and Calvin are not rejected outright; instead what is best in their work is extracted, and resown in Catholic earth. Jansenism, Pascal and Racine are examples. However, it is in the life-work of the painter, Nicolas Poussin (1594–1665), that the fullest and greatest Counter-Reformation vision is to be found. A complete theological philosophy was projected in visual images. Although Poussin was born in France, studied in Paris, and found many of his patrons amongst the higher French bourgeoisie, from the age of thirty he lived almost without break in Rome. Here was his homage to the South, his establishing himself unambiguously in a Catholic milieu. Rome also had a strong classical association for Poussin, the presence of antiquity and its reworking in Italian Renaissance art, but that influence generated the weaker side of his own work – academic bacchanalias and scenes from Greek and Roman mythology.

It is deeply perplexing that the commanding visual representations of *sola fide*, of saving grace, should not have come from a great Protestant artist, a Rembrandt or Vermeer, but from a Catholic. Luther's rallying cry finds its concrete form in Poussin and the early Poussin at that, notably in two works painted respectively in 1631 and 1641. Here is a sign already that the gap between the two Western branches of Christianity is far less than the institutional, visible Churches have ever allowed.

The first work, *The Plague of Ashdod*, is in the Louvre. Rats run about the town. The citizens mill in confusion in the square outside their temple, where the statue of their god, Dagon, has shattered in the night. They defeated the Israelites in battle, took the Ark of the Covenant, and placed it in their temple. Now plague has struck. Corpses lie around. People are dying. A baby is being pulled away from its dead mother's breast. Children are being shielded from the contagious bodies of their parents. The architecture of the town is severely rectilinear and claustrophobic. Leading townsmen stand bewildered as their community decays around them. However, through the chaos there is an overriding order. A triangle of vectors, of invisible lines of force, controls the painting. Two vertices are inanimate, the top of an obelisk in the background which indicates a brightly coloured sky, and the Ark of the Covenant itself, on the top of which are two golden angels, bowed down, wings stretched forward shielding the lid.

Nicolas Poussin, *The Plague of Ashdod*, Louvre, Paris

From each of these vertices long lines run down to the bottom right of the painting where they meet at the third vertex, the source of order. It is a young boy. He tiptoes into the scene from off-stage right. He is naked apart from a loose white shift. His skin is white and his chubby cheeks are rosy – there is none of the green hue of the plague-stricken. His right hand is in motion, coming up from his side, it has not quite reached the horizontal. The index finger is pointing in the gesture of authority. He gazes with a radiant demonic intensity into the scene. A man covering his own face against infection attempts to keep the boy away, to save him. He need not concern himself, for the one person who will not catch the plague is this boy.

The Plague of Ashdod is a difficult work. Like many of Poussin's complicated paintings it has many layers. It strikes the viewer first as a cluttered mess with overbearing architecture – which, after all, is the scene. Once the viewer takes in the boy, however, the work seizes hold with extraordinary force. The story is an Old Testament one: there are therefore no explicit associations with Christ. This is just a boy. He sees and he knows. He will restore the town of Ashdod. He is its future. Already, from his right hand we see him taking command. He is a figure of pure grace: he both has it himself and is the agent bringing it to save the town. He is a gift from outside, a gift from God. With his faith anything is possible, mountains may be moved. He is literally the death of death, bringing an end to the death and dying that litters the canvas. The painting could have been titled *Sola Fide*; it is the incarnation of Luther's paradox, and it is visually coherent. At the same time it is, incidentally, anti-humanist. Reason and Will get the citizens of Ashdod nowhere. Salvation is wholly with the rosy-cheeked boy tiptoeing barefooted into the scene. The townspeople do not see him. There is no image of such powerful life in our culture as this Ashdod boy. Poussin's unique gift has been to transform a mere painting into an active agent of sacred force. Once you have seen this boy he will not let you go: you will not forget him.

The second great work by Poussin on the 'faith alone' theme

is *Matthew and the Angel*, in Berlin. Unlike *Ashdod*, here is a simple image. Matthew sits centre-foreground in a landscape. There are ruins of a classical temple around him. He is near the bank of a river which takes up most of the centre of the work, winding through the painting into the distance where there are further ruins, mountains, and a partly cloudy but vivid sky. A golden-haired angel stands next to Matthew. His robe is white; his wings are white. His arms and right shoulder are bare, a beautiful pale flesh. His left hand lightly holds the top of Matthew's page; the right points to the text. He is the inspiration, bringing to the ordinary mortal the holy word. The pen is in Matthew's right hand. He looks up into the angel's face. The angel looks down joyfully. Matthew is concentrating on the most important work in his life, what he was called to do, finding the appropriate voice to describe the life of his Lord. Grace has come. Now he can fulfil his vocation. The mood is reverent and peaceful. The landscape itself echoes the mood, a tranquil alert clarity. Even the ruins of human creation are a part of the divine harmony, with their double symbol of the transcendence through grace of the profanely human, and the taking of the Greek classical through Christ into a higher plane. Here is revelation, but not with blinding lightning and thunder. Poussin's angel is gentle and helpful. The whole work has icon intensity: this is what it is like to be visited by the angel. This is grace, and grace is all. Matthew could be a self-portrait of Poussin, painting *Ashdod*.

The simple message is faith alone, which is given by God's grace, saving grace; there is no free-will. It was not because of Matthew's good works, as traditional Catholicism would have it, that the angel came. This, however, is where the Protestant imagery stops. The torment and the strain are not there. Matthew has nothing in common with Rembrandt's broken old men, burdened by their fallen state, desperate for a blessing. The bleakness of the Protestant fall is absent, as it was in *Ashdod*. The air is Catholic. Vocation is relaxed; man is at ease in God's landscape; if there is grace there is harmony. In mood there is little of Luther and Calvin, although they provided the seed. Poussin is producing an integrated Protestant-Catholic vision.

In the period of *Ashdod* and *Matthew* another Frenchman, Georges de la Tour, was painting his own great Calvinist readings of vocation. Like Poussin he refused to secularize the religious core. The key work is *Joseph the Carpenter*, in the Louvre. It is night. Joseph stands, bent double over a beam into which he bores a hole with his gimlet. His huge form in the shadows takes up half the surface of the painting. On the right his son holds a candle to light his work. The flame is unusually long and bright. The boy Jesus' face is brilliantly illuminated. His father looks down with frenzied concentration. He works as if his life depended on it. Why? In the darkness of the floor we see the clue. What he is making is the Cross. His vocation as the father of Jesus has as its highest element to meditate through his trade on the tragic climax of his son's life, twenty odd years later. That boy lights his work; without the son's help it could not be done. The father does not know what he does. If he did he would be paralysed. If he knew the future he would be turned to stone – rational consciousness again being the Medusa. His vocation is a state of grace, for it gives him unconscious access to the tragic destiny he was chosen to father. The gimlet itself is in the form of a cross, and it defines the central axis of the painting. Joseph's hands are clamped so tightly on the handle that they look like they are themselves extensions of the wood, as if he were himself attached to the cross.

True vocation can be terrible. Not the serenity of Matthew, but the other, darker side, that of tragedy. Who would choose to be Joseph? He is beside himself with a dreadful foreboding, only kept sane by his work, that work enabled by his son whose agony it prefigures, that son who understands in the way the Ashdod boy understands, he strong enough to shoulder it, and not just that, but gaze radiantly, smiling on his father's work. Joseph keeps his almost demented eyes on the boring gimlet. The important thing is to keep going, not close the eyes, stop in panic and flee, not pretend all is rosy, life a breeze, death nothing. With the help of Jesus the father keeps his conscience on his awful fate. It all depends on that son, who has his place to stand, and holds his father's hand, so to speak, through the dark night of the soul. The son is very fine.

What an extraordinary moment in our history was this! It may have been the same year that to the north Rembrandt was painting his *Sacrifice of Isaac*, perhaps the same month. It is, of course, the same problem. The Catholic, de la Tour, chooses the Gospel story of father and son. The Protestant is condemned to the much harsher Old Testament one. Both men are wrestling for their lives with faith alone, grace, the call, vocation and guilt. The difference that makes all the difference is that Isaac is not Christ. He cannot help his father. Abraham, as human, cannot survive faith alone on his own. Joseph can, but only just, and because his son is there to hold his hand, to illuminate his work, to whisper that he understands, and all is well. This is the Ashdod boy again. *Joseph the Carpenter*, unlike Rembrandt's *Isaac*, achieves the death of death. It is in the Catholic Counter-Reformation that Christianity becomes livable again.

In his middle period Poussin painted a fuller amplitude of the revised Catholic possibility. This is at its prime in the two series of the Seven Sacraments, painted in bursts in 1636–40 and 1644–8. The great work from the thirteen that have survived comes from the earlier period, the first *Confirmation*, painted a year or two before the *Matthew*. It hangs in Belvoir Castle in Leicestershire. A new theme is added, that of community, made sacred by the Church. *Sola fide* is maintained, but here brought within the circle of human society. The central figure is a little boy, strongly reminiscent of the Ashdod boy, naked apart from a loose blue tunic. He has golden hair, his hands are up in prayer, he stands in front of the sitting priest, who has his right arm outstretched, his open hand delicately touching the boy's forehead. Everything this priest represents, all he is as a man, is concentrated in the right hand, which shimmers with its holy mission. The boy is extraordinary. His stance is nonchalant and motionless, yet we can feel him leaning his whole being forward, his head slightly back, eyes closed, releasing himself into the power of the priest. He has achieved a state of complete trust and receptivity. He is open to grace, which now comes, its agent being the ordained hand, its context the ritual of Confirmation. This is initiation. This is the rite of passage from boyhood to adulthood, at its rarest and most sublime. This is the most important moment in the boy's life. He has found his vocation.

The Protestant stress on faith alone is modified. The boy's state of openness is made possible by help from others, and especially mothers. Poussin explains. Behind the boy there are other figures. Firstly there is another boy, in a bright red tunic, back to us, kneeling. His mother, in gold, kneels next to him, her right hand gently touching his back, steadying him. She is one of the anchoring points in the painting, being the one figure whose body is erect. Her head is turned to the left, away from the priest. She carries us to a third boy, in white, who is himself vivid with conflicting emotion. He looks forward at the Confirmation, understanding, but his response is to sway backwards in bashful reticence, his left hand covering his mouth, stricken with both a boyish shyness and sacred fear – at the enormous significance of what faces him. His mother is right behind him, leaning in reassurance over him, her right hand squarely planted in the middle of his back, in support and to stop his motion backwards, her left hand stretched forward pointing authoritatively, redirecting her son's movement back towards the Confirmation. The woman in gold, with the boy in red, by turning back towards the hesitating child also helps reunite him with the ceremony. A group of secondary figures reinforces the powerful circular motion in the painting, away from the priest and then back in towards him. He cannot be escaped.

Poussin thus brings back the Catholic element, the vital role of the Church and its rituals. An ordinary community of fathers, mothers and children is transformed into something higher, and thereby bound together and to its everyday tasks with an inspired sense of purpose. We have the Protestant notion of vocation without the punishing Protestant loneliness of the individual lost in his subjectivity. Man is reunited with his fellow-man. The Lutheran Ashdod boy here becomes a Counter-Reformation figure, joining a sacred community, and that is a big difference.

In the second series of the Sacraments, now in Edinburgh, a further element is added. In his *Penance*, or *Confession*, Poussin focuses on the archetypal penitent in the Gospels, Mary Magdalene. The scene is Christ dining at Simon the Pharisee's. Guests recline around a low rectangular table covered with food which occupies the centre of the painting. The large figure of Simon sits front-right. Christ, in bright crimson robes, lounges on the left. The fleshy Magdalene is on the extreme left, golden robes slipping off her right shoulder, thick long golden hair loosely bound by a white ribbon. She is opulent sensuality incarnate, now bent over, weeping, caressing Christ's foot, wiping it with her hair. His right hand is raised over her bowed head, in blessing. Everything important is happening in the left third of the painting. Simon sees what is happening and is reprimanded for his moralizing against Mary, who is a whore. He remains outside the holy triangle. His own feet are being washed, by a servant, but this is a merely profane cleansing. He is being taught, about penance, about openness to grace. So is the young John, sitting right next to Christ, and he will tell the finale of the story, years later, in his Gospel. Judas sits next to Simon complaining that the precious oil that Mary is wasting on Christ's feet could be sold, and the proceeds given to the poor.

Mary Magdalene is a central Christian figure, the great sinner who, once she sees Christ, recognizes her transgression and prostrates herself at his feet. She is the commanding figure of transgression, penance and forgiveness. It is through her sin and reconciliation, through her guilt, that she finds her vocation, as Christ's leading disciple – it is she who is in the Garden to meet him after he rises from the tomb, it is to her that he addresses the intimate prohibition, 'Touch me not!' She becomes his messenger to the world. Protestant theology was severely impoverished by its neglect of women, and above all of the two Marys central to the Gospels.

Poussin's final vision is of a marriage of earth and heaven, of sensual and spiritual. The indicative work is the *Annunciation* of 1657, now in London, just around the corner from *The Ambassadors*, a powerful counter to Holbein. The young Poussin, in his *Golden Calf* and *The Crossing of the Red Sea*, both from 1635, had imposed a Puritanical opposition between salvation and the pleasures of the flesh. The *Annunciation* is quite different.

Down on one knee, the angel confronts Mary. Apart from bare arms and delicate feet he is clothed, in an elaborate white garment. His head is inclined forward, directly at Mary's lap and womb. He points with both hands, arms outstretched like a pair of godly dividers. The right hand is horizontal, straight at Mary's breast. The left points diagonally upwards. With the right he commands, with the left makes the sacred connection. Mary's response is to rock backwards, as she sits on a low platform, her legs crossed, her knees wide apart opening her lap. Her arms move out and back from her sides, and she bares her palms to the angel. Her head inclines backwards, her mouth slightly open, her eyelids down. She is in a state of complete receptivity. Even her bare feet, visible under her gown, evoke her surrender. The painting has powerful erotic undertones, set by the force of the angel, his penetrating right arm, and the intense way he looks straight at her womb. The woman is in a state of ecstasy, open to the seed.

This angel is beautiful and terrible. The folds of his white garment fall in harmony to the body's nonchalant authority. The feet and hands are fine. But his wings have brilliant crimson orange tops, deep royal blue in the middle, and white ends to the feathers. They rise up behind his head with a violently rich potency, of passion and royalty. There is a trace of wicked earthiness in his angelic face. Nor is Mary the usual chaste, otherworldly figure. She is flesh and passion and spirit, a full-blooded woman. It is out of the fusion of body and soul, articulating both, addressing both, that the messenger of the sacred speaks. Poussin paints the release of the two explosive forces that govern human life, in a precariously controlled situation, depending on the forces remaining in balance. Where there is sacred command there is seduction. Where there is seduction the sacred must rule, otherwise it is transgression – back to Mary Magdalene. The *Annunciation* is another image of 'faith alone', but with disturbing elements not conventionally represented in Christian art. Mary is an ideal of the receptivity to grace, which comes through the angel. This is not purely a spiritual matter. Openness to grace, on earth, requires the fusion of the forces of earth with those of heaven. Poussin is literal: Mary's spiritual openness, which is total, without the slightest reserve or self-consciousness, depends on her sexual accessibility. She is in a swoon.

There is a final twist. Mary, in fact, rules. It is she who has allowed the angel in. Her arms encompass him. The crimson wings pin his back. A huge white dove is positioned over Mary's head, to counter the force drawing the white-clad angel into her lap. Poussin almost always made women the redemptive figures – apart, that is, from Christ.

What, at the other pole, of death itself? In *Ashdod* we have the boy killer of death. The theme reappears in the mature painter of 1658, in the *Holy Family in Egypt*, in the Hermitage, what Poussin called in letters his Egyptian Madonna. In the background is a pagan funeral, restricted to a thin horizontal plane, but set off by two obelisks, symbols of pagan authority. Here they have no weight. The painting is dominated by the family group in the foreground, the figures large. Joseph in the shadows quietly takes the water. The donkey drinks. The baby Jesus lunges for figs. Three helpers serve with an infectious reverence and joy. The central figure is Mary, square shoulders, erect torso, but sitting easily. Her left hand touches the figs, both blessing the gift of food and offering thanks. She is serene. Yet she is the authority that overawes the painting. This is the Egyptian Madonna, fulfilling the vocation to which she was called in the *Annunciation*, painted one year earlier. The pagan coffin is directly over her head, a trivial empty box next to the true sacred presence. She is the death of death. Grace has come to the three helpers, who have been given the divine call.

In hard theological terms Poussin adds four elements to the faith alone, no free-will, responsibility, guilt and vocation of the Reformation. They may plausibly be called Catholic. The first is community. The task of the Church, as in the Sacraments, is to infuse human community with sacred community, thus binding and securing it. Grace may come alone, but the preparation of each individual is the task of the community, and furthermore, that grace must be used to help the human group into which the individual is born.

The second element is the rehabilitation of the sensual. The flesh is not necessarily evil, the source of transgression, as in Paul, Augustine, Luther and Calvin. Poussin's most memorable male figure of evil is his Judas, in the second *Eucharist*: a man alone and without grace, bitter because there is a better man than he, Christ. His sin is not due to a temptation of the flesh. In general, for Poussin, the pleasures of the body are among the gifts of God, and should not be denied, although it is true that they harbour forces of potential devastation. The third element is exemplary women, and above all the two Marys. Mary Magdalene embodies a more Catholic fourth element, that of the holy sinner, of the redemptive force unleashed when great transgression is truly repented and forgiven.

There is a possible gap in Poussin's vision. There is no great crucifixion. Is there, then, a decisive answer to *The Ambassadors*? The Ashdod boy and the Egyptian Madonna do not confront the skull directly. Indeed in this vicinity Poussin at times wavers. The first sign is in the second *Extreme Unction* of 1644. In reality this is a death painting rather than a sacrament: there is little transcendence. The imagery darkens further in the greatest of Poussin's last works, *Winter* or *The Deluge*, in the Louvre. This painting is bathed in a lurid, incandescent grey. The flood is killing off all humans, good or bad. Parents futilely pass their child onto a rock infested with snakes. A man prays desperately in the prow of a boat which has just plunged backwards over a waterfall and is already half submerged. Even Noah's Ark is closed and black, a funeral barge. There is no way out. *The Deluge* is a hauntingly beautiful nightmare of death, in which there are no redemptive elements, apart from the mood itself.

This is not the whole story. In two works, *The Landscape with a Man killed by a Snake* of around 1648, and the *Lamentation over the Dead Christ* of around 1657, Poussin did take on the question of death, in his own way. In the *Snake Landscape*, in London, we can make out obscurely in the shadows in the foreground a man wrung to death by a gigantic python. The scene is observed by a man running past. His expression is of stark terror. He has seen the demonic underpinning to reality. Just ahead of him, on a track, a woman is alerted by his state. She sits up, mouth agog, arms raised in shocked surprise. She cannot see the corpse and the snake. Although she is a stranger, in an instant she becomes an intimate companion of the horrified man, helping earth his terror. She welcomes him, accepts him, is with him. Behind her the top half of the painting opens up into a sublime landscape, centring on a lake. City, nature, men working and at leisure, all fit into a harmonious whole, one which has an extraordinary luminous depth. Companionship connects the terror to the possibility of grace, of a happy idyllic life. Poussin here unites the demonic with the sublime, each living off the other, an alertness to one necessary for contact with the other. The demonic, however, is only bearable with the help of others.

The *Lamentation* was painted in the same late period as the *Egyptian Madonna* and the *Annunciation*. It hangs in Dublin. This is the really serious work. It is Poussin's crucifixion, his taking up of the question of whether death can be transcended. He chooses neither of the conventional subjects, the crucifixion itself nor the *Pietà* – mother cradling the body of son. The corpse of Christ is flat on the ground, evenly lit, horizontally across the bottom front of the painting. At its feet Joseph of Arimathea leans forward out of the dark opening into the stone sepulchre, his left hand forward, palm open towards Christ's head. The gesture welcomes, beckoning him into the tomb. It is at the same time hesitant, perplexed, asking for salvation, asking the question, is death merely death? Joseph's face is the only one in the light, not blotted out by shadow. It asks the great question. Joseph is the onlooker, who does not know. He is you and I.

There are four other figures. Mary the mother stands, her black face wracked with pain, a towering silhouette of grief. That she stands is ironical: her spirit is in a state of collapse. John kneels behind the head of Christ, gently lifting it with his left hand, his right delicately supporting Christ's elevated left forearm. It is elevated because Mary Magdalene has hold of the limp hand, which she caresses and kisses. Her white shrouded head is down over the hand, itself in the horizontal. The last figure is the third Mary, behind Mary Magdalene: she leans forward clasping her hands together, her gaze fixed on the face of Christ, gesture and expression revealing shock, consternation, beseeching and pity. She is about to topple forward, but the intensity of her concentration builds up so much spirit that she hovers there, anchoring the top right of the mourning group.

The corpse is relaxed, at peace. This is because of the three mourners. They have drunk of the sacred force which was their Lord. Now they redirect it back at his lifeless frame, in grief, and thereby they impose an upwards vertical motion on the scene, in spite of all the weight of mortality. The centre-point is Mary Magdalene caressing the left hand. As once she wept copious tears over his feet, washed them with her hair, anointed them with oil, and she was forgiven, now she returns as the redeemed mature woman, sure in herself, knowing where she stands, and hence she is free to pour all that she is into the limp left hand. John helps her, and the third Mary too. In another Poussin miracle, the placement of the figures, their tones, what they do, and above all the constellation of their hands, the vibrancy of those hands, all combine to begin to lift the corpse. Mary the mother is too sunk in her own grief to help, but she acknowledges, with one outward gesture. Her left palm, wide open towards the viewer, is directly above the unified hands of Christ and Mary Magdalene, in the exact centre of the painting.

This is not quite the end of this part of the story. The Counter-Reformation did provide its own explicit crucifixion. It was two

Nicolas Poussin, *Lamentation over the Dead Christ*, National
Gallery of Ireland, Dublin

hundred years ahead of its time. Donatello was the master. Appropriately enough it stands, in the place for which it was sculpted, through the doors behind the Gattamelata, in Padua, in the dark. To see it requires a guard to unlock huge iron gates. It is the centre-piece of the High Altar of the Basilica of St Anthony. Just as Donatello anticipated humanism in his equestrian statue, he anticipated the Reformation in his Altar. There is nothing medieval about this work, although executed around 1450. And it is deeply, vitally unhumanist. Outside the Fourth Gospel itself, it is the master-work of Christian tragedy, Christianity's reply to the ancient Greeks. Donatello had provided his own counter to the Gattamelata, his explanation for the great warrior's melancholy face.

The bronze Christ on the Cross is very high. He looks down. His face is harrowed with anguish, with both the pain of the slow torturing death, and the recognition of the tragic completion to his mission – 'My God, my God, why hast Thou forsaken me.' It is a wracked inward face, the brows furrowed, the eyes heavily lowered, the mouth open, grimacing, gasping for breath. This is a man, and he is dying a terrible death. The body is in the prime of manhood. Although the ribs show, as the breath is drawn in, the beautiful arms and legs are not tense. However, the open palms have thick steel nails through their soft centres, spiking the sacred source from which the blessings streamed. There is no sublime transcendence here, no immediate release to sit in peace beside his father. This is mortality. There is kinship to Holbein's *Christ Corpse*.

At the foot of the Cross, directly under Christ's feet, is Mary, not the older Mary of the *Pietà*, but the young Madonna, his mother. She sits on a throne holding the infant Jesus, but this is no conventional Madonna and Child. She sits forward, her face tense, her slight head carrying a heavy crown. She senses what is above her head. She knows the fate of the baby she holds. Indeed she thrusts it forward, in an instinctive maternal attempt to save it from the tragic destiny that looms overhead. But the infant Jesus is himself secure and confident, itching to begin his mission. Christ looking down sees not only you and I, the viewers: first and foremost he sees his mother, as mother. His look is not entirely inward: he grieves for her. In his agony he is with her, just as years earlier he had been with his father, Joseph the Carpenter. She in turn has accepted her vocation, and what mother would choose to be her? She steels herself, her narrow shoulders are there to help carry his burden, as it weighs momentously over her head. Just as she nurtures the infant she will be there for the grown man. He is not alone.

Here is death full on. It is a horrifying death, the worst imaginable. There is no magical resurrection. It is a man dying. The awfulness of it unnerves the viewer: he can as little escape the look of this Christ as he can Holbein's corpse. But here it is all right. Christ, with the help of Mary, says Yes, in spite of all. Mary too, the most cursed of mothers, not having the relief of blindness to her son's fate, says Yes, I can take it, I shall not turn to stone. Again the angel is terrible. This is the Mary of Poussin's *Annunciation*; the infant is the Ashdod boy. We have the completion of the human cycle, with the death of the man. Because of her son above, Mary can bear it. Through Mary we too participate. She is our guide, as with the Egyptian Madonna, our way in. She teaches vocation, terrible vocation. At last Luther and Calvin have become concrete, real flesh and blood, images that can hold. The soil is Catholic.

So it was: in the same few decades in the middle of the seventeenth century in which the masterpiece of cultural subversion appeared, and Rembrandt wrestled through a long attempted Protestant revision, and failed, a new Christian response to humanism was formed, harnessing the strength of both the Protestant and the Catholic lines. Here also it was that the peerless Donatello finally found his place.

6

THE BOURGEOIS FUSION

The Counter-Reformation vision was complete. However, it did not take root. No theology or philosophy appeared to map intellectually the territory staked out by Poussin. At the decisive moment the great opportunity was lost, and the main current of Western culture took a different turn. What followed in France was the legacy of Descartes and later Rousseau, not a Catholic Luther or Calvin. In Italy, the Spanish Inquisition stifled any new possibilities. In England the Anglican Church was ideally placed, with its moderate Protestantism and its Catholic tendencies, to provide an institutional basis for an integrated Christianity. In this it failed completely. After Milton, English culture produced no Christian theorist of any distinction. In practice the Anglican Church quickly degenerated into a bastion of upper-class complacency. Radical Protestantism itself moved in quite the wrong direction, giving birth to Methodism.

Probably the momentum towards secularization, led by the glittering humanist ideal, was already too great. The combination of reason and free-will was starting to bear fruit, above all in the successes of science. By the late seventeenth century a great individual like Newton, using no more than his intelligence, had been able to discover the laws of gravity and plot the motion of heavenly bodies. Concurrently a new cultural form was emerging that would predominate for the rest of the humanist epoch, establishing its own practical way of life. That was the bourgeois form. In essence it was the product of the fusion of secularized Protestantism with humanism. The Protestant–Catholic union was not to be.

Jan Vermeer, *Woman with a Water Jug*, Metropolitan Museum,
New York

Home and family are the hub of the bourgeois ideal, to which all other elements connect as spokes. The home is the sacred site of the culture. It is the domain principally of the mother, her spaces, the world within which she nurtures and instructs her children, and is companion and wife to her husband. The father is the head of the household and the principal agent of discipline, yet much of his time is spent away from home, at his work, which is a vocation. In the full bourgeois ideal work should take the form of a profession. The cardinal virtues are honesty, sobriety, reliability, industriousness and duty. Education and culture are valued.

These are the bare bones. To get a fuller picture we need to separate the constituent elements. Let us consider the Protestant contribution first. In some places in fact there was a Puritan bourgeoisie without significant humanist influence. Max Weber described as much in his study of the Protestant Ethic. There is no clearer picture of this social type than in Vermeer's work, idealizing the seventeenth-century Dutch middle class.

Vermeer paints the home as sacred. His middle-class interiors are a world unto themselves, complete. The light filters in through lead-lighted windows from the outside, but the outside world is unimportant, unnecessary. Within the rooms it is women who impose a tranquillity and reverence, whether they hold a water-jug, work at lace, model, or play musical instruments. The women themselves are exemplars of vocation, as in the lace-maker of 1665 with her head bowed over her work, her whole being concentrated on her hands, in the physical work which doubles as a spiritual discipline. In this Puritan domain the state of grace of the individual within her sanctuary – the home not the church is the sacred ground – invests everything she touches with her higher conscience. The profane water-jug becomes a holy chalice. Moreover, for Vermeer there is no social hierarchy. His kitchen-maid has a rough complexion and a stocky figure, like the earthenware she uses, but she too, in her humble vocation, has found a state of grace which the painter conveys by bathing the objects around her in a luminous earthy intensity. The bread is realistic enough to pick off the canvas and eat.

Vermeer is so rigorous in his emphasis on home as sanctuary that he depicts his representatives of male vocation – astronomer, geographer and artist – as working in middle-class lounge-rooms or studies. The ethos is strictly Protestant, whatever Vermeer's own religion. The astronomer and the geographer embody the Puritan ideal of vocation. Both men use their work to meditate on the secrets of heaven and earth, to wonder at the glory of God. This work involves them entirely, body and soul, a means of integrating the unconscious passions from below with the light from above. The right hand in one case holds a pair of dividers, in the other acts as dividers itself. Here is the point of union of physical and spiritual, of inner and outer, taking the measure of things, seeking their balance and thereby establishing it. For both men work is prayer, a state of concentrated meditative openness to grace. The Puritan bourgeois ideal thus focuses on revelation and salvation, but in the ordinary, private everyday world. The things usually taken as significant in life – romance, adventure and crisis – are not specially important. Neither are such distinguished locations as palaces and cathedrals. The events that occur, great or small, are taken by the individual as fate, predestined, to be digested in the same manner as astronomer or lace-maker work through their simple piety. Inwardness is all, but it requires both a sanctuary and a vocation.

The place that bourgeois culture found to stand was thus Puritan, a derivative of the Reformation, or in the French case, the Counter-Reformation. As Vermeer showed so brilliantly, it was a secure place, as long as the Puritan core remained, with its intensity. Critics of the bourgeois have usually typified it as materialistic, obsessively attached to profane routines in work and family life, driven by fear, greed and a need for status. Their caricature is in essence false. Bourgeois culture got its strength from precisely the opposite, that it managed to find a sacred core in the daily practices of home and work. A man's armchair and a woman's favourite fruit-bowl became emblems of the divine presence, objects of deep and lasting attachment.

The middle-class Puritan ideal was too one-sided to succeed

on its own. There was too much in both human nature and social life neglected by it. We saw these limitations with the *Jewish Bride*. Vermeer himself saw another flaw in the vision, that the heavily meditative image of vocation could combine with the conviction that events are predestined to produce a too passive or resigned response to fate. In his *Man and Woman Drinking Wine* he shows a woman slumped in shame because she has tacitly agreed to a seduction by a black-hatted stranger which she knows is wrong, and the signs are that she does not even want. It is as if the man is fate, which she must accept, with resignation. Then afterwards she must devote her spiritual energies to accommodating what she has done, to try to turn guilt into penance and restore the balance. Her philosophy seems to have undermined her capacity to say No. In a number of works Vermeer paints the vulnerability of his closeted middle-class women to temptation. He prefigures the fascination of nineteenth-century bourgeois literature with adultery.

Moreover, Vermeer only paints individuals. The home is sanctuary, but there is no family, no sacred community. Rembrandt was closer to the ideal, especially in his various Holy Families – he used very ordinary men and women as models for Joseph and Mary, thus implying that every family should contain some of the essence of the formative sacred community. Vermeer had already intuited the loneliness of the Protestant, and later bourgeois, reality.

In bourgeois culture this Puritan individual, bent on the solely religious goal of salvation, concerned about his soul not his **I**, fused with a worldly individual whose concern was rather with his **I** – his ego. The ego's goals were the age-old ones of wealth, status and power, its pleasures mastery over others and over the material world, and prestige in the eyes of men, being looked up to as somebody, having social eminence. Bourgeois culture could not admit that the ego's goals were what they were, and introduced a brand of vulgar Calvinism to rationalize them as having a higher spiritual end. The argument went that worldly success was a sign of God's approval. God showed the elect that he had chosen them by predestining their success in business and society. Conversely, the poor were poor for a reason, as a sign of spiritual damnation. Here was the source of that hypocrisy for which bourgeois culture soon became notorious, the moralistic self-satisfaction in which confidence of election, stripped of humility, combined with brash egoism.

It was at this point that humanist metaphysics entered the fray. The ego was active in its pursuit of its worldly goals. For material success the 'I am' had to flex its muscles. In bourgeois neo-Calvinism we are back with Erasmus: God decides events but he leaves the **I** of the chosen individual to will its glory. The bourgeois took pride in his position in society, for he had achieved it – it was not merely predestined. 'Self-help' was a part of his ethos, or as the adage put it, 'God helps those who help themselves.'

The second humanist fortifier followed. The willing ego, using its supreme faculty, its reason, working hard at its vocation, could create a world in which man was better and happier. The bourgeois social world's own view of itself was that it *was* better than any other, past or present. Within it the individual was happier, and more virtuous. Thus followed another humanist axiom, the belief in progress. At its height this cultural form did fulfil in its members a secure satisfaction about their condition. This is well caught by Georg Lukács in his 1909 essay on 'The Bourgeois Way of Life', taking a German focus, and finding the beauty of this world exemplified in Theodor Storm's short stories, in 'a lyrical description of a quiet, warm, simple life-mood'. There is a contentment in simple things. However, on this as other fronts, there was an uneasy alliance between the gregarious humanist optimism of the self-made man and the pious Puritan fatalism that Vermeer had seen.

In the dynamic bourgeois mode the value-creating **I** would typically devote itself to building not just a home, but also a place in society. The self-made man would use his fortune to establish himself in a part of town or country suitable to his means, and then attempt to buy the accompanying style of life, manners and education for himself and his family. He would build solidly, to last. It was a central but unacknowledged part of the bourgeois reality that its members came from nowhere, socially speaking, but once they had arrived they worked relentlessly to consolidate their legitimacy, their right to belong. They were particularly keen to give the impression that they were a part of a tradition. Thus in its public dimension the bourgeois family aped the aristocratic mode, with the difference that the lack of name and blood was compensated for by a greater emphasis on good breeding. Out of social insecurity it attached itself with anxious devotion to a cultural creation, proper behaviour, and became far more keen on manners than anyone with actual breeding.

The new social hierarchy was not aristocratic. Blood and name could not be bought. The "gentleman" was therefore redefined in a less aristocratic manner. His breeding was learned rather than inherited. A greater emphasis was placed on cultivation. Education becomes the key to creating a privileged caste, when blue blood is missing. Children sent to the right schools and then university can be taught to look and behave like aristocrats. As a result the humanist ideal of education, of using knowledge to make man better and happier, was fused with a snobbish ambition to employ education and culture as a means of discriminating those of superior class. Culture becomes a marker of bourgeois prestige.

The bourgeois enthusiasm for education and culture was not, however, in essence a social affectation. It had a deeper drive, and again its source and its rationale was a hybrid humanist-Puritan one. On the one hand humanism placed central emphasis on education as the means for exercising and training man's highest and defining faculty, his reason. The improvement of the world depended on trained intellect. Protestantism was no less keen on education, but on the separate grounds that every man must be literate to understand the Bible. Conscience, the mediator between God and man, could not evaluate daily conduct unless it knew the laws by which a man should live on earth. They were to be found in the holy scriptures. Even in predominantly

Catholic France it was Protestant schools in the seventeenth century that led the way in educational reform.

Once bourgeois education developed its full form, its ultimate goal, if usually unstated, became the pursuit of "truth". This vaguely mystical grail beckoning to the prosaic material world was itself a humanist-Puritan hybrid, combining the rationalist faith that clarity of mental insight brings virtue and happiness with the Protestant focus on revelation, the journey after spiritual knowledge. These quite distinct worldly utilitarian and religious strains have nothing in common, but as "truth" was not examined too closely it survived as the Siren song of bourgeois culture.

It was in France that bourgeois education was pioneered. Well before the Revolution of 1789 humanist ideals had come to dominate educational practice. The ultimate goal was "general culture", with special emphasis on teaching children to think logically and to write graceful prose. The curriculum concentrated on the Graeco-Roman and also the French classics. Under the influence of the Enlightenment there was already a sprinkling of more utilitarian subjects like science, history and geography. The *Collège de France*, founded in 1530 by François I to promote humanism, had by 1770 seven of its nineteen chairs devoted to science and mathematics. The Revolution itself merely underlined this humanist practice, and especially the guiding ideals of Reason and Progress, as its official doctrine. Napoleon then completed the model by building a strict hierarchy of institutions under central bureaucratic control. Apart from reforms in the 1850s which increased the status of science, the system remained basically unchanged until 1960, by which time something resembling its structure could be found in all Western countries.

The picture is complicated in an intriguing way by the English case. In England the middle class developed earlier, and expanded more rapidly and extensively than anywhere else. After Cromwell it became integrated into a political and social order of unique stability, to the evolution of which it increasingly contributed. Yet English education, dominated by Oxford and Cambridge, and the Public Schools, remained essentially aristocratic until well into the twentieth century. For instance it was not until the 1930s that the humanist value on "culture" made any headway in the Public Schools. A key difference in England was the enduring vitality of a social hierarchy led by a confident upper class, one which was open to the middle class with money. Entry was through sending sons, and eventually daughters, to Public School. Those elite schools had the aim of developing "character", which they did mainly through an emphasis on sport and a Spartan disciplinary regimen which had special effect because they were boarding institutions – they had total control of their pupils. They were not greatly interested in whether their students learned much – their curriculum until well into the twentieth century was devoted to the rote learning of the ancient classics. The main nineteenth-century reform, exemplified by Thomas Arnold's Rugby, was the addition of a severe evangelical Protestantism, infusing the character ideal with piety: the School's task was now to turn out more godly, morally superior gentlemen with a strong sense of civic duty.

The Public Schools retained their aristocratic goal of reinforcing the class hierarchy. Character was not simply to be pious and good: it should have "tone". There was an inviolable code of how to speak and behave, what views to hold, and with whom to associate. Here was the crucible for the intensely coercive formation of the small, exclusive caste that dominated English society and occupied almost all its important offices. In this system there was no need for the humanist ideal of Culture. The thrall of the aristocracy was enough, and it was invigorated from the 1820s by a radical Protestant zeal whose image of virtue also had nothing to do with Reason. There was thus a divide between French education, soon followed in Germany, which devoted itself to developing a humanist elite centred on Culture, in effect stressing talent and merit, and English education which retained an aristocratic aloofness to ideals of cultivated learning.

The humanist university, while in its early stages a creation of Renaissance Italy, from the eighteenth century was consolidated in France, following the same principles as the schools. It centred on the Humanities, its guiding ethos being to transmit a general culture and develop mental excellence. As its full bourgeois form developed during the nineteenth century the professional schools gained in importance, notably, law, medicine and engineering – Napoleon himself had already established the training of engineers, for his own military purposes. The quintessence of a bourgeois education became to balance a general familiarity with the Humanities with the practical training in a profession. In the American system the latter often followed the former at a separate institution. The pillar of bourgeois society was to be the cultivated doctor, lawyer, or engineer, regular in church attendance, and devoting a significant part of his leisure to honorary work for the community.

Another bulwark of the bourgeois achievement was its politics. The form was parliamentary democracy, and here England led the way. Its evolution took most of the humanist epoch, being largely complete by 1867 when Walter Bagehot published his enduringly insightful analysis of its workings, *The English Constitution*. Parliamentary democracy is bourgeois in its form, although not in the manner in which it came into being. The middle class played but a minor role in its formation. The steady development from the absolutism of Henry VIII to the constitutional monarchy of Victoria was largely due to the success with which the aristocracy steadily wrestled power from the monarch, and then consolidated that power in parliament. A parliament is quite unlike the typical aristocratic model of governing, the oligarchy or federation of powerful nobles. Its executive and legislative decisions are made by a committee, the Cabinet, under the charge of a powerful chairman, the Prime Minister, who is elected by the collegiate of the majority party in the parliament. The Cabinet is served by an independent bureaucracy.

The democratic part came with citizens electing their representatives, and having the further check on those in power of a free press, public opinion, and free associations or pressure groups – as de Tocqueville stressed in his great study contrasting aristocratic and democratic political forms. This was a humanist derivative, in giving special power to each **I** among the citizenry. It depends on "liberal" assumptions about the capacity of every adult to reason, to think intelligently about how he is ruled, and about him being free to will what he thinks right. The Protestant stress on the pre-eminence of the individual's conscience also played its part, especially in the turbulent seventeenth century. A further humanist derivative, the belief in merit, was also important, leading to ability rather than social background or personal patronage being the factor deciding who should occupy public office.

An ethic was still required in politics, and this was Protestant. A just politics depends on conscience, men acting honestly for a good higher than that of their own egos, that of the nation. It depends on vocational commitment. The heroic figure of Abraham Lincoln in American political imagery illustrates the point. Moreover the Protestant ethic became the more necessary as the traditional aristocratic code of honour receded, with its obligation that nobles devote some of their time to politics in an honorary capacity. Without either ethic, politics degenerates into a chaos of competing pressure groups, deals, buyings off, and before long corruption. Bourgeois politics was in essence neither corrupt nor Machiavellian; it was honest and just.

Parliamentary democracy depended for its success on one further factor, a respect for tradition, and the practical manifestation of that in an independent judiciary – the legal system free from the political one, with its own history and tradition, and its own collective conscience. In the crises of English political history it was usually reliance on a long established constitution and its legal forms that thwarted any tyrannical moves by the monarch. This factor is neither Protestant nor humanist. Indeed it is at odds with humanism, as Edmund Burke pointed out in his polemic against the French Revolution. The wisdom inherent in the English political system by the end of the eighteenth century had little to do with reason or ideals about progress and the "rights of man", or the arrogance of the humanist 'I am'. It had rather to do with good instincts and healthy prejudices, a respect for what generations of fathers and their fathers had slowly and sometimes painfully built. In other words bourgeois politics depended in good part for its stability on an anti-humanist scepticism about the power of human reason, a conservative warmth and attachment to custom and tradition.

The European aristocracies had a real culture, with authority and weight. It was founded on ancestors, their blood in the veins, their portraits on the walls, the swords and decorations from wars, and the stories of generations of valour. This was clan culture consolidated in property, the ancestral home, a horde of dependents, and the status of the family title, all engraved in a fixed social hierarchy with king above and commoners beneath. The Reformation created its own quite different real culture. Humanism, however, never succeeded by itself. While it had its own unique and trenchant ideals it never managed to grow roots. It was a parasitic form that to survive had to feed off strengths external to it. There had been Christian humanism, still tied to the Catholic umbilical cord. There was aristocratic humanism. This is in fact the case of Brutus. His code of honour is an inheritance from the nobility. The Renaissance created the glittering humanist fantasy, but once it lost its Christian root the ethic it sought to ground itself in was not its own. The ideal of the gentleman is in fact another hybrid, of humanist notions integrated into an aristocratic core.

The third and last parasitic form was Puritan humanism, the case of the bourgeoisie. Bourgeois culture had a tendency to swing backwards and forwards between Protestant and aristocratic poles, especially in England where the class organization of society survived longest. In the nineteenth century sons from hard-working middle-class entrepreneurial families would often, on entering Oxford or Cambridge, soon distance themselves from their Puritan home backgrounds and take to aristocratic habits, under the influence of the poise, confidence and style of the upper-class gentlemen. Their fathers usually approved – for them the harsh Calvinist God was now little more than a distant ancestral ghost. By this time in France and Germany the aristocratic presence was weaker, and the bourgeoisie compensated by making Culture a much stronger ideal. As a result humanism was more central and vigorous there, the university more culturally significant, and indeed the bourgeois ideal itself more creative and independent – it was, however, less stable.

When bourgeois culture moved away from its Reformation root it did not necessarily move in an aristocratic direction – that aristocracy being itself in decline from at least the eighteenth century. It was inevitable that worldly success would, as it always had, tend to undermine piety, weakening the need for serious religion. It became a standard pattern in bourgeois families for an early Puritan asceticism to give way over time to a self-satisfied materialism. Here too, however, the humanist 'I am' proved to lack the internal strength to move into the cultural vacuum and impose its own form. As a result once the bourgeois lost his Puritan soul he found the solid order he had so laboriously built to be hollow, comfortable rooms echoing coldly with a brittle routine snobbery and a wooden and weary self-importance. Often as not psychopathology of one type or another took over, Vermeer's *Woman with the Water-Jug* turning into the neurotic housewife obsessed with cleanliness. In the place of Oliver Cromwell appeared the secular entrepreneur accumulating wealth for its own senseless sake, or the bureaucrat dedicated to his own rules, absurd in themselves.

What I am arguing here is that in the Western tradition since the Middle Ages there have been three distinct real cultures, Catholic, Protestant and aristocratic. Humanism attempted to replace both Catholic and aristocratic, and failed – as a separate culture with its own roots that is. Almost immediately it found itself confronted by a new cultural force, Protestantism, with which it ended up going into alliance. There is one complication to the argument: to know a culture means to know the sacred site on which it was founded. In the case of Catholicism there is the crucifixion, the Gospels and the establishment of the papal church in Rome. In the case of Protestantism there is crucifixion and Gospels, reoriented by the metaphysics of Homeric Troy and Greek tragedy, as articulated by Luther and Calvin. The aristocratic case is more difficult. Its origins are in warrior clans – hence the role of honour. However, its oath of loyalty was not simply to King and Country, but rather to God and King. The Middle Ages was its formative period, during which the exemplary figure was the Christian knight, and the exemplary war the crusade against infidels. In strict terms then, aristocratic culture is only partly independent from Catholicism. Nevertheless, by the time of the Renaissance it had established its own integrity of form.

In *Mansfield Park* Jane Austen painted a brilliant picture of an aristocratic family in decline. The argument works just as well for the bourgeois family. In the novel it is a timid, physically frail girl from the middle class, Fanny Price, who restores order. She has an indomitable Calvinist conscience, and her judgment is always right. However it is a special Puritan mood that is the secret of her influence. That is intensity. It is Fanny's intent resoluteness in what she knows, the backbone of her extraordinary fortitude of character, that wins through. It is the same intensity that saves the bourgeois family from the aimless monotony of the prosaic everyday life that its critics have emphasized. Indeed, at Mansfield Park once Sir Thomas, the head of the house, returns his rather severe presence makes the evenings dull. Intensity versus pleasure. Fanny's intensity is linked with her shyness. Jane Austen was herself to remark: 'What has become of all the shyness in the world.' Without the shyness and the intensity we are back with the ambassadors, in whom learning is a deadness – they are the antithesis of Vermeer's astronomer. Without the shyness and the intensity the sacred turns to the profane and the women began to feel trapped in their lounge-rooms, restless and bored, the chain on their instincts losing its sense. The bourgeois family in decline has its untethered passions bolting into fantasies of adultery, its own pious culture subverted by Romanticism.

Where there was the intensity, faith and fate still ruled. As with Vermeer's women, as with Fanny Price, the individual soul was inviolable. Life was under the thumb-screw, men with severe, rigid faces, stiff of movement, their characteristic dress the high starched collar with tie, the black suit and black top hat, women tightly laced and intent in their interior domestic spaces, lost once they relaxed. While all this presided, humanism was saved from the skull. In turn humanism saved the bourgeois from a demented fanaticism or a disconnected inwardness. It softened the sense of iron predestination. But here was the problem that in the end would tip the equilibrium. The inviolable Soul needed an implacable and inexorable Fate, the two great polar forces living off each other. Tame one, and the other would wither, in the end – Luther had seen this. An intense bourgeois culture had created comfort as an incidental: once, however, the intensity dimmed, the surface habits and rituals of that comfort, the plush rooms, became the last hope of a sinking culture, while increasingly anxious passengers clung to the broken spars of the wrecked ship.

Puritan intensity had its own internal problems. Apart from Luther, it lacked an active engagement with the demonic, and especially with death. We saw this in the case of Rembrandt. The problem became aggravated in the bourgeois adaptation, in that humanism led in quite the opposite direction, itself being completely at odds with the metaphysics of Greek tragedy. Its worldliness was not that of Poussin. Indeed from a bourgeois perspective his *Annunciation* is immoral, even disgusting. In Vermeer, to take one of the highest examples, there is no terrible angel. Nor is there any tragedy.

7

REASON AND ROMANCE

Humanism did finally make the attempt to go it alone. The time was the eighteenth century, the place France, and the movement the Enlightenment. At last the ties to Christianity were cut, Catholic or Protestant, and indeed the leading figures turned with vehemence against all religion, denouncing it as superstition, a barbarian shackle on the triumph of rational humanity. Moreover, the attempt to graft humanism onto an aristocratic morality was also ditched. Reason was enough, able to create its utopia on earth out of nothing, with no more to lean on as an ethic than Voltaire's advice to the individual, 'Remember your dignity as a man.' The very term Enlightenment said it all: the bright midday sun of the Renaissance was now a complete and perfect reality. Where truth illuminated the way there was no need for religion. Nor was there need for morality. This was to be culture without shadows.

The Enlightenment was the fulfilment of humanism. It was the purest and most single-minded embodiment of its ideals, the most energetic, optimistic and successful of its children. The eighteenth century was the age of Reason. Its hero was Sir Isaac Newton, Voltaire merely setting the tone by eulogizing him as 'the greatest man who ever lived'. Its method was "critical intelligence". It formed and developed the major sciences of physics, chemistry and biology. It did the same with the new sciences of man, psychology, sociology, history and economics. Intellectual progress was the presiding ideal, and it proved brilliantly successful in practice. For the first time the scientific method was abstracted from non-rational interests: the study of facts, as Hume urged, was separated off from values, theology, aesthetics and metaphysics. Mind was applied to the analysis of all things. The aim was no longer to explain the ways of God to man, but to understand the nature of man and his world. Pope put it that the proper study of mankind is man. No one disagreed, and Diderot went further, arguing that it is only the presence of man which gives the world meaning. Man was unambiguously at the centre, and he was on his own there. Furthermore, from Locke onwards, the doctrine of original sin was rejected: man is freed from his past, from transcendental determinations. Bacon had already asserted that science can free man from the Fall. In tandem the belief in free-will was radically generalized into the ideal of "freedom". Kant in his 1784 essay, *What is Enlightenment?*, wrote of man's final coming of age, his maturity as a free and rational being, under the motto *sapere aude* – dare to know.

In fact what happened was as Luther had predicted. Reason and free-will were on the other side of the scales from faith. Emphasize them long enough and the scales would tip, as they now did. Luther's outraged cry against Erasmus, 'You are not devout!' came to fulfilment with the Enlightenment. This was in part necessary, for the root of Christian faith was fast withering, leaving humanism either to graft itself onto another culture or go it alone. For the moment it went alone, and took the other cultures with it. In France a high proportion of the more literate of both aristocracy and clergy had Enlightenment books in their libraries, and Enlightenment ideas in their heads. What Luther had not foreseen was that reason and free-will in practice would produce the steam-engine and penicillin, and that material abundance and the conquest of disease would weigh the scales for a very long time against the darkness of faith.

While the men of the Enlightenment themselves looked to Newton, the post-Renaissance figure who had pioneered the metaphysical way for them was rather Descartes, the father of modern philosophy. It was Descartes who enshrined Reason as the presiding god of modern culture. The utopian simplicity of his pure rationalism established the new authority that made the Enlightenment possible. At this level Newton had merely refined Descartes' method and then executed it with superhuman effect. The key work is *The Discourse on Method*, published in 1637. Descartes was an exact contemporary of Poussin, but whereas the great French painter exiled himself to Rome in the south, the philosopher and mathematician moved north, to Holland.

For Descartes Reason is all. The world can be recreated anew, by mind. Descartes provided the philosophy for Bacon's assertion that knowledge is power. He himself embodied the life of heroic reason. In his *Discourse* he makes much of the story of how he came to his method, spending an intense day of thought alone in a heated room. He states as his aim to spend all his life cultivating his reason. The essence of man, and especially of Descartes himself, is to be conscious. The method that follows is radical, starting with a clearing of the decks of inherited beliefs, all of them. The task of reason begins on *terra nullius*, to create the world again from the ground up. The building blocks themselves must also be created out of nothing, by the power of mind alone. Unless reason has demonstrated it to me incontrovertibly I shall not believe it. Descartes' own portentous criterion is "clear and distinct", without doubt. The palace of Reason will be constructed only from propositions that are clear and distinct. The rest is rubbish.

The most important application that Descartes himself made of his method was to himself. The question was 'What am I?', what is the nature of being, how do I even know that I exist? The answer, stated as the first principle of the method, was that the one thing I know clearly and distinctly is that I myself am conscious. The incontrovertible manifestation of my being conscious is that I doubt, understand, will, imagine and sense. Thus the first principle of philosophy is 'I think, therefore I am.' The literal translation from the original French is 'I am thinking, therefore I exist.' The defining feature of man, what distinguishes him from the beasts, is that he thinks. Here is the new Archimedean rock. I am, not because God made me, but because of my own innate capacity to reason.

The Cartesian method is deductive. There is no barrier between geometry and physics. An uninterrupted chain of deduction leads from the mathematical origin to revealing the entire natural world. It was at this point that Newton, in his *Rules of Philosophising*, reversed the method, to start with the facts and then move to the theory, the method of induction. According to Newton the laws of nature are not *a priori* but are in things themselves. In this the Enlightenment, and subsequently most of modern science, followed Newton rather than Descartes, but as much for another reason, the dazzling pre-eminence of the man himself – in his laws of gravitation Newton had shown for the first time that there are general cosmic laws, not just particular ones as with the orbits of the planets. If there are general laws, accessible to the human mind, then man can understand everything. Thus the 'I am' through the 'I think' could gain power over the universe. Descartes himself had been boundlessly confident about the results of practical science, and especially medicine, that it would in time make men 'the masters and possessors of nature'.

It is in Descartes' twin formulation, the 'I think' and the "clear and distinct", that the humanist antipode to Luther's darkness of faith and no free-will is finally established. Erasmus' feeble defence of free-will is no longer necessary. Descartes himself simply posits unbounded free-will, the one thing man has infinitely. It is the instrument of Reason: 'I can do whatever the intellect presents.' As a result it is impossible for me to do wrong.

The unshackling of Reason was the palpable result, and like a young stallion locked up in stables for winter set free in spring pasture, it galloped far and wide with a wild and virile exuberance. The main shackle to be cast off was that of religion. Although Descartes had retained a rather formal deism, the central eighteenth-century men of reason turned with venom against Christianity. Hume and Diderot mocked the resurrection as mere illusion; Voltaire made his warcry *écrasez l'infame*, crush vile superstition. Out of the scientific explosion the decisive blow against religion was struck by history, which now replaced myth.

It overthrew the traditional way man had viewed and valued his past, as a repository of magical stories about ancestors, the formation of the world, the defeat of monsters, and the heroic foundations of peoples. It thereby undermined the traditional Christian orientation, accepting the Biblical chronology from Genesis to Christ as gospel, and devoting scholarship to the venerable inspection of the sacred texts in order to illuminate the holy law and its saintly bearers. Rational, critical methods came in, and before long the authority of the Bible began to diminish. Once there was history then, as Hume demonstrated in his *History of England*, the facts became supreme. Bayle wrote of his ideal historian: 'Truth is my queen; to her alone have I sworn the oath of obedience.' The Bible suffered from internal contradictions. It also suffered at the hands of the new sciences, discoveries in biology and geology being at odds with Old Testament chronology. Once the past was rational history, subject to the methods of the clear and distinct, then Christian culture had lost one of its main supports. God was in process of being reduced to a god of the gaps in understanding, gaps which would be steadily closed. The way was prepared for the progressive view of evolution, that the history of man and his cosmos was one of continuous progress, reaching its high-point in the eighteenth century with the emergence of the free rational individual. Of course, this was just another myth, the liberal one, which reality in the next two centuries would tarnish, but at the time of the Enlightenment it seemed another glorious jewel in the crown of the 'I think therefore I am.' As we shall see later in our story, the cultural consequences of the replacement of myth by history were to be profound.

In its exhilarated rampage Reason trampled religion into the ground. Morality suffered a similar fate. Here the story is more complicated, with a number of threads weaving together to produce a vision of a human world beyond good and evil. The first thread was the ancient Socratic one, that it is ignorance that generates evil. In the utopia of rational adults men will be too enlightened to do wrong. Descartes put it that if he saw everything clearly it would not be possible for him to sin. This was extended in the economic liberalism of Adam Smith with the notion of the "invisible hand", a principle in the free market that automatically corrects imbalances. It was complemented in the utilitarian view that the free man pursues his pleasure, and this pleasure is his virtue: morality is thus collapsed into the category of happiness. This thread ended with Bentham's 1776 formulation that the measure of right and wrong in a society is the greatest happiness of the greatest number. In effect morality has been eviscerated into a technical computation of units of pleasure. It has been rendered rational. Ethics, if it is anything, is a derivative of reason and pleasure. The one theory of punishment celebrated by the Enlightenment, that of Beccaria, was wholly utilitarian, only interested in deterrence, with no notion of retribution, that a crime sets up a moral debt that must be paid off.

The last thread in the Enlightenment "beyond good and evil" was material determinism. Reason rampant, following Newton, was discovering laws of nature in every nook and cranny. The inevitable result was that the free play of critical intelligence destroyed the newly won freedom. The life of plants is determined, just as the orbit of planets is determined; the nature of animals is determined, so too must be the nature of man. La Mettrie provided the metaphor, in the title of his book, *Man the Machine*. Holbach saw everything in nature determined by its essence. The direct conclusion was that there is only determined being, and therefore no morality, only necessity. Man is a tool of the laws of nature. Diderot put it that all a man can say is that he was born fortunate – call that virtue – or unfortunate – call that vice. Nothing is "against nature", so there is no point moralizing against the facts. The facts are simply facts; accept them. Deformity is a fact, homosexuality is a fact, incest is a fact.

In this manner the Enlightenment watered the seeds of its own destruction. Unbounded Reason is restless, it fidgets, it cannot sit still. Remove the traditional limits and it will pry in every drawer. Exploring every logical possibility it becomes perverse, perhaps out of boredom with itself, and finds its greatest pleasure in contradiction – this is the masochism of Reason. From Descartes' arcadian palace it soon bolted head first into the wall of material determinism. From that impenetrable barrier it rushed straight into another, the sceptical one championed by Hume, built on the thought that if we can trust only the senses and the method of induction then we cannot be sure about anything. That the sun will rise tomorrow is merely a supposition based upon past experience. We cannot be certain. There is no clear and distinct knowledge except in the remote and exclusive world of mathematics. Not only is the moral code a convenient fiction but even the so-called laws of nature are provisional. Starting with the 'I think' and being ruthlessly consistent leads you to the 'I doubt'.

In the wake of the Enlightenment, science continued to prosper. The Cartesian ideal survived and its authority held through the demonstrable success of practical science, although it would never again throw off the shadows of either determinism or scepticism. The consequences of rampaging reason for morality were, however, more grave. A hint of things to come was provided by the most dizzily acrobatic of all eighteenth-century minds, that of Diderot. Here was chatterbox reason incarnate. Diderot's reduction of virtue to fortune, and his biological determinism, that nature gives us our character and there is nothing to be done about that, leads him on the one hand into a primitive utilitarianism, if it brings pleasure do it. It also brings him to advocate new titillations for playful man. Why should not the man of reason, for whom scientific experiment is a pleasure, try out cross-breeding? Would it not be fascinating, for instance, to create a man-goat? What fun! Diderot was entirely naive, without any idea of the monstrous world with which he was flirting. It would not be long, however, before another Enlightenment disciple of 'I think, therefore I am', the Marquis de Sade, was taking this line of thought one further stage, that of deliberate depravity.

Reason also moved into politics, creating the form that would dominate the West for the remainder of the humanist epoch – liberalism. Here the ideal of freedom combined with the 'I am' to enshrine the autonomous rational individual as the central unit of society. Liberal political theory leaves individuals free to pursue their own happiness. It entrusts power to those elected by the autonomous citizens choosing of their own free-will. Socialism, in terms of these first principles, was to prove no more than a sub-species of liberalism. In practice, Reason's politics worked in England, where its ideals were gradually integrated into institutions whose stability had, as we have seen, strong aristocratic and Protestant roots. When, however, it tried to go it alone, with a full utopian surge driving to build a liberal system out of nothing, the result was the French Revolution. Here was Reason's greatest test: it had the chance to show what it could do left to itself, what it could create once it had annihilated the prejudice, superstition, intolerance, gross inequality and exploitation of the existing European social order. The greatest happiness of the greatest number was not the result. No rationalization could excuse the Terror, followed by the Napoleonic devastation of the entire continent – the sacrifice of French lives alone through this period being of the order of two million. We are back to the fact that humanism on its own is not a culture, and the attempt to make of it more than it was opened the way for demonic forces that only real cultures can check.

For Descartes, the humanist 'I am' was not enough. He had to predicate it on the 'I think'. He thereby inaugurated radical rationalist humanism which drove the extraordinary burst of intellectual enthusiasm which was the Enlightenment. Its greatest gift was science, and above all medical science. Its greatest immediate curse was to give authority to the childlike utopianism that spawned the French Revolution. The 'I think' had severely limited the 'I am' in spite of all the gushing about freedom. The deification of Reason leaves much in human nature in the dark. The Enlightenment was in fact rather narrow-minded, naive about human motivation, about society and about politics, always in danger of barricading itself inside an arid and abstract intellectualism. It was from within its own ranks, and early in the day, that it produced the first reaction against itself – Romanticism.

Already in 1750 Rousseau wrote that reason corrupts us, the arts and sciences degrade all that is sacred. His alternative god was to be passion, his riposte to Descartes, I feel therefore I am. Rousseau himself set the mood with his own delight in nature, his rhapsodic description of being alone at night in a boat, on a lake in moonlight. Wordsworth would prefer storms and mountains, as would Byron, adding adventure. Romantic love was the golden path to the experience of full passion, the more turbulent, intense and anguished the better. Actually, love needed to be unrequited to generate the intensity of longing that gave the Romantic hero his aura of poetic sensitivity, of all-absorbed dedication to his love. From one extreme, of deified Reason, Western culture jumped to the opposite, deified passion.

Romanticism shared with the Enlightenment a radical individualism, valuing autonomy, hostile to custom, tradition, and above all the bonds of human community. It kept freedom as its pivotal ideal, an unbounded free-will. At the same time it had no sense for the normal business of society, including politics. Its other-worldliness, absorbed by the personal, the intimate and the private, was however the complement to the Enlightenment, starting where the other stopped. Whereas the Enlightenment was reason, light and optimism, Romanticism was emotion, darkness and pessimism. It was heir to a curious cross between Calvin and Hamlet. Its individualist intensity, obsessed with the inner self and its emotions, was a sort of degenerate Protestantism, with salvation displaced into passionate ecstasy, moral conscience into an intoxicated reflection on self and its sensations. Many Romantic artists, poets and philosophers were the sons of Puritan clergymen.

The Hamlet lineage is the more revealing one. For the Enlightenment there was no cognisance of death. The brightness of the rationalist noon removed the shadows. Death was simply out of mind. In eighteenth-century France, in general, Hell became unpopular, and the Devil was turned into a comic figure. However, the repressed returned in force in the Romantic reaction. Byron, Keats, Shelley, Schubert and others all died young. The formative German Romantic work, Goethe's *Werther*, had as its climax the young hero taking his own life once he realized his love would be eternally denied him. Death becomes more explicit in late Romanticism, its imagery prevalent in the paintings of Caspar David Friedrich and differently the Pre-Raphaelites, the 'love-death' central to Wagner's *Tristan and Isolde*, and a similar focus in Tennyson, in *Morte d'Arthur*, *In Memoriam*, and *The Lady of Shalott*. In the earlier Romanticism of Wordsworth it is the violent passion of nature that infuses enough vitality into the sensitive anti-social individual, now without God, to keep Death quiet. This is short-lived. The next move, once awakened Romanticism has turned to face the skull, is to give a mysterious transcendental quality to death, the corpse of the pale and beautiful Lady of Shalott drifting into Camelot, or the fantasy left with Keats' knight-at-arms, 'alone and palely loitering'. The heartland is melancholia. We are back with Hamlet's 'absent thee from felicity awhile'. And of course it was the Romantic movement that enshrined *Hamlet* as the central imaginative work in Western culture, replacing the Bible. Just as the French Revolution replaced the Christian calendar with its own secular one, starting at the Year One, so too the alternative messiah had been found. It was not to be Socrates, the more obvious choice – a neglect which further indicates the emptiness of humanism as culture. It was Hamlet, and he proved an enduring icon, casting his baleful authority across two further centuries. Thus we have arrived at the true Romantic ideal, to experience a beautiful death. Moreover, this beautiful death was to be humanism's own last ideal.

Behind the scenes the eighteenth century was directed by the problem caused by the loss of faith. It was the decline of Christianity that led to the schism between reason and romance. Poussin's late union had been of the spiritual and the sensual. Now the spiritual floundered without its animating faith, and sought its substitute in enchanted Reason. This degradation of the spiritual, aggravated by the neglect of the sensual, immediately produced a counter-solution, that of enchanted romance. Fate and soul still survived, although the former was in danger of the profane transformation into material determinism, and the latter of either the banalization into ego or the madness of being housed in unstable isolated individuals addicted to emotional chaos. Reason and romance were opposites that needed each other, just as the bourgeois needed the bohemian. (The bohemian was, by the way, Romanticism's most stable child.) The schism remained, and in the nineteenth century, when Reason was not prospering in natural science it began to inflict its own curse, the rationalization of the world, just as Romanticism turned increasingly towards the skull, and became nihilistic. In the eighteenth-century prime we witness both the high-point of humanism and the beginning of its decline, as things fell apart, and into fragments none of which were able to stand alone and command the world.

There was one serious attempt to save the Enlightenment, right at the end. Kant realized that it was not true that Reason could survive without a moral foundation. He further realized that the liberal utilitarian reduction of virtue to pleasure merely displayed the shallowness of reason on its own. In *The Groundwork of the Metaphysics of Morals* of 1785 and *The Critique of Practical Reason* of 1788 he developed his response, a rationalist ethics. Kantian ethics is the masterpiece of the Enlightenment, and it gave humanism its one real chance to stand on its own two feet. Moreover, with Kant we are back with Brutus. Already in the late 1770s in his *Lectures on Ethics* he had stressed that the universal end of mankind is moral perfection, and that in morality honour is pre-eminent. It is not necessary that I should live happily, but it is that I should live honourably. The dishonourable life is not worth living. This time, however, humanist ethics is independent of the aristocratic root.

Kant's system centres on the moral law. This is distinct from the natural law, the laws of nature which science studies, the domain of pure reason. It is a universal code of morals, given *a priori*, not dependent on human experience, not a derivative of human nature. It holds for all men at all times who have reason and will. The principal task of human reason is to understand the moral law, which it serves – this is practical reason. The moral law is opposed to self-love; reason is opposed to instinct. In illustration of how seriously reason takes its moral task Kant notes that the one subject of enduring interest when mixed company gets together in conversation is the moral worth of an action and how this reflects on character. Humans take a keen interest, whether in gossip or serious discussion, in evaluating good and bad behaviour.

The moral law has in effect replaced God, centre-stage for Kant. God is an abstraction, not essential to the system, although Kant himself does keep him in the wings. 'The moral law is holy.' Known through reason, it acts through will. Will is autonomous, that is free. Man as a rational being may act against his impulses. Man knows what he ought to do, and is free to do it. Freedom is the condition of the moral law; conscience is impossible without free-will. Free-will is thus the sole principle of ethics. It is what makes man more than animal. It is determined by reason, but reason in turn acts in obedience to the moral law. Finally, the motive for obeying the moral law is not egoism, that is pleasure, but reverence. The moral law is holy. Its subjective, psychological correlates in the individual are shame and duty, not happiness. Its reward is that it opens up revelation of an intelligible world.

There are two further principles of Kantian ethics. Firstly there is the categorical imperative, which virtually follows from what has already been stipulated. In practice a man should always act in the same way he would judge it right for every other man in his situation to act. In other words act in obedience to a universal law, irrespective of the consequences of the act, irrespective of personal interest. The act is good in itself. Kant's suggestion is that in reality this is precisely what good men do – only listen to the everyday conversation about the action of others in ethically difficult situations to understand this.

The second principle Kant calls the practical one. It is independent from what has gone before. Man is an end in himself. He should never be treated wholly as a means. Man as a rational being with an autonomous will is a member of a kingdom of ends. To treat another as a means is to treat him as an object or a slave: it is to deny the key to his humanity. 'Morality is the only condition under which man can be an end in himself.' That is, his dignity is dependent on morality, on him being treated as an end in himself.

Kant knew well the foundations of humanism. He knew Pico's axiom that man can do whatever he wills, that he is free. He knew that an ethics is necessary, that its principle should be honour, and that the 'I am' must be subordinate to it. Working within the parameters of the Renaissance, but adding his notion of a universal moral law, he developed a system which is coherent, comprehensive and plausible. It both disdains the immoralists of the Enlightenment, like Diderot, and pitches itself directly against utilitarian liberalism – reason is counter to instinct, the moral law to pleasure or happiness. In fact Kant gave liberalism a moral future, by investing the autonomous individual with an ethical dignity, a place to stand as a rational man with free-will respecting the law. Humanism had at last found an ethics worthy to counter Luther and Calvin, one that was profoundly to influence subsequent Western assumptions. If liberal humanist culture has any gravity of its own it is in what Kant spelt out. Just one piece of simple, late Kantian advice, anti-utilitarian, is enough of a sign to us of the wholly different calibre of his meditations on ethics: 'emphasize the shamefulness of vice not its harmfulness.'

Kant, like his great German predecessor, Luther, knew that free-will was the crux. He went the opposite way. His conscience is at odds with that of Calvin and vintage Protestantism. It depends on a paradox, as Kant himself admitted. Will, being autonomous, is a law unto itself. Yet it obeys laws. Kant assumes that the rational man, knowing the moral law, will obey it. This is the core axiom of rationalist optimism, to be found originally in Socrates, and later in Descartes. Without it the Kantian system collapses. Experience suggests that it is a false optimism. From *The Iliad* on, the greatest of our literature has regularly portrayed men knowing what reason tells them they should do, not doing it. Achilles knows he should not get carried away in a man-slaughtering rampage, he knows he should respect the corpse of

129

Hector: in the heat of his rage, his passion for revenge, he takes no notice of reason's supplication, nor does he later regret his excess. Hamlet knows perfectly well what he should do, kill Claudius, but his will refuses to obey his mind. Hamlet cannot control his own Will. As a result of his lack of free-will, his inability to act, just about everybody gets killed, guilty and innocent alike. The consequences *are* important. Moreover, the fact that modernity should have chosen such a strong embodiment of no free-will as Hamlet as its messiah is a sign of how unconvinced it was by the Kantian line, beneath the rational surface.

In reality reason does not determine will. We do not need Homer or Shakespeare to tell us this. At the end of the day the brilliance of Kantian ethics suffers from a superficiality, its failure to take account of the power of the demonic in human nature, the weak, subsidiary and circumscribed role of reason, and above all that, as Luther thundered, faith is only to be encountered in the dark, where man is in chains, without freedom. That the moral law is universal and holy is all very well, and true, but to know it in the vital sense of coming under its thrall is not within the power of reason. The forces which determine goodness, that is whether men obey the moral law or not, have little to do with either reason or will. They have to do with faith and its obscure minions.

Kant was deaf to the death of death. Indeed this admirer of Rousseau, even after he knew about the Terror, continued to defend the French Revolution as the sign of the progressive triumph of reason. He continued to defend the men who had made it, for according to his moral logic because of their high-minded ideals they were good men, excusing the reality that in the name of freedom they had carried out untold atrocities. Descartes, the modern founding father of Reason, had spent years alone by himself wondering whether anything exists. His greatest son, Immanuel Kant, for all his rectitude and shrewdness, could not face the truth about the clear and distinct in political form, and so he too finally retreated inside the floating glass balloon of pure reason.

PART III
Fall

8

MOCKERY, MOCKERY
EVERYWHERE

With the end of the Enlightenment the spell breaks. The clear and distinct light of naive Reason is eclipsed. Worse, the eternal quest to achieve a death of death, and gain life, is completely abandoned. Holbein's corpse rises and begins to haunt the darkening world. Humanism's second movement has started, its descent into oblivion. Reason survives, but without honour, and it turns nasty. In its prophets a new unconscious current surges, driving Reason to profane and to mock. All that was fine and beautiful and good in Western culture is turned upon, with malicious intent. The demons awake and grope towards the surface. We have entered the period of the wrecking.

At the concrete historical level what breaks the spell are the events in France between 1789 and the defeat of Napoleon in 1815. It is ironical that Kant should have completed his ethics on the eve of the French Revolution, the event that was to compromise his system fatally. 1789 to 1815 destroyed the cultural ideals of the Enlightenment. Naive Reason was no longer possible, except in the narrowly circumscribed domain of science. In fact science was forced into a cultural vacuum, sealed off from moral issues, where it was left to its own logic. It continued to prosper. Indeed the same period that saw humanism's political ideal shattered in practice witnessed across the Channel the Industrial Revolution, the pioneering phase of technological innovation and factory organization that would transform the material life of the West. Very soon this economic revolution would begin its own eating away at the foundations of the old cultural traditions, by generating vast quantities of new money, and

Edvard Munch, *Madonna*, Munch Museum, Oslo

creating entirely new processes of work and leisure. On its own narrow liberal-rationalist front it revitalized the Enlightenment, giving it authority through major segments of the middle classes, ones that had lost contact with their roots and yet were unaware of the darker developments at the cultural frontier. In the nineteenth century, in other words, the main span of middle-class culture continued happily on in a liberal, rational and optimistic manner, flirting with Romanticism, but all the while the illusion had cracked, and where it mattered in the long run, at the cultural frontier, the wreckers were advancing furiously.

Solidly grounded culture is only marginally vulnerable to material change. The size of the impact of the French and Industrial Revolutions was possible because the old authorities were already tottering, under threat from within. The main reasons for weakening authority were, as we have seen, that the humanist ideal in its Enlightenment form had gravely loosened both Christian and aristocratic roots, and been unable to establish itself on its own. The only form remaining at the start of the nineteenth century with some vitality was the bourgeois one, the Protestant-humanist hybrid, that is with the partial exception of England where the aristocracy retained some of its traditional confidence and authority.

The weakening of cultural authority had two consequences. The first was rancour. When the gods fail the leading believers, inevitably highly-strung, emotionally wrought, sensitively intense characters, turn in rage against them, as did Milton's Satan. Christ's 'He that is not with me is against me' applies to the intellectuals, the priests of culture. This is son against father. As the old cultures falter they are turned on viciously, and ground into the dirt. The sons smell blood. First come the beasts of prey, then the vultures. Such are the simple mechanics of rancour, and they are universally to be observed when cultures go into decline. We have already examined the most subtly brilliant harbinger of this, Velázquez.

The second consequence was chaos, which in the nineteenth century had two faces. One of them was honest: nihilism. The last places to stand, the rocks of Christian salvation and aristocratic honour, had splintered, leaving nothing under the feet. Voltaire's 'your dignity as a man' and Kant's 'dishonourable life is not worth living' were soap-bubble ideals. The reality was Nietzsche's "death of God" and Dostoevsky's "everything is permitted". The other face of chaos was the liberal pretence that it is possible to live according to reason and free-will. Bourgeois culture in decline was redirected along these lines, imagining that the mansion of the clear and distinct, of wealth and status, would keep one secure and content at night. It would not. Under the liberal surface the demons were astir.

The extent of the degradation of Western culture brought about in the nineteenth century is illustrated in a painting with which the century closes, Edvard Munch's *Madonna*. The woman is naked. Long black hair swirls crazily, a red beret mimics a halo, red lips, black closed eyes, she is caught in a dreamlike vortex of helplessness and anguish. In the face there is a shade of peace, of the end of torment, but it is the peace of a corpse – as Munch himself made clear in an accompanying text. The colours are those of a lurid, perverted sensuality and death. Nothing matters, apart from a peaceful death, Hamlet's felicity. Yet this is no longer Romanticism's beautiful death. She is a profane soulless animal in an empty world, simply wanting to escape her torment. At issue is the inversion of one of Western culture's central icons, Mary the Madonna, as representative of the holy vocation of motherhood. Munch is painting against Raphael. His Madonna is framed by spermatozoa, and at her bottom left is a hideous embryo: all she can give birth to is death. She cannot even nourish herself. It is hardly two centuries since the high point of Poussin's *Annunciation* and what we have reached is dead culture, culture whose mission is to disenchant, saying that this is the true Madonna, life is no better than death, join me in despair. It is Velázquez, not Poussin, who has gained sway. Munch pictures one of the victims of dead culture. Even the mocking is over. It has won, and all there is left to paint is the nothing.

The story of the nineteenth-century demolition of its inherited culture could be told through painting. It could be even further focused down, onto the progressive desecration of the female body. Such a narrative would start in the late eighteenth century with Goya's *Maja Nude*, a stiff blank-eyed body stripped of the constraints preserving the sanctity of woman, vital to the classical genre from Titian to Rembrandt. Goya's nude is frigid flesh with a brazen stare. The story would continue with the exquisitely crafted pornography of Ingres: his nude *Odalisque* is pure flesh, an object for voyeuristic male indulgence. It would reach its climax with Manet's deliberately shocking masterpiece of 1865, *Olympia*, the naked whore who stares mockingly out of the canvas, goading the viewer. Without shame, she too is a spiritless object, in whom the sensual decays into an unblinking indifference. In the painting both black cat and African maid are terrified by their mistress. Manet, who referred to Velázquez as "the painter of painters", had made his intentions explicit in 1863, with his *Picnic on the Grass*, and even more with his *Christ Corpse* of 1864, an echo of Holbein's profane messiah. Within this history it is notable that the last great work in the classical mode, defending the Law, was painted in 1824 – Delacroix' tragic *Massacre at Chios*.

Such an overview would provide vivid illustration to the attack on the Old Masters, and the remarkable success of that attack. The result is Munch's *Madonna*, followed a decade later by Duch-amp's *Urinal*, the piece of plumbing exhibited as a work of art, asserting its own profane self to be of equal value to a Raphael *Madonna*. These two works speak for themselves. However, painting did not play a central role in the nineteenth-century fall of European culture. It merely provided one of the ancillary battalions. As a subversive agent Manet, for instance, produced nothing of the force or calibre of *Las Meninas*, nor of his revolutionary contemporaries, Marx and Darwin.

Humanism's second movement, its fall, is to be located squarely in the nineteenth century. By 1900 it is all over, and where twentieth-century culture remains in the humanist mode, as it largely does, it does no more than continue to work through a destructive logic already well established. There are three quite distinct phases to the humanist fall. The first stage is the active demolition of the old cultures, the period of the mockers. The second stage is that of the recognition of nihilism, one that produces resistance, a fight against it – what might be termed dynamic nihilism. The third stage is the acceptance of the inevitability of nihilism, and the giving in to it – what might be termed resigned nihilism. It led to a withdrawal into the unconscious, a surrender to oblivion. These three stages will be dealt with respectively in the next three chapters.

The key wreckers were Marx and Darwin, although the latter was unsuited temperamentally for the unwitting role he played. There were, of course, hundreds of others, in all cultural areas. It was these two who grasped hold of the holy tablets of the Law and smashed them so comprehensively that they could not be pieced together again, at least not in the humanist epoch.

Marx was the chief mocker. Three aspects of his character combined to make him ideal for the role: an instinct for where the enemy's strength lay, an intelligence that in its learned incisiveness made him tower over other radicals, and an unscrupulously violent and malicious temperament. The key to understanding Marx is the third aspect. He was driven by his own extraordinarily aggressive disposition to imagine the total destruction of Western culture. His true pleasure and goal was in annihilation for its own sake. His work is full of emotionally charged images of devastation, and a mere handful of pages in the many thousands is devoted to the communist utopia that would grow out of the ashes of revolution. When asked by a journalist late in life what was the essence of human existence, Marx answered 'Struggle.' What he really meant was anticipated in a poem he wrote when he was eighteen, in which the hero, Oulanem, asserts:

> The world which bulks between me and the abyss
> I will smash to pieces with my enduring curses.

Marx saw that the cultural form which still had strength was the bourgeois one. So he set out to destroy it. His main tactic was rancorous, that of malicious gossip, to attribute mean motives to the object of attack. The key work is *The Communist Manifesto* of 1848, the handbook of revolution, socialism's sacred text. Bourgeois society is based on greed; it is avarice projected as a social principle. It reduces personal relations to self-interest, to the 'callous cash principle'. Its method of operating is 'naked, shameless, direct, brutal exploitation'. Its culture is hypocrisy, with ideals of law, morality and religion merely prejudices cloaking self-interest. It has destroyed all that is honourable in work and soaked it in 'the icy water of egotistical calculation'.

In other words the bourgeois is mean and selfish, with no higher motives than his own material gain. The caricature goes further, into the inner sanctum of bourgeois culture, the family. It too is based on gain. The wife is merely an instrument of production, a possession, little more than a prostitute. The greatest pleasure of bourgeois men is in seducing each other's wives. Marx in effect takes the Romantic contempt for the bourgeois, as a boring and hypocritical mediocrity, several stages further by introducing moral categories. The bourgeois is the force for evil in the modern world.

As the bourgeois is driven by one motive, greed, he has reduced all social life to one dimension, the economic. Here Marx produces his most important observation, a true one, that in modern times the great revolutionary force is the economy, capitalism itself: it is the remorseless process of industrial creation and destruction that is undermining all traditional beliefs and customs. Marx blames the bourgeois for the supremacy of economics. Then in a curious identification with the enemy he asserts as an objective law that history is dominated by economics, and can only be understood by his method of dialectical materialism. Economics becomes god, for Marx as for his postulated bourgeois. He has two motives for this move. The first is that he has correctly observed that economic change has become the great cultural destroyer. The industrial revolution is doing the dirty work itself.

The second is that economics is impersonal. Marx was profoundly misanthropic and it would not have suited him to have found revolutionary heroes amongst despised humanity. He took special pleasure in using terms like "scum". The view that men were merely the pawns of world history, its tools and victims, suited his disposition. The Economy is an avenging god, and it is just, the engine of the apocalypse. The last element in this vision of negativity is that while the present is diabolical the past was no better. Just as men are scum, they have never created a golden age. What comes before is oriental despotism, the idiocy of rural life, and various other modes of exploitation usually held together by that opium of the people, religion. If Marx had had a personal motto it should have been that of Sorel: 'Kill, Kill!'

The orgy of violence that Marx projected into history, both as the principle of the past, exploitation, and that of the future, revolution, had obvious personal sources. A Jew himself, descended from a long line of Rabbis on both sides, he was explosively anti-Semitic. In his theory bourgeois greed has Jewish origins. Indeed the Christian was corrupted by the Jew, whose worldly god is gold, whose worldly cult is haggling. Marx wrote of the German social democrat, Lassalle, a man who had been a generous host to him, as 'the Jewish Nigger . . . a greasy Jew disguised under brilliantine and cheap jewels.' Again and again in his letters he spits on the graves of his ancestors. The Russian, Pavel Annenkov, observed his public attack on Wilhelm Weitling and remarked on his proud and faintly contemptuous manner, the persistent jarring tone, his lack of manners, and that his 'sharp, metallic voice was well suited to the radical judgments he was delivering on men and things'. In 1860 he wrote three hundred pages of bitter and sneering polemic, *Herr Vogt*. One of his targets was the Jewish publisher of the London *Daily Telegraph*, someone who in fact had done him no harm. Marx wrote:

The great art of Levy's nose in reality consists of cozying up to foul odour, to smell it out hundreds of miles away and bring it forth. Thus Levy's nose serves *The Daily Telegraph* as an elephant snout, insect palp, lighthouse and telegraph. One can therefore say without exaggeration that Levy writes his newspaper with his nose.

It was Nietzsche who postulated that the mood of modern culture, set by the intellectuals, is rancour. He could have found no better case-study than that of Marx. There was not just the sneering vindictiveness. There was also deceit and hypocrisy. He scrutinized his daughter's suitors with a bourgeois strictness. He never acknowledged his own bastard son. Even his own beloved scholarship was tainted. He never tired of dismissing the work of his fellow revolutionary intellectuals as "unscientific". He prided himself on his Doctorate, his scholarly qualification, and considered his own work thorough and rigorous. Yet there is now evidence that Marx systematically falsified evidence and misquoted to support his arguments. He was never interested in considering alternative hypotheses. His lack of interest in the truth is illustrated by him never having visited a factory, in spite of invitations from Engels. The pursuit of truth was not his motive. Perhaps the most striking example of this was his dependence on reports from the factory inspectorate on cruel working conditions. The very existence of that inspectorate, and the continuing reform of factory conditions through Acts of Parliament that their reports produced, directly contradicted one of Marx's leading arguments, that under capitalism exploitation of workers must increase. Needless to say that the prophet of equality, of the free relations between man and man, was no democrat himself. He scorned elections, and any organization he had anything to do with he tried to take over and run in a ruthlessly dictatorial way.

Marx is perverted humanism. On the one hand he asserts that 'Religion is only the illusory sun, around which man revolves, until he begins to revolve around himself', and he gives pride of place in human activity to science. The works of Shakespeare were the family Bible in his home. On the other hand he is the father of social determinism, according to which man is a feeble pawn in the hands of history, the creation of the society in which he was born. Individuality is an illusion; man is a social product.

One of Marx' own examples is that a painting by Raphael is merely the product of the material circumstances of the age and place in which the artist lived. This is a tellingly rancorous example, reducing one of the sacred objects of Western culture to profane economics. Marx would have admired Duchamp's *Urinal*.

The very ideal of "equality" is rancorous. What it really means is tear down everything superior, starting with Raphael. Marx himself was not the slightest bit interested in democracy: "equality" is simply ideology with which to profane the existing order. The "dictatorship of the proletariat" is a rationalization for smashing everything that is right and good, put into practice in the Russian Revolution, which is symbolized, as was its French predecessor, by the ransacking of the palaces.

The degree of Marx' identification with his caricature of the bourgeois is shown by the hallmark of his ideal society, the communist utopia, which is material abundance – goods will be plentiful, there will be no scarcity, no need for private property. Thus the man who falsely identifies the essence of bourgeois culture as a mania for possessions has as his own dream a world of plentiful commodities. What the dialectic boils down to is that Kill, Kill, the turning of the West into rubble and corpses, will see a miraculous inversion, the transformation into a land of milk and honey, without struggle. The personal twist to this is Marx' own pitiful incompetence with money: a spendthrift, he never showed any inclination to earn a wage himself and spent his adult life sponging off friends and acquaintances, borrowing without any intention to repay, and in the process condemning his own family to a squalor that was responsible for the death of three of his children. In his ranting about the bourgeois obsession with gold there is more than a little envy.

Dostoevsky observed that the essence of the revolutionary idea is the negation of honour. This is rancour, the mockery of honour and what it serves, the Law. The Enlightenment, with the late exception of Kant, had neglected honour. Kant had been right, the dishonourable life is not worth living. But not all villains kill themselves: rather, they embark on a systematic programme of destruction, aimed precisely at eliminating everything honourable, what shows them up for what they are. Humanism could not hang on to honour, unable to ground it in its own soil. So, in the end, it turned against it. The specific target was the one remaining cultural form with weight, the one remaining house in which honour dwelt, the bourgeois one.

It did not need to be like this. There are elements in the revolutionary movement driven by a genuine compassion for the wretchedness of the poor, and the callous working conditions in some factories – in short, by a concern for justice. The most endearing quality in Marx himself was his kindness to children and his spontaneous response to suffering. These fine feelings, however, stayed private. They did not feed through into his work which is underlaid with the stridency of resentment. The tone gives it away. It is coursed with hate. The difference becomes clear by making the contrast with the way Dostoevsky, for instance, describes the life of the poor, or with Simone Weil who in her simple Christian manner outlines the inhuman conditions of factory-labour – she actually worked on a car assembly-line.

Although Marx' own mission was single-minded, it would not be right to see the movement he inspired, socialism, as solely driven by rancour. It had another root, the liberal one. Socialism has been half resentment, against anyone who was better or who had more, and half the liberal pursuit of freedom, the 'I am' freed from all traditional limits of blood, class and wealth. In itself socialism does not play a significant part in the story of the rise and fall of humanism. It was too much a sub-species of the genus that did, liberalism.

Liberalism was not rancorous, yet it was to prove a great destroyer of culture. It was rather naive, in the Enlightenment mode. It did not itself mock, but it cleared the decks for the mockers, as Marx himself perceived. In the cultural battle it played the role of the "useful idiot", doing the job for the vandals, but in all innocence. The devil never had a better hench-man than liberalism, because its heart was pure.

Humanism

There were areas in which liberalism was benign. There still are. Three stand out. In politics, the liberal ideals of freedom and the responsible and rational adult, grafted onto two real cultures, two ideals with depth, Protestant vocation and aristocratic honour, helped develop the parliamentary democratic system that has remained the backbone of Western society. Second, experience has shown that the free market, theorized in the liberal tradition from Adam Smith on, for all its imperfections, has produced greater prosperity, and with a reasonably fair distribution of goods, than any other form of economic organization. Third, the liberal ideal of the autonomous individual, articulated by Kant in the imperative to treat every man as an end in himself, has in the bourgeois mode produced an everyday life which is tolerably just. These are considerable achievements.

Let us now turn to the other side of the scales, and the greatest example of liberal vandalism, at the hands of the most brilliant of the offspring of Descartes and Newton, Charles Darwin. For Marx the world is ruled by economics and the iron logic of History. For Darwin it is Nature that rules, through the mechanism of natural selection. Biology replaces theology, and indeed it also replaces the Humanities. Once upon a time it was God who created the earth and the species that dwell upon it. Now it is evolution which is the creative agent. Its principle is functional: if it works, it will survive. The existence of things on earth has nothing to do with either their beauty or their goodness. It has to do simply with their power. It is the strongest within a given environment which survive. Weakness means extinction. If it is powerful it is good. The new god, Biology, recognizes only this one quality.

Darwin is a child of Enlightenment science, and he becomes its greatest exponent, the Newton of the biological sciences. This is now science in a moral vacuum, pursuing its rational ends without heed of the wider consequences. Darwin himself was a narrow man, his whole mind focused like a powerful spotlight on the patient observation of nature, and theoretical extrapolation from what he saw. He was cold to art, poetry or music. The time

144

of the Renaissance man is past. On the other hand there is no rancour in Darwin. His masterpiece, *The Origin of Species*, is written with a clear and honest enthusiasm. It is argued with a lucid, systematic elegance, quite the opposite of the flagship of Marxist science, *Capital*, which is wildly uneven in tone and thematically jumbled, with its major theses of little enduring significance. Darwin is the master of the clear and distinct.

It is the consequences of Darwin that are grave. He joins the mockers with his reduction of man to a plaything of Nature. Within evolution man is merely a passing part of a continuum between the amoeba and some futuristic mutation. His ancestor is neither Adam nor Brutus, but the monkey. As much as Marx profaned his own Jewish ancestors, Darwin went further, laughing at mankind and its veneration of the past, saying if you really want to know where you come from, go to the zoo, and study that parody of yourself, the great ape. He is your true father. Darwin's mockery is the more devastating in that it is not grounded on personal prejudice, nor on a bogus science like dialectical materialism, but on the most powerful and enduring theory produced by modern Reason, one which millions of subsequent studies and experiments have only strengthened. It is a simple theory too.

That man descends from the monkey has had two major effects on Western culture, both crippling. Firstly, it knocked the stuffing out of the humanist 'I am'. It means that man stands on nothing. The material determinism of the Enlightenment is trivial next to Darwin. Man exists because he does what every creature does, struggle to survive. So far the environment has been kind to him, so his species has flourished. This is temporary, as is his position at the top of the evolutionary scale. At some point in time it is inevitable that some chance mutation or some chance change to the environment will exterminate him. There is no place for free-will. Nor is there much dignity: in terms of the new sacred, Biology, the amoeba has greater distinction than man, for it has survived far longer than he. All that remains of orthodox humanism is that man's reason allows him to plot his own evolutionary path, in retrospect.

Not only is there no free-will, there is no responsibility, no morality, only power. Darwin himself argued that man's moral code has evolved from primitive forms in lower species, from the social instincts that are necessary for the survival of some species. This means that any law is provisional, to be kept while it is useful, entirely relative to the moment of evolution. No such law can be incontestably binding. If such utility is the foundation of the law, men will soon stop obeying it, for one man's use is another man's nuisance. Everything can be disputed, for everything is relative. There are no absolutes. Darwin thus provides the tank corps of modern relativism. What follows is one of the central axioms of Western nihilism, that life is absurd. Natural selection works through chance variations in a species. Man is thus the product of a myriad tiny changes from the amoeba. Each one of those changes was random, purely due to chance, before a favourable environment, as a second stage, determined that it would survive. In other words I am the product of a million years of myriad accidents. Moreover another such "accident" will eliminate me and all my kin, ancestors and descendants. What then is the point of it all? Darwin's answer is, Struggle to survive. This is precisely where we are not animals. For us the biological imperative is not enough. Moreover, Darwin himself has so demoralized us by pointing out who our great forefather was, the founder of our race at one remove, that the absurdity has tended to undermine the will, the will to survive.

Darwin protested that his theory was not incompatible with religion. His hunch was that at the start of evolution there were very few primordial forms – perhaps only one – from which all plants and animals descended. His theory did not explain the creation of these primordial forms. Perhaps God? He misses the point. The theory of evolution was so comprehensively successful that it made the humanist faith in science impregnable. If Darwin himself had not explained the creation of the first form of life on earth, some other scientist soon would, and so on, to the creation of the earth, the solar system, and finally the universe. It would be the scientific explanation that would be believed. After Darwin, supernatural causes were finished, for the remainder of the humanist epoch.

The second effect of Darwin on Western culture was the deeper and darker one. The theory of evolution tapped directly into the unconscious. The huge public response to Darwin was due to the association of man with monkey, the "ape theory" as it was popularly known. The search for the "missing link" took off, and has continued unabated with the search for early forms of man, for signs of the transitional species between ape and man. The first publication of Darwin's theory roused no popular interest – it was only when the implications for the origin of man became clear that Darwin became a household name. What was it that really riveted the public, that stopped it in its tracks, and drew its interest hypnotically towards this new idea? The answer is in what features in much of the scientific literature and even more in the many popular articles and cartoons: the image of the monkey, and especially its head, and its resemblance to man. But what the monkey head resembles is more precise. It resembles the human skull. Its lack of long hair, its pronounced eye sockets, its prominent teeth, and its bulbous jaw make the skeletal form more obvious. There is some affinity too between the monkey's bulbous jaw and the similarly rounded protruding human cranium, although one is at the lower front of the skull and the other at the upper rear. With eyes half-closed, gazing intently at the monkey's head one is caught by a dream image, blurred and distorted, of the human skull. We are uncannily transfixed into the shoes of the Ambassadors. Here is the focus of Darwinian research, under the unconscious equation, ape equals skull. There is a double reference, indirectly in the resemblance, directly in that the study of skulls becomes central to the Darwinian enterprise. The thousands of subsequent books on human evolution are full of diagrams of skulls.

Reason here bares its fangs. In Darwin the demonic returns,

with the imagery of a medieval hell sublimated into modern scientific forms. The agent was an honest, good and gentle man who could not have hurt a fly. If there is any personal element it is in the chronic sickness that dogged the second half of his life. Unwittingly, Darwin pioneers the scientific worship of death. This sleight of hand is accomplished by shifting the sacred site from the cemetery to the academy. The horror is kept under strict control, only let loose in the most civil and disguised sublimation, the study of the origin of species, or the Descent of Man, as Darwin put it in another title. The invitation to modernity is to join me in the museum, in the laboratory, in the lecture hall, for the scientific study of the skull. Through this study revelation will come. There is no threat, for man's supreme faculty, his reason, is in command. Let us worship at the temple of Nature; the skull is our holy relic. Science shall neutralize the fear of death.

This was all a lie. What Darwin did was clear the cultural decks for the emergence of the demonic, unchecked. He did once admit that his theory was like a murder. Reason lights the tunnel housing the monster, Luther's monster, opens the gate, but has no means for taming it, merely providing quaking humans with the delusion that to study its habits is to draw its teeth. Your original father is the gorilla: look again, and see what he represents, death. Once there is Darwin then there is the terror, and apart from it, nothing. Science, as Marx saw, is the agent of nihilism, the destroyer of culture. The title, *The Origin of Species*, is deep with double meaning. Without God, the ultimate question is on what do we stand, a question about ancestors. Here is Darwin's quest, his search for origins, and he is frank and direct about it, as he is about the simple answer: the skull disguised as the great ape. So it is that in the post-Darwin West the slightest allusion to the gorilla has sent a hideous shudder through us all.

Natural Selection not only knocked the stuffing out of humanism. It eliminated religion. Man has no divine origin: he was born in the primeval swamp. Christ is merely the member of a species, five stages removed from the squid, and further evolution will some day make him obsolete. The Catholic Church made the appropriate reply: let science explain the history of the human body, as long as it does not include the soul. Its reply was to fall on deaf ears, as far as the direction of Western culture was concerned, and Darwin was left with a free hand to degrade the metaphysics of man even lower than Hamlet's "quintessence of dust". *The Times* in London recognized the new cultural order, welcoming the burial of Darwin's body in Westminster Abbey: 'The Abbey needed it more than it needed the Abbey.' After Darwin, Munch is free to paint the Madonna as neurotic, in a traumatized swirl of reds and blacks, able only to create a dead embryo, itself an image out of a Darwinian textbook.

The Darwinian view is refutable by example. That view would hold that there is no essential difference between a group of men abducting a teenage girl, assaulting, raping and murdering her and a pack of wolves attacking a deer. Both acts are driven by violent instincts, with the partial contrast that in the human case the aggression is against the same species, and may contravene some collective survival need. Any self-respecting human community recognizes the two cases as fundamentally different. There is a brutality to what the wolves do, but no culpability or guilt: animals are innocent, which gives their behaviour an honest simplicity. In the assault on the teenage girl there is not just the extreme breach of the collective conscience of the community, but more significantly the violation of what is holy in the victim. The act is quite explicitly a desecration. After the event the entire community is contaminated by spiritual pollution, something wolves do not spread.

The new scientific picture of the world is utterly dispiriting. Darwin himself in his *Autobiography* recalled how once standing in the midst of the grandeur of a Brazilian forest he was filled with wonder. He was convinced there was more in man than the mere breath of his body. 'But now the grandest scenes would not cause any such convictions or feelings.' It is Natural Selection. Gone too is the hushed awe at the curtain to *Julius Caesar* as Antony hymns to Brutus, This was the noblest Roman of them all. Gone is the haunting imperative to human transgression, Mary Magdalene, as she lies prostrate at the feet of Christ washing them in her gushing tears. Gone are all heroes of conscience, all images of courage, honesty and fidelity. For what we see is merely the acting out of social instincts that man has inherited from the ants, instincts which are there because they serve a survival function. The crucifixion is itself superfluous superstition: we live on in the genes inherited by our children. Modern art, literature and philosophy that portrays life as a dismal wasteland, as a sort of living death, is a direct amplification of Darwin.

Darwinism harmonized with liberalism. Indeed, the latter's classic text, John Stuart Mill's *On Liberty*, was published in 1859, the same year as *The Origin of Species*. Both were English and both were blithely ignorant of culture, somehow assuming it unnecessary. The liberal model of society is a benign survival of the fittest, blind to the demonic, leaving all men free to their own individual devices, and all will be well – sweetness, light and progress. Both saw morality as a sort of awkward encumbrance. Moreover, both played a similar role as cultural destroyers, pitting reason and the striving individual against the forces of tradition, honour, authority and revealed religion. History turned out to be on their side. Their utopia would be realized, for good and for ill. Its benefit was the conquest of most of the traditional sources of human misery – squalor, hunger, disease and brute labour – but not warfare. Its cost was that life in the palace of reason became typified by the banal bureaucratic routines of the office and the depressive leisure routines of television and overeating. On the one hand comfort, on the other a disenchanted world emptied of meaning, with the one remaining limit on freedom, death, unanswered and therefore rising to the surface to cast its chilling shadow across life.

In this the heritage of Marx combined neatly with the liberal-rationalist one. The attack on the bourgeois helped turn him into the Marxist caricature, only interested in material things, believing in science, liberty and progress. The ideal of progress was itself reduced to the purely material, as comfort – rationalized in the twentieth century as Gross National Product, the key indicator of social well-being. In short, science and liberalism provided the new ideology for the middle class, once its Protestant root had withered, and the vertex of that ideology was economic progress. Marx had some sense of these affinities, writing to Darwin to ask him for permission to dedicate the second volume of *Capital* to him. Darwin declined.

What we have been considering in this chapter is one of the darkest episodes in the long and turbulent history of Western culture. It was the episode in which humanism turned nasty. There is the sickly, gentle Darwin, in retreat from the world with his large family, like a child in his patient devotion to his studies of plant and animal. In truth he is another Holbein ambassador, with narrower interests, unmusical, glimpsing an obscure image of his holy grail, the origin of origins, and it is the same one, only this ambassador is going to convert the whole of Western culture to his quest. He is prophet as well as ambassador of death, his book the most influential in the nineteenth century, side by side with *Hamlet*. Then there is rancour incarnate, Marx, projecting onto the honourable, pious, middle-class gentleman the low passion to seduce his neighbour's wife. No honour, no trust, no fidelity – nothing but greed. Kill, Kill!

The cultural consequences of Darwin were, consciously, that religion and honour are irrelevant, we should ignore them and continue on in the enlightened pursuit of comfort; unconsciously, that the origin of origins is death, and it rules. The cultural consequences of Marx were, consciously, that selfishness and economics rule, and culture is merely a cloak disguising base bourgeois motives; unconsciously, the gods of culture have betrayed us so let us annihilate them. Under the powerful influence of this last element, Western High Culture since the middle of the nineteenth century has devoted itself with hardly an exception to the demolition of the traditional moral law, especially in its bourgeois guise. Flaubert's *Madame Bovary* (1857) was merely the leading example among thousands of the parody of middle-class life as empty and hypocritical, clutching at possessions and status, titillating hysterical women and strait-laced men with Romantic fantasies. The mockers had won the field. What had started two hundred years earlier in *Las Meninas* with the needling away at the powerfully authoritative King had been developed into a comprehensive victory by Marx and Darwin.

9

INTO THE HEART OF
DARKNESS

So it was, the two high cultural works to preside over the nine-teenth century, *Hamlet* and *The Origin of Species*, focus on the skull. That Hamlet is invited to take centre-stage is a sign there is nothing left to mock. The old order is wooden. In the chiller air, the spectre of Holbein's corpse steeps the atmosphere for the first time, no longer a marginal shudder, and it balefully redirects the mocking drive into a slide into the heart of darkness. On the frontier the wild charge of the vandals is already over. The mood is rather that of Shelley's Ozymandias, the tyrant doubling as Western culture itself:

> Round the decay
> Of that colossal wreck, boundless and bare,
> The lone and level sands stretch far away.

After the mockers, there is nothing. The West has entered nihilist modernity, humanism's last site. The man who understood its nature best was the German philosopher, Nietzsche. With an unerring nose for first principles he saw into the humanist test of finding a place to stand: 'Since Copernicus man has been rolling from the centre toward X.' He saw that by his own time the task was hopeless. His Zarathustra exclaims: 'Who will hereafter raise high the image of man?' Nietzsche was the last of the humanist philosophers, seeing the end but still trying to save the order. In his 1882 parable on the Death of God he outlines the implications of life without a religious, sacred beyond. A madman runs into the marketplace screaming that we have killed God. In a series of demented questions he spells out what follows:

How were we able to drink up the sea? Who gave us the sponge to wipe away the entire horizon? What did we do when we unchained this earth from its sun? Whither is it moving now? Whither are we moving now? Away from all suns? Are we not perpetually falling? Backward, sideward, forward, in all directions? Is there any up or down left?

Without God, life is either horrible or absurd. There is nothing more.

Joseph Conrad, in his own 1899 wrestling with the same question, *Heart of Darkness*, symbolizes modern civilization by the city. Life in the city is absurd, full of stupid importance, meaningless petty routines, the butcher on one corner the policeman on the other, a healthy appetite and filching a little money, order kept by holy terror of scandal, the gallows and the lunatic asylum. Life is 'that mysterious arrangement of merciless logic for a futile purpose'. Nothing survives Conrad's relentless nihilism: he portrays the highest and the best only to ruin them. And his juicy little tale is littered with skulls.

Once the nihilist metaphysics was perceived, and that its time had come, the first response was to fight. This is the phase of resistance, of dynamic nihilism. It produces the two great pieces of modern theory, the ones that got a firm and direct hold on the crisis of late humanism. Their authors were Kierkegaard and Nietzsche.

There had been an earlier phase of resistance, of a different sort, born in immediate response to the French Revolution. This was conservatism, with its founding work, and enduring masterpiece, Edmund Burke's *Reflections on the Revolution in France*. Burke recognized the mockers, correctly predicted the results of their acts, and he chose rather than wrestle with nihilism to fight against its advance, by restoring the old order. He fancied neither reason nor romance. Conservatism has remained an opponent to the humanist mainstream, has an achievement or two to its credit, and is worthy of some passing attention.

Burke saw the barbaric consequences of utopian Reason applied to politics, of trying to build a new social order on "clear and distinct" Cartesian principles, founded on abstract ideas about the rights of man. He knew the weakness of human intelligence in relation to the demonic outrages of which man is capable when unchecked. He knew its weakness too in understanding the nature of the institutions which check such forces, institutions which take generations to build, and thereby contain within them the accumulated wisdom of legions of forefathers. Social order depends on custom, tradition, authority and hierarchy. Burke saw that it is deep cultural roots which anchor things. Thus he strove to preserve the aristocracy, and in particular its structural role in the political system of Constitutional Monarchy. He himself was the great theorist and defender of the hybrid aristocratic-Protestant English parliament. His guiding principle is finely caught in his advice that one should approach the faults of the State as the wounds of a father, 'with pious awe and trembling solicitude'.

Long before Marx, Burke saw that Enlightenment modernity is at odds with tradition. His *Reflections* are written with the feverish pungency of wounded rage, of a man fighting for his honour, violated, outraged, helpless. Conservatism has been largely reaction, futile reaction against the juggernaut of modernity, a series of last ditch stands here and there, on occasion successful for the moment while the war was steadily lost. Its one great success was Burke's own, the preservation of parliamentary democracy. That masterful English creation would prosper for the rest of the humanist epoch, while all around it religion waned, courtesy declined, a law-asserting High Culture turned into a rampaging desecrator, and most of the social hierarchy and its complicated tiers of obligation was flattened.

One strand of conservatism was not reaction. There was the recognition of the dogged narrow-minded virtue of the common man, that in spite of being encircled by celebrated mockers, an entire educated elite of nihilists, he would cling to his traditions and stick to what he believed to be right and wrong. Burke on the strength of the English:

Thanks to our sullen resistance to innovation, thanks to the cold sluggishness of our national character, we still bear the stamp of our forefathers . . . We know that *we* have made no discoveries; and we think that no discoveries are to be made, in morality; nor many in the great principles of government, nor in the ideas of liberty, which were understood long before we were born, altogether as well as they will be after the grave has heaped its mould upon our presumption, and the silent tomb shall have imposed its law on our pert loquacity. In England we have not yet been completely emboweled of our natural entrails;

There is a desperation in this, of knowing the cause is right, but fearing it is doomed. It is a time for extremes, which is more obvious in the case of Burke's French contemporary, Joseph de Maistre. De Maistre believed the only hope of preserving the old order lay in the abolition of education, and the instating of the sacred altar and the executioner as the two pillars of society. Jane Austen too saw the precarious state of things, describing in her sociological novel, *Mansfield Park* (1814), how one foolish generation under the influence of the new ideas could destroy an age-old great house – authority was that weak. A generation later de Tocqueville answered in the negative his own question as to whether democracy and stable culture are compatible.

The problem for conservatism was that the tide of modernist humanism was far too strong, and neither aristocratic nor Protestant culture were rescuable in their existing form. While a second Reformation was required, conservatism at best staged a series of holding operations, directed by an unworldly vision of the future as a hazy nostalgic recreation of an idealized past. It lacked the colossal initiative that the task demanded, and tended to withdraw into cogent, pessimistic analyses of decline.

Nineteenth-century conservatism would soon focus on a more specific theme, the loss of community. It saw in the steady erosion of strong unified belief and local ties, symbolized in the traditional village, the essence of modernity. It plausibly found the cause here for the emerging social pathology of lonely individualism, of senseless mobility from place to place, job to job, relationship to relationship, commodity to commodity, idea to idea, in short of a rootless and restless existence, absurd in its busyness. This view would become axiomatic to the mainstream of Sociology, theorized most fully by Durkheim, in his study of *Suicide* (1897) – the title itself an unintentional metaphor for the state of Western culture. I shall return in Chapter 12 to the community theme.

Kierkegaard and the Second Crisis of Protestantism

Both grand theorists of the cultural collapse of humanism were of Protestant stock. The Protestant root had gained a singular strength in the West. Furthermore, the orientation of the two exemplars of English conservatism, Edmund Burke and Jane Austen, while being contextually aristocratic, was directed by a Protestant ethos. It is Kierkegaard, however, who senses that he has to restore his religion, work a second Reformation, or all is over. It is only Kierkegaard who dedicates his life to achieving the death of death. He returns to the Protestant heart, by his time its own type of darkness, to search for the faith that eludes him. In the process he finishes the job Rembrandt had started, in the shadows of Luther and Calvin, to confirm whether or not there is a place to stand. We recall that Rembrandt failed, principally because man was not up to the divine call. The father of faith, Abraham, lost his mind because of the personal and ethical violation of him demanded by God. Kierkegaard goes the next and final stage with Abraham. Bypassing the question of his sanity, he wonders whether he had faith at all. Kierkegaard was a man of his time, unable to retreat into the secure and unproblematic Christianity of the past, desperate to find a path he could take seriously, given what he knew, back to faith. The result is late humanist modernity's one great piece of religious wrestling, and Protestantism's second crisis.

Kierkegaard's argument is that human experience in modernity has broken down into three distinct spheres, the aesthetic, the ethical and the religious. They have become stages in cultural decline, with the religious collapsing first, followed by the ethical, reducing life to the aesthetic plane. Kierkegaard attempts a restoration. The major works are *Fear and Trembling* of 1843 and the *Concluding Unscientific Postscript* of 1846, although fragments of the picture appear elsewhere.

What then are the three spheres, or stages? The aesthetic is the sphere of pleasure, of the individual's pursuit of temporal happiness. Kierkegaard's repeated example is a love affair. The hero of the aesthetic is Don Juan, who dedicates his life to the art of arousing passion, of orchestrating seduction. An aspect of this is the psychological observation of mood and motive, in self and other. It is the sphere of Romanticism, of concentrated indulgence in feeling, in beautiful pleasures. It values artistic expression and individualism.

The second sphere is the ethical. It is universal, determined by laws higher than the individual. It depends on action, whereas the aesthetic may be largely conducted in the imagination. If an affair or a flirtation is aesthetic, then marriage is ethical. It is not to be ended once the individual's pleasure diminishes. There is duty and obligation. The ethical places limits on pleasure. The ethical is the domain of the tragic hero. Antigone sacrificing herself for the Law is an ethical heroine. Brutus and Uriah are ethical heroes; Hamlet fails in these terms. The ethical is the sphere of the bourgeois, of marriage, vocation and duty, all in obedience to universal law.

The third and highest sphere is the religious. Like the aesthetic it is individual, but that is the only similarity. It is based on suffering and its characteristics are subjectivity, inwardness and guilt. There are three different types of religion. There is primitive religion, in which the sacred is pure and direct. Man is bathed in the presence of divinity. This is the world of the child, of simple guilt, in which punishment works: a smack from the father and all is better. We have lost this world. What remains is either Religiousness A or Religiousness B. "A" is having faith that faith exists, but not having faith itself. God is indirect and invisible. He has no outer presence, unlike in primitive religion in which he is entirely external to the individual. Man is shut up in himself, locked in subjectivity, in dread yearning for the only escape, revelation. The greater the dread the greater the man. Neither beast nor angel have dread, for neither have guilt. Inbetween is man. Religiousness A is an absurd condition, in which what a man cannot know, but only believe, is the object of his faith, which necessarily eludes him. This is Kierkegaard's own condition.

Religiousness B is faith. A miracle occurs and there is a leap of faith, from A to B. Again the outer calls. This faith is like being in a ship that has sprung a leak, enthusiastically pumping while not trying to find a harbour. In the same situation the understanding, unlike faith, stretches its arms towards the shore, and sinks. Religion is man's relationship within himself to eternal happiness. The path to it is through dread, distress and paradox. Whoever arrives is higher than the tragic hero. Mary, for instance, is higher than any heroine. She was entirely alone in her mission, foreseeing the dreadful fate that would befall her son. And that son: 'Was it not dreadful that this man who walks among the others – was it not dreadful that He was God?' And what of the disciples: 'Was it not dreadful to sit at table with Him?'

The problem here, for Kierkegaard himself and all modernity with him, is how to achieve the leap of faith. All else is trivial. But Kierkegaard is beside himself with doubt, a doubt we observed in Calvin. Kierkegaard is at least open about his doubt, placing it at the centre of his spiritual quest. It is the monster without whose killing he cannot live. He longs for the simple world of the child, or the Catholic, for whom punishment works. His own guilt is unquenchable. It is laughable that God, moreover, should be moved by human suffering. How petty that would make him. There is no remission of sins. The role of guilt now is to bore into the soul to make a man deeper, more inward, more pitiful, more dreadful. And then the paradox: out of sheer tormenting inwardness comes faith, out of the ashes new life. Such is Kierkegaard's hope. He even creates a method, a discipline to replace fasting and chastity. So burden yourself, he says to the individual, so burden yourself with inwardness and guilt, that the paradox will explode into faith. This is hard-core Calvinism taken to its logical extreme. The only anchor in a chaotic and ephemeral world is my inner self and my conscience. Intensify them!

Kierkegaard devotes his *Fear and Trembling* to the question, Is faith possible? He poses the question through meditating on the strongest conceivable example, the father of faith, Abraham. Like Rembrandt he concentrates on the testing of Abraham's faith, through the sacrifice of his only son, Isaac. In Kierkegaard's categories, what God asks of Abraham is that he attain the religious by annihilating both the aesthetic and the ethical. He is required to destroy his own happiness, by murdering his pride and joy, the pleasure of his life, his reason for living, Isaac. Furthermore, he will ruin his marriage, turning his wife in uncomprehending hatred against him. He is also required to break almost every major moral law, thou shalt not kill, thou shalt protect the innocent, especially your own children, thou shalt not betray trust – son loves and trusts father – not to mention the laws of the tribe and its patriarch, to continue the blood line. Abraham is neither an egoist pursuing pleasure nor a tragic hero – he renounces the universal laws of ethics. The knight of faith gives up both wish and duty, unlike the tragic hero who gives up wish for duty, and gains the universal. For Kierkegaard, Abraham is utterly alone with his act, his three day journey, his setting up of the sacrifice, his response to Isaac's troubled question about the location of the sacrificial animal. No one can understand Abraham. His wife certainly cannot. No one can know what drives him, that intimate private word of God. Abraham is silent, absorbed in what he does, and the nightmare dread of it, of his own right hand plunging in the dagger, of how he will live after this act, day after day, night after night, overwhelmed with grief and terror. So it is that God loads his knight of faith with dread, distress and paradox. So it is that he deepens his inwardness. Abraham has 'the terrible responsibility of solitude, of unutterable sighs'. He is the loneliest man.

Again and again through his meditation Kierkegaard asks whether it is possible to believe in Abraham. Is such faith plausible? What of the enormous paradox which is Abraham's life, that is the question? Think how strong that faith would have to be, to keep him warm at night after the deed, to hold his hand, to keep him sane. Kierkegaard's timid answer, endlessly repeated, is 'Abraham I cannot understand.' I cannot think myself into his state, for I do not have the confidence of faith. No! it is not possible to believe in him. 'Is faith I wonder to be found on earth?' Kierkegaard swings between adulation and contempt: Abraham offers so much, but he leaves so little. He leaves nothing. But if Abraham did not have faith, then he was a simple murderer, a rogue, and of no interest metaphysically speaking.

If faith is not possible, if the father of faith was a fraud, then ethics too soon collapses and all that remains is a debased form of the aesthetic. This is modern life. Kierkegaard finds it a joke, typifying it by those people in their twenties who believe they have achieved their utmost. There is no inwardness, no seriousness. Dread is interpreted as a disease of the body. People don't call the priest any more lest the patient die of fright. Religion becomes like using a jack in a bog. Passion too dies, for it has lost its root: faith is the highest passion in man. Kierkegaard pits himself against the times. Unlike the modern hero whose task is to make things easier, he aims to make them more difficult. His ideal sermon would counter the restless, fidgeting world of entertainment and journalism by returning every Sunday with the same originality to the same theme. So speaks a great Protestant conscience, at its wits' end because it sees clearly the precarious state of its faith and the increasing frivolity and emptiness of the world in which it dwells.

What then is Kierkegaard's solution? There is a new Protestant agony. Kierkegaard accepts Luther's darkness of faith. He is not interested in the light, for that is at best the plane of the two English lords wagering on the runaway horse, at worst life determined by indifferent pleasures, cushioned in sedative comforts. In the darkness, however, he cannot find faith. He is willing to descend beneath the ethical, like Abraham, but he does not have the firm cord of faith to lead him, only the agitation of unquenchable dread. There is the mental torment of paradox, infinite guilt and no faith. Either one believes in Abraham or nothing. Therefore it is nothing, and Luther's monster roams in the dark, untamed, untamable.

The old Protestant contradiction, that I have no free-will but am responsible, was unproblematic, once logic had been relegated to its rightful minor place in human conduct. The new contradiction, however, is serious. Kierkegaard's own attempt to reach Religiousness B, to make his leap of faith, is through thinking. It is not any old thought. With peerless ironical wit and ethical-psychological insight, Kierkegaard maps the condition of Western culture and the havoc it is wreaking on the individual doing his best to live within its crumbling structure. On the plane of knowledge his challenge is to think in the categories in which we live. No more rationalist fantasy about the goodness of man or idylls of social progress. No more other-worldly pretence about happiness and virtue. No more Romantic haze. Just the hard facts. For the first time since the seventeenth century a depth returns to the consideration of the central metaphysical questions. Kierkegaard does think in the categories in which he lives.

His solution, which is the new Protestant contradiction, is to think his way to faith. The hope is to take the path of knowledge in order to reach the path of faith. But Kierkegaard himself knows as well as Luther and Calvin that this is impossible. Faith and knowledge occupy separate universes. Reason is useless as a means to grace. 'Faith alone' is a gift of God. Kierkegaard's attempted compromise is through a certain type of thinking, one designed to accentuate guilt, heighten suffering, intensify inwardness, bring on the loneliness of Abraham, and focus on the paradox which cannot be thought. Indeed he asserts that great thought depends on being centred on paradox, that which cannot be thought through – he may well be right about this. His next move is to glorify paradox. Faith becomes 'the objective uncertainty due to the repulsion of the absurd held fast by the passion of inwardness, which in this instance is intensified to the utmost degree.' His logic echoes that of the early Church father,

Tertullian: Because it is impossible, it is certain. Kierkegaard puts it:

A revelation is signalled by mystery, happiness by suffering, the certainty of faith by uncertainty, the ease of the paradoxical religious life by its difficulty, the truth by absurdity.

Here is Protestant modernity's last statement. Faith depends on a miracle, to cut through the paradox to revelation. We do not believe in miracles any more. Kierkegaard does not believe in miracles. Kierkegaard's solution is absurd, pursuing knowledge in order to believe, knowing full well that the mission is hopeless. But he must stick to his mission, for the alternative, what he sees around him, is beneath contempt. At least Kierkegaard has his inwardness to keep him warm, and he has thought in the categories in which he lives, honestly, to the ultimate point, where there is nowhere left to go. Faith eludes him.

While Rembrandt's doubt was that man is not up to the divine call, he is made of too poor stuff, Kierkegaard's is that he is no longer able to hear the call. He is lost in his inwardness, trapped in subjectivity. The monster which he glimpses in the dark, which he cannot kill, is the Medusa. There is nothing beyond, and therefore nothing under the feet. The shades of the skull start to materialize in front of the eyes. There was to be no serene old age for Kierkegaard, young kin around him. He died a bachelor, aged forty-two.

Nietzsche: Prophet of Nihilism

Nietzsche's diagnosis of nihilistic modernity is similar to that of Kierkegaard. However, he twists the judgment and inverts the solution. Protestant Christianity becomes the main cause of the problem. It must be killed off completely, allowing a rebirth of the great Renaissance individual. Nietzsche is a humanist, although a most peculiar one.

The opening gambit is Nietzsche's first and finest work, *The*

Birth of Tragedy (1872). The focus is culture. Human life is lived on the surface, driven by a substratum of demonic instincts, nightmare fears, and a barbaric will to lust and sadism. This is the unconscious, Dionysian basis of reality. Culture's task is to transform or sublimate these Dionysian drives into harmonious and beautiful images that capture the mind and give an orderly direction to how men conduct their lives. Nietzsche's example is Raphael's *Transfiguration*. The bottom half of the painting is the dark and turbulent world of man, a mad boy possessed by demons, his family distraught and helpless. The top half is the transfiguration of Christ, a haunting image of transcendence, which the boy sees and thereby regains his sanity. The greatest example of culture was Greek tragedy, in which the Dionysian is encountered at its most demonic, the individual is annihilated, but out of the ashes rises an intoxicating sense of the elemental oneness and significance of existence.

In modernity culture has failed. Either there are the uncontrolled Dionysian excesses of Romanticism, without any ordering principle, or the banal pedantry of rationalism, which closes its eyes to the demonic. The result is nihilism. The second aim of Nietzsche's work is to explain how this came about. One side of the story is that God is dead. Therefore there can be no transfiguration, no faith, no ordering principle from above. Culture depends on a "redemptive illusion" to sublimate the night demons, to give a man a strong enough sense of a fixed and stable order around him to release the anarchic forces within. Christianity was the last such illusion, and it has gone. Already Hamlet was without illusion, and he saw the truth clearly and distinctly – not the Cartesian illusion. The truth he saw is that life is either horrible or absurd. His knowledge paralysed him. For Nietzsche, Hamlet is the embodiment of modern nihilism.

There is another side to the story. It is developed most fully in the *Genealogy of Morals* of 1887, the work of the "mature" Nietzsche in which he is at his most pungent, lucid and concentrated. Under the influence of Christianity the West had experienced a steady disciplining of the instincts, a repression of

Dionysus. This has led to an increasing bad conscience, mounting guilt. Through this process man has lost his spontaneity, his gaiety, and his ability to make decisions without a laborious moral conflict in himself about what is right or wrong. He has lost his very zest for living, to the point of becoming sick of himself. He has become cautious, timid, bored and boring. Instinctual control makes for frustration, and the disease of modernity, rancour. Modern man is malicious bad temper mixed with an obsession about comfort. The psychology of rancour is that the pain of guilt is deadened by the letting off of savage emotions against those who are still active and decisive.

This progressive enchaining of the instincts has gone hand in hand with a growing intellectualism. The pioneering culprit in this history of the deification of Reason was Socrates, who rejected Greek tragedy, true culture, as primitive and replaced it with the first rationalist ethics. Nietzsche pits a powerful psychological argument against the Enlightenment: the real basis of the modern faith in reason is to allow over-repressed individuals who have lost the spontaneous ability to act, who find that whatever they do they feel guilty, to allow them to rationalize their behaviour as good. We love reason because we need excusing reasons. To have to rationalize every move, out of guilt, makes a man particularly rancorous against anyone less inhibited. Rancour is the disease of the impotent, made sick by bad conscience. In modernity the sick take over, and the emotions of pity towards those who are worse off and nausea at life replace what is healthy and vital, an unselfconscious pleasure in power. Nietzsche's contrasting ideal of an undecadent people was the ancient Athenians, with their "hair-raising cheerfulness". He sets gratitude, the predominant emotion of Greek religion, opposite the misery of Christianity.

Nietzsche attempted a series of solutions. The first, in *The Birth of Tragedy*, was to urge a return to the metaphysics of Greek tragedy, to myth against reason. Ironically, in this instance he was on the same side as Luther, whom he hated, "this calamity of a monk". The position could not hold for long, for it depended on faith in a higher order, and Nietzsche had no such faith. With time he became more and more contemptuous of the darkness of faith, more virulently anti-Christian.

Nietzsche's second and most sustained solution is the humanist one of the cultivation of great men, of the self-assertive, confident 'I am'. The Renaissance was the last period of vital culture, in which larger-than-life individuals acted and created at will. Napoleon is the last descendant of this tradition, the last Roman, and Nietzsche lionizes him as such, the man unchecked by a bad conscience who proved that we can do anything we will. Napoleon is an example too of the incompatibility of freedom and morality: Nietzsche went straight to the flaw in Kantian ethics, highlighting it in the most autonomous man of the nineteenth century, that he was only so because he acted beyond good and evil. The Renaissance for Nietzsche was not Reason. It was purely Will, the Will to Power. If he had known it, Nietzsche would have found in Velázquez' self-portrait in *Las Meninas* the perfect incarnation of his ideal humanist, indeed of himself and his own mission.

Nietzsche's "superman" turns out, however, to be grotesque parody of the humanist ideal, a sign of how close to the end of that culture the West had moved. There is not much difference between Napoleon and the next historical incarnation of the value-creating hero, Hitler. Just how unfanciful these connections are was illustrated in the title of the propaganda film made of Hitler's 1934 Nuremberg Party Convention, *The Triumph of the Will*. In this Nietzschean phrase is the finale to humanism's opening 'We can become what we will.'

Dostoevsky was alert to this ghastly emanation of late humanism. He made a sequence of Christian attacks on humanist monsters. There is Raskolnikov, who theorizes Napoleon as the extraordinary man who for the sake of destiny is permitted to be above the moral law, to kill tens of thousands without a second thought. There is the nihilist, Stavrogin, a nineteenth-century Hamlet, who out of boredom seduces a twelve-year-old girl and then listens indolently as she commits suicide. There is the revolutionary, Verkhovensky, enacting without conscience the ideals of the French Revolution, who has two passions, eating and destruction. Raskolnikov finds that he cannot become what he will. After murder he is paralysed by his conscience. He is not Napoleon.

If Nietzsche's second solution is horrible, his third is absurd — a mark of his singular brilliance as a diagnostician of culture is that he keeps getting trapped in his own categories. Nihilism is inevitable. Let us then welcome it, embrace it. It will help us get rid of all the moralistic, hypocritical, sanctimonious dross of civilization. Let us join in the destruction of all values so that we can start anew. Nietzsche produces his third and last ideal, the value-creating philosopher, and he resurrects Socrates as its first representative. The villain of *The Birth of Tragedy* becomes the hero of the late work. The mission of the philosopher is to tap the ideals of the time to see how hollow they ring, as if with a tuning fork. This is what Socrates did, the stinging fly as he called himself, a cultural irritant to all complacency. The principal task is introspective, what Nietzsche calls "self-overcoming", for the philosopher to destroy his own values first. This is a new version, an intellectual's one, of 'We can become what we will.'

There is bad reason and good reason. The bad is the usual pursuit of knowledge as rationalization, in order not to see the truth. The modern intellectual's real fear is to regain consciousness. Good reason has the nerve to endure the awful truth about man. It is Dionysian, in method akin to dancing, productive of full-bellied laughter. It forces a man to think in the categories in which he lives. Nietzsche was himself master of this virtue, the most insightful psychologist the West has produced.

So Nietzsche's third solution is a new Enlightenment, of ruthless psychologizing after the truth. It hinges on new values. What will they be? Where will they come from? The philosopher is not a man of action, a Renaissance man, nor even a Don Quixote, whom Nietzsche admired greatly for his ability to move in an absurd world. The restoration of culture through mind is impossible, as Nietzsche himself stressed from the outset by castigating Socrates as the great destroyer. The new values do not come. Psychology, however lucid, cannot generate an ethics. Hamlet is paralysed by what he sees, the truth. The man who shouts in the market-place that God is dead is mad. And Nietzsche himself, ever the victim of his own categories, after the coherence of *The Birth of Tragedy*, steadily became more strident and erratic. Finally there are the unrelieved delusions of grandeur of his last work, *Ecce Homo*. Not long after, he collapsed into a catatonic schizophrenia from which he never recovered.

The last words of *Ecce Homo* are 'Dionysus versus the Crucified.' The first letter of his madness was signed 'The Crucified.' His late works are full of vitriolic attacks on Christianity, one itself titled *The AntiChrist*. We are back with Luther and Kierkegaard: faith is all. Nietzsche knows that if he cannot find a replacement for Christ, he has had it. He will have become like Don Quixote at the end, a normal man, his only wish to die – Nietzsche hated this ending. It is Me versus Christ, the humanist I as God, or nothing. But who am I? I have tried Socrates, but I better than anyone have seen through the emptiness of Reason – 'knowledge never creates values.' I have tried Dionysus, but without Greek tragedy he is a berserk demon destroying all in his path. I myself have to become God, or succumb, like Hamlet, to the horror and absurdity. Nietzsche manages it finally, but only in his demented imagination. His third solution is psychotic.

In his madness he confirms his lunatic identification with Christ, and gives away the source of his rage, that he himself cannot become God. The theorist of rancour was himself the most rancorous critic of his own Protestant, Christian roots. His hostility to Luther stems from affinity: his diagnosis is the same, only the path is barred to him. He takes the alternative, humanist course, rightly seeing Socrates and not Erasmus as its pioneer. What results, his whole work, modernity's great introspective autobiography in the form of philosophy, demonstrates that the humanist path is a dead-end, one that has now been reached. The philosopher hero destroying values is hastening the very nihilism that Nietzsche has charted as the stagnant hell-pit of the time. There is no way out.

In a footnote to his 'philosopher as hero' Nietzsche launches his last value, *amor fati*, to love fate. From the superman, the value-creating great man, Nietzsche swings to the opposite extreme. We have no will, we have no freedom, we have no values. All that is left is Necessity. Let us worship it. Thus he ends by echoing the instability of Enlightenment thought, one minute total freedom, the next total determinism. By this stage his categories are no longer interesting.

For Nietzsche, no holds were barred. His philosophizing with a tuning fork discovered that truth itself is an illusion. There are merely mental perspectives on reality. What we see are conjuring tricks of consciousness. Emotions govern the eye, and they are subjective. "Evil" is merely an interpretation; so is "sin". Even our assumptions about events being caused is a convenient fiction, as for instance in the saying, 'It rains.' What, asks Nietzsche, is the "it"? The single truth is that existence is either horrible or absurd. All is appearance, all is relative: there are no fixed points. Nietzsche drags out the motto of the Assassins: 'Nothing is true; everything is permitted.' He is left with a Darwinian "will to power" driving man. The real constraint is Necessity, not culture. Culture merely inhibits the will, making man sick. Thus Nietzsche's own position shows where you end if you wed yourself to the humanist ideals of reason and will, and you are rigorous and honest.

Nietzsche's significance to the story of the rise and fall of humanism is as the last humanist philosopher. He is also significant for introducing the psychology of guilt into the analysis of Western decadence. In particular he stresses that increasing levels of instinctual repression have progressively reduced confidence in the 'I am', have inhibited the will, and have cultivated the intelligence as an agent of rancour. As a consequence man has become tired of himself, hypersensitive to pain, obsessed about his comfort, unadventurous, and lacking much desire for anyone or anything. In all of this Nietzsche was right. He was partly right too in blaming Christianity, and especially Protestantism, for radically increasing the cultural war against the instincts. He was signally wrong, however, not to recognize the other side of Luther's heritage, its serious attempt to address the problem of guilt, reading it as a religious and not a psychological phenomenon, the only answer to it through faith rather than knowledge. Here Kierkegaard was the true prophet, even to the point of praising the Reformation for augmenting the burden of guilt in order to focus the spirit religiously. The crisis for Protestantism came when the theology weakened, leaving the guilt without any cultural forms to sublimate it into images of salvation. Nietzsche and Kierkegaard provided a similar description but an opposite response, Nietzsche arguing that it would have been better without this assault on the instincts, sticking with the glory of the Renaissance, Kierkegaard following Luther, dismissing the Renaissance as childish, spiritually speaking. Nietzsche tried to get the last nourishing drop out of humanism, Kierkegaard to turn the tide.

Either way was closed. The Renaissance man on his own proved not to have the resources to found a new culture. In any case high levels of guilt had made him culturally obsolete. The value-creating philosopher is a contradiction in terms. It was only in literal madness that the Nietzschean I was able to emerge. Nietzsche collapsed in the arms of his own categories: without God, life is either horrible or absurd. Kierkegaard did a little better, in his own wrestling with nihilism. Left to the path of knowledge as the only way to the summit of faith, he found that he did achieve greater inwardness, deeper guilt, a more tormented solitude, and an all-pervading dread. What he gained was depth. Kierkegaard is deep. Compared to him other nineteenth-century figures appear like flotsam. There is a type of anchoring in this depth. The paradox, however, failed. He got no closer to the state of grace which is faith. The path of knowledge leads in circles, spiralling down, into the heart of darkness.

10

UNCONSCIOUS

'For in that sleep of death what dreams may come . . .' Again it is Hamlet who gives the cue. After the struggling resistance of dynamic nihilism comes the torpor of resigned nihilism. The humanist **I** survives as a shadow, lonely, mournful, isolated from community, restless, no place to stand. It makes its final move, withdrawal into self. Kierkegaardian inwardness rules the world, but it has lost both its religious and ethical content. It is narrowly psychological. Guilt pervades everything, and it is a sickness. Locked in subjectivity means dominated by the unconscious. The turn inwards is to embrace the unconscious, hoping for the return of the long lost father, hoping to find a light in dreams. Will and Reason have lost their sense. The active life is an absurd waste of energy and time. The last of the great painters, Cézanne and Van Gogh, try to find some order in this retreat from the world. The last of the great theorists, Freud, centres his work on the concept of the Unconscious, and tries to find a small part for reason to play.

Freud attempts to reconcile reason and romance. He is a tough realist about the nature of romance, seeing its instinctual basis in the unconscious, driven by the demonic forces Nietzsche called Dionysian. His patients are trapped in unconsciousness, instinct and repressive character becoming the new agents of Necessity. It is a psychological necessity that now rules life. Freud pulled no punches in his case-studies, liking the short-hand, "wolf-man" and "rat-man", to describe two of the definitive ones. The majority of his female patients were suffering from "hysteria", which he attributed to sexual frustration and analysed without any

Paul Cézanne, *Lac d'Annecy*, Courtauld Institute Galleries, London

reserve. All proprieties are scrapped in approaching the unconscious: anal compulsion, frigidity, premature ejaculation, sado-masochism become the stock-in-trade of psychoanalysis. Indeed propriety itself becomes a cause of neurosis, politeness and reticence symptoms of "civilized nervousness". Nietzsche's 'morality makes us sick' is extrapolated on an imperial scale.

Freud is doctor-confessor to the decadent bourgeoisie, once their lives have been flattened to the psychological plane. His theses echo Nietzsche: the bourgeois temperament has become too severe, producing bad conscience and guilt. The result of over-repression is that individuals become locked in their unconscious, traumatized by fantasies of being chased by wolves or indulging in riotous sado-masochistic orgies. Bourgeois culture in decline produces hysteria, obsession and depression. Freud himself described the typical middle-class marriage as 'spiritual disappointment and physical deprivation', the frigidity of wives and the impotence of husbands being endemic.

Freud offers knowledge as cure. Knowledge can make you happy. The final representation of this stock humanist illusion is psychological knowledge: Know thyself and you shall become well. The object of Freudian therapy is to discover the origins of neurosis, that is of psychological inhibition, bring them to consciousness, and then hope that awareness will free the patient from the bonds of his necessity. Freud was a sober optimist. He did not go as far as the second half of the Socratic credo, that knowledge will make you more virtuous. He had no expectation that his patients might become morally better. Indeed his hopes were at times disarmingly modest, as he put it 'to turn hysterical misery into common unhappiness'. The movement he founded tended to be more naive in its optimism, as he himself was at other times, foreseeing a future in which reason had reshaped the instincts. The Enlightenment faith in progress had found one last protagonist.

The main structure of Freud's work is of little significance for our story. It is hardly more than a dated humanist optimism wedded to Nietzsche. The theory of repression and the unconscious is pure Nietzsche, extended and turned into a system. The main theses are also familiar, repression makes us sick, religion and civilization are the main culprits in increasing guilt, religion belongs to the childhood of the human race, and morality, history, philosophy are all reducible to psychology. Even Freudian therapy is the turning into a practical method of Nietzsche's philosophizing with a tuning fork, coming to know yourself by destroying your illusions. Both stress intellectual self-overcoming as the way to undermine the last repressive authorities over the individual, and set him free. Freud's humanism is more simplistic, in its half-belief that a free, autonomous individual, master of his own instincts, was possible. Freud also held to the standard Enlightenment view that science and truth are adequate replacements for religion and faith, and that High Culture is capable of serving as a source of moral order. Here Nietzsche was more troubled, his metaphysical wanderings deeper. He would have granted one of Freud's sceptical themes, that psychological therapy is "interminable": the patient is never completely cured, that is never completely free.

The most that can be claimed for Freud as philosopher, in spite of his rightful status as the most influential theorist of the twentieth century, is that he systematized parts of Nietzsche, developing a wide-ranging and penetrating theory with some new areas of psychological detail. His greater urbanity, the stability of his own stoic character and the high rectitude of his bourgeois life gave him an equanimity that on the one hand made his work impressively clear and distinct, with a masterful accuracy of insight. On the other hand it blinded him to the emptiness of the metaphysical world he inhabited. Freud prided himself on his honesty, but in fact he was far less honest than Nietzsche. Once he stepped outside the confines of psychology he was all at sea, unable to think in the categories in which he lived.

Where Freud is significant to this story is in playing the Pied Piper, leading the modern middle classes in droves, with haunting music piping to the rats in the unconscious, leading them to an illusion of redemptive freedom, but in reality drowning them in the very unconscious from which they imagine they are being saved. Freud continues the new, Nietzschean reading of inwardness. It is no longer the domain of spirituality, of conscience grappling with wish to produce right action in the world, or when that fails transforming guilt into dread. Inwardness is now neurosis, an instinctual bog in which the modern secular individual is stuck, an entirely psychological bog. The doctor's task is to overpower the gaoler, conscience, by means of reason. In fact, what the patient gets in his therapy is a beguiling mixture of narcissistic psychic massage and liberal illusion. The poor patient, rattled with anxiety, suddenly finds that an intellectually gifted analyst, a figure of authority, is willing to spend hours every week discussing his every nuance of sordid and petty feeling. Here is the true Freudian sublimation, every repressed instinct may be enjoyed intellectually, in warm and tender talk, as the phalanxes of guilt are disbanded by the ethic of therapy, in which all may be revealed, there is no evil, no bad character, just nasty repressions for which others, notably parents, were responsible. There is some genuine progress here, for psychoanalysis recognizes the demonic, to which the surrounding liberal culture had remained tenaciously blind. But the method is perverse: one carefully timed hour lying on a couch, devoted to polite chat about the demonic, in controlled intellectual tones, the control possible because of the bourgeois limits of authority and courtesy, limits as repressive as those the session is meant to be exploding. This is not at all to do with cure. It is rather Kierkegaard's wager, providing those incapacitated for living with a more stimulating view of themselves. Their psychic discomfort is glamorized as a bolting horse. The ride was in the past, at least an interesting, adventurous past. The engaging question is whether the rider fell off or not. The irony is that the psychoanalyst, who prides himself on his ability to reveal everything, cannot answer the key question, cannot tell you the simple and important truth, whether you have fallen off, never mind whether your neck is broken and you are dead.

The truth is not told. Only trivia are revealed, but magnetized by the analyst's authority they carry such an unconscious charge they do not seem to be trivial. The whole show is kept on the road by the redemptive illusion that at the end of the analysis there will be no more repression, you will be freed from your past. You will be liberated. Free for what, is the next question, to which there is the simple reply, free to enjoy yourself. Thus reason frees us for romance. At this level Freud is a relic of the eighteenth century, captivating a philosophically dim and personally desperate West with this obsolete hope fortified by an intellectually commanding psychology.

Patients were not cured. The reality was that the typical Freudian subject simply became more introspective, his life unchanged apart from the expenditure of more and more time dwelling on self, exactly the opposite of what might make him better, a more active involvement in life. Freud's updated Socratism that guilt is a failure of self-understanding was proved a lie in practice. All that happened through interminable talk was that the guilt was articulated, provided with conscious hooks on which to tie its grievances. This seemed to make little difference to the constitution of the patient. The devastating example of this was the wolf-man, whose case-study is the most important in the whole Freudian literature. In 1980 lengthy conversations with the wolf-man himself were published. Coming across, late in his life, as engagingly urbane, honest and sane, he describes his sessions with Freud as enjoyable discussions with a cultivated man, ones that had no long-term effect on his character whatsoever.

Here was a comprehensive empirical falsification of Kantian ethics: reason does not control will. You can know what is wrong with you, but being able to act on what you know, setting yourself free, is another matter. Character is destiny, or, more precisely, necessity. The figure we are reminded of is, of course, Hamlet. Modern culture is Hamlet writ everywhere. Freud would have been closer to the truth, unwittingly so, if he had followed one of his impulses and called the Oedipus complex the Hamlet complex. Hamlet is far more hopelessly neurotic than Oedipus, more guilt-ridden in a modern way, and his attempted self-cure is through endless talk, a "cure" that makes him worse, serving as a rationalization for impotence – as theorized by Nietzsche, but not in the case of Hamlet. We should not understand the *Hamlet complex* as the problem of a man who wants to kill his father and marry his mother, but as that of one whose last passion is to think himself sane and free, who tries it and fails, and is left with one felicity, unconsciousness, which means death. Here is one of the many reasons why Freud the humanist had the greatest of all humanists, Shakespeare, as his favourite writer.

So the Freudian patient became more and more in love with his own embattled unconscious, proud of his sickness. He was not alone. All of the educated middle classes who have read Freud with held breath, but not invested in therapy, all those who have watched quasi-Freudian films, scanned quasi-Freudian newspaper articles, or bought books titled *How to Become a Better Person*, all have come under the thrall of the new authority. In fact the cultural air the twentieth century has breathed has been inescapably Freudian. The authority is unconsciousness. The ancient Greeks, who were wiser, called it oblivion. Freud was himself wiser than his English translator: in the original German it is the "unknown".

Take the rat-girl. Herbert Hendin describes her in his 1975 book, *The Age of Sensation*. She is a 1960s American college student. She dreams of a glass of water, clear and calm on the surface, with a rat at the bottom, bleeding at the tail. She is the dream, with her life well-organized and successful on the surface. She fears that her inner self is rapacious, a rodent that if set free will gnaw to death anyone close to her. The demon is her femininity, the female erotic, symbolized by the bleeding at the tail. In reality she broke off any relationship with a man once it threatened to become intimate, fearing that if she opened herself to her instincts what would come out would be the rat. She vowed never to marry. However, she was finding less and less pleasure in her studies, the safe area of her life. She is a case of modern repression, trapped in inwardness to such a degree that the outside, her active life, is cut off from feeling, and brings her no pleasure.

177

What could an analyst do for her? A lot of talk about vermin, and where they come from psychologically speaking, is not going to give her the one thing she needs, faith in a stable world predicated on a fixed higher order strong enough not to come tumbling down if her rat starts to run amok. Freud, and for that matter Nietzsche, could tell her all about her demonic unconscious, but they have nowhere to lead the rat once it is out – Nietzsche lamented exactly this in his Death of God parable. She is right not to trust them. But she cannot live the way she is. She is a victim of humanism. Indeed she may even be beyond the Freudian illusion: her unconscious is so horrible that she may refuse the invitation to study it, to look into the glass.

The cultivation of the unconscious is explicit. The patient lies on a couch, is invited to relax and put himself in a trance or dream state. Day-dreaming aloud is the approved method. Furthermore, the most prized subject matter is night dreams. The patient is encouraged to dig into the caverns of his sleep, to find the gold nuggets. 'To sleep perchance to dream . . .' Life is richest in sleep. In sleep the true meaning is revealed. During the day one puts up with sterile bourgeois routines, drab and frustrating marriages, but at night life comes alive. This is the heart of darkness tamed: even nightmares become bearable, ultimately precious. Daytime may be at best "common unhappiness", but there is compensation. The last glorification of the humanist I is psycho-biography, pieced together from dreams, the one story left that has meaning, kept safe and intact in the unconscious. It provides a sort of place to stand, if only in the imagination, giving sense to the quest of knowing the unknown. Hamlet's dying request to Horatio, 'tell my story', expresses the same hope, that there must be a logic hidden there somewhere to make sense of the mess I have lived, to give a sense to the 'I am'. But Nietzsche had already exposed this hope as empty.

Freud was not alone in piping modernity towards the river of the unconscious. Painting had preceded him. In the chaotic fall from the great tradition of the Old Masters that is nineteenth-century art, enough of the authority of the past survived to make possible in the 1880s and 1890s a brief recandescence. On the edge of the plunge into rank nihilism stand two great painters, Cézanne and Van Gogh. Both, however, had made the fatal concession, and sought to embrace the unconscious, as solace. They stood, oblique to each other, on the same precipice, but with a different outlook. They instruct us of an important conceptual distinction, between two kinds of unconscious, one sublime and one demonic.

Cézanne represents the sublime unconscious. With unusual self-awareness for an artist he had as two of his sayings, that I want to do Poussin again after nature, and I want to make Impressionism more solid and enduring like the Old Masters. He achieved both. Cézanne starts the breakdown of form, with a deliberate purpose not found in Turner or the early Impressionists. Nietzsche's relativism, that truth is illusory, that there are merely perspectives on reality, was concurrently being worked in art. Cézanne experiments with fracturing forms, breaking reality down into abstract components. However, he always put it back together again. He was no relativist. In the long tradition of Western culture there is little to match the intensity with which he concentrated on the re-establishment of order. It is as if Cézanne were one of the citizens of Poussin's Ashdod: having contributed to the devastating plague, he now dedicates his life to finding the hidden order of forms. In his greatest works, the landscapes, the forms are so precariously built up from dabs of paint, smudges of colour, snatches of shape, so delicately and accurately placed, that the viewer can feel the wind in the trees, the warmth of the sun shimmering on the houses. Things lack solidity: there is none of the heavy rectilinear architecture that Poussin deprecates in his buildings. Things are fleeting, but so sensitively vivid that the fear that there is no substance to reality is transmuted into an illumination about an underlying order. Just as Poussin has the fresh-faced boy tiptoeing into *The Plague of Ashdod*, establishing a series of powerful lines of force to anchor the scene, Cézanne managed through great labour so to proportion and place his forms that they tapped an underlying, invis-

179

ible order. There is no terror here, just the sublime intoxication of an idyllic dream.

There is a fundamental difference to Poussin. Cézanne has removed the people. Humans do not inhabit his natural utopia. His world is sublime, but it is abstract, excluding all moral content. The Old Masters painted scenes of human crisis, of temptation and disaster, stories, and they instructed us how to behave, which Law to obey. Cézanne withdraws from all of this. He invites the frazzled modern soul to dream with him, to escape from hard reality into an unconscious world made conscious. His genius was to reveal an elemental order to the unconscious. This revelation enabled a flight to a sort of Western Nirvana. Its message is do not put up with the dismal, profane world of ugly and nasty people, escape with me. It is another couch, with a more uplifting outlook than the one provided by psychoanalysis. Here is Romance's greatest moment, its swan-song, and it is a truly beautiful death. In the *Lac d'Annecy* of 1896, for instance, one is wooed into a complete and perfect order, which is a state of grace.

The argument is starker in the lesser painters. In Monet there is not the intensity, the rugged ascetic wrestling with forms. What results is an easier, more relaxed and sentimental beauty. In the *Rouen Cathedrals*, *Westminster Bridges* and *Water-Lilies* the images are more pleasantly dreamy. With half-closed eyes the viewer can swoon away. Monet helps him retreat into the sublime unconscious, as with a light hypnotic tune, and linger awhile in the smoky blurred forms of harmonious inwardness. Monet too had his iridescent moments, the extraordinary luminous light of *Verteuil in Summer* (1880), brilliant moments which, however, burn out, leaving no trace. In literature the same retreat was worked by Proust, a man without an ounce of active life left in him, writing from the sick-bed, his vision that life is a continuing sequence of beautiful dreams. The source of felicity is again the sublime unconscious.

There are two ways from Cézanne. There is the wall-paper effeteness of Monet and other Impressionists. Then there is the more radical continuation of the breakdown of forms. Cézanne himself initiated the move with his late *Bathers*. Picasso and Braque followed, one step further over the edge, Braque retaining the beauty of line and colour, but with the meaning gone. Finally came the intellectually rigorous Duchamp. Duchamp's 1912 *Passage from Virgin to Bride* deliberately takes one of the two moments in a woman's life which should be most rich in ethical and religious emotion and abstracts it into an incomprehensible muddle. Here, however, we are straying into the territory of the demonic unconscious.

Van Gogh represents the demonic unconscious. In his great works there is a terrible intensity, the forms with jagged edges, rickety planes and swirling shapes at the moment of disintegration. The painter just holds them together, and in that *just* is a breath-taking cultural force for order. Van Gogh makes clear what a life-and-death struggle is culture, and what its breakdown means. It is through his own work that he clings on to sanity, furiously resisting the waves of psychosis. The parallels with Nietzsche are obvious, the dates almost identical. Van Gogh, however, is not on the side of nihilism. He is a lonely knight of resistance. It is a compromised resistance, for as with Cézanne there are no people, no communities, no human ethical domain. The battle is conducted on the plane of perception, and it is the world of nature and inanimate objects that provides the subject matter. Nevertheless Van Gogh finds an order in the mind, out of the unconscious projected onto thatched cottages, poplars and cypresses. This time the unconscious is demonic, threatening madness, a tormented horrific madness, which can be felt in the major works, for they take a direct look into the eyes of that Medusa, and just manage to hold their footing.

A procession of modern artists follows in the shadow of Van Gogh. There is Munch, with his hysterical women and depressed men, his *Madonna* entangled in her own neurotic nightmare lifelessness, sister of the rat-girl. There is the Austrian, Schiele, and the harsh, violent world of German Expressionism. In literature there is Kafka, taken over by paranoid guilt fantasies of being turned into a bug, or depressive guilt feelings of not being bothered to turn up at his own wedding. Guilt has shed its explicit Greek sublimations, and turned itself into a huge, shapeless and all-encompassing chamber, the demonic unconscious. This is the modern hell. Freud theorized it, Brecht dramatized it, and most contributors to twentieth-century High Culture have embraced it.

The climax to all of this was Picasso. The man whom the twentieth century has celebrated as its greatest genius reveals through his long life and vast work what scavenges around in the wreckage of humanism. Picasso incarnated the Nietzschean superman. His egocentricity was mammoth; he was driven by a tempestuous will to power, and especially over his women. His *Weeping Woman* portraits, for instance, show the reality of the demonic unconscious free from all limit. The subject is Dora Maar, whom Picasso often beat, and into unconsciousness. He felt compelled to destroy the very things in Dora that he admired. In the end she lost her mind. The portraits are typical of Picasso in their flatness of feeling, apart from a horror that lurks in the faces. The abstracting of the subject kills off any normal projection of female grief or sadness, a repressive distortion that likely indicates the painter's own guilt, his need to blur the reality of why the woman is at her wits' end with despair. What comes through is his own terror of the emptiness of existence.

Picasso lived "beyond good and evil". He lived "freely", obeying only his own pleasure, and especially a capricious sadism. His response to the one woman who ever escaped from him, Françoise Gilot, was to burn a lighted cigarette into her cheek and ensure that no art dealer handled her pictures. He was not only mean-spirited, and resentful of the success of any of his friends, but also a coward. In court he disowned his friend, Apollinaire; he refused to intercede with the Nazis to save the life of an old Jewish friend, Max Jacob; and during the war when a pot exploded he dived under the table, leaving his wife and daughter unprotected. The rationalization was the modern nihilistic one, 'I am against everything.' The artist is the great man, whose genius allows him beyond all petty moral constraints. The notable

thing is not that someone should have lived out Nietzsche, Dostoevsky and Conrad's "everything is permitted", but that Western
elites should have bowed down at his feet for having done it.
Picasso is emblematic.

Picasso is reminiscent of Marx, in his satanic character and
mission of destruction. He is also reminiscent of Velázquez, of
the triumphant value-creating artist – Picasso was, by the way,
obsessed by *Las Meninas*, painting his own version again and
again. The difference here is that the twentieth-century genius
had very little to say and no values to create. In the end it was
a curse that he was born with such a prodigious technical talent,
and such a lust to paint, for apart from occasional moments of
childlike gaiety his vision was merely of disintegration – rampant
cubism. At the time of the *Weeping Women* he painted a crucifixion
in which Mary the mother drinks her son's blood and Mary
Magdalene clutches his genitals.

In the aftermath of humanism, with all cultural barriers
smashed, 'We can become what we will' is simplified back to the
jungle, in which lust and sadism rule, the "Triumph of the Will".
Yet even here man is not just animal, for he has consciousness,
which means ultimately, consciousness of death. Free-will has no
answer to the skull, and so out of an odd mixture of childish exuberance and anxiety the genius of the twentieth century churns out
fifty thousand works. To live freely, by one's own will, means to be
drowned in one's own unconscious, in its demonic form.

Once the individual is submerged in his own unconsciousness
there is the question of what happens to society. The modern
experience has been bureaucracy. As Romance degenerated into
caged subjectivity, Reason degenerated into the sterile order of
the office, and what Max Weber called "mechanized petrifac-
tion". With individuals in total retreat from the world, their private lives all, the public world was rendered profane, in the first
step losing its traditional spiritual and ethical underpinnings, in
the second losing its emotional ones. The caricature of the bourgeois became reality, as Freud found out. Thus the outer did
become absurd, as Nietzsche and Conrad had seen, as Hamlet

had experienced it. Or it became persecuting, as Kafka imagined it in the paranoid imagery of his *Castle* and *Trial*. The rationalization of life also swept through art, in surrealism, in Bauhaus, in the arid geometry of Mondrian, and later in even more brittle banalities.

In short, the heritage of the death of culture in the humanist mode has been a routine public life, and a retreat into the individual unconscious in the hope of staving off madness or melancholia. That unconscious itself becomes more and more an inescapable pit, a devouring demon. There are the occasional consolations of the sublime, with the help of a Monet, or of intellectual clarity, with the help of a Freud. There are sorties to idealize the demonic itself, in order to recapture lost vitality, as in D.H. Lawrence, for instance, gushing lyrical enthusiasm over charging bulls, rearing stallions, homosexual wrestling or female fecundity. The rat-girl is, however, the reality. She is the true child of modern culture.

The deceit of Freud was that he made things worse, becoming a far more influential prophet of nihilism than his more perceptive, more satanic and more tragic predecessor, Nietzsche. Freud's concern was individual health, what he called normality, the pursuit of pleasure his criterion of value. According to his disenchanting psychology the child is under the thrall of its genitals and its anus, there is no difference between Napoleon and Christ, both were "father figures", and a story like the repentance and forgiveness of Mary Magdalene is a piece of primitive, irrational delusion. Mary Magdalene would have been better off undergoing psychoanalysis to cure her of her guilt. Munch's Madonna could easily have been a patient of Freud, a fate no doubt to which she would have remained indifferent. Why not, she might have said, if it helps to pass the time. Freud, in his own personal life, was much better. In response to the slings and arrows of life's hardships he aspired to a state of resignation. Resignation to fate he held in the highest ethical regard. He thereby adds a second dimension to his role as prophet of resigned nihilism.

All is silent. All is still. Coleridge's earlier guilt imagery has become the reality on the frontier of Western culture:

> Day after day, day after day,
> We stuck, nor breath nor motion,
> As idle as a painted ship
> Upon a painted ocean.

That ocean is flat, grey and boundless. That ship is ghostly, ghastly. It is Holbein's blurred skull. In a late shift in his theory, Freud introduced a notion that worried and baffled his followers: rather than counterpoising an "aggressive instinct" to the life-creating erotic one, he chose the term "death instinct". Freud postulates an impulse within us all towards death, a wish, a desire for extinction. Was there not some obscure inkling here of the truth of his own mission, that in cultivating Hamlet's 'to sleep perchance to dream' he was acting in the service of the forces of destruction, that to turn the unconscious into god was to paralyse humanity, seducing it with psychological knowledge, turning it through interminable sophisticated chatter to stone? There can be no surprise that after Cézanne, Van Gogh and Freud Western High Culture – its art, literature and philosophy – was to portray life as a sterile promontory, as worse than death. The coat-of-arms of this culture displays a rat bleeding at the tail under an owl's face doubling as a skull, the motto NOTHING. The humanist epoch ends with Hamlet, Hamlet, and more Hamlet.

PART IV
Posthumous Trials

11

THE SACRED RAGE OF
HENRY JAMES

The story of the rise and fall of Humanism is not complete without consideration of two later attempts to build anew within the wreckage. They use what was there, introducing no new materials. They take us over the frontier into a post-humanist domain. Both come from the New World, America, and they draw their strength respectively from a Protestant and a hybrid Protestant-Catholic root. While most that has passed for High Culture in the twentieth century has merely shone a spotlight on different corners of the ruin, mounted a fragment or two, perhaps touched it up a bit, or chipped some more pieces out of it, there have been two grand trials at reconstruction. I am not taking account of two other trials, at a new religious vision, those of Rilke's *Duino Elegies* and Simone Weil's essays, for neither have cast significant ripples in the wider culture. In contrast Henry James has been applauded as the last of the great novelists, his work the highpoint of Western fiction. John Ford is the most important contributor to that major genre, the Western, within the new art form of the twentieth century, the film. His main work spans almost exactly the twenty years between 1940 and 1960 that mark the classical period of the cinema, its great Hollywood era. Both Henry James and John Ford create visions that are realistic to their own time and have metaphysical weight. Both were in search of a place to stand.

The work that is definitive to the vision of Henry James is *The Ambassadors*. Although it was the second published of the three great last novels, it was the first written (1900–1). James himself assessed it as 'quite the best, "all round", of my productions'. It stands in relation to our story here as the second *Ambassadors*, a reply to Holbein, as to much else with which we have been engaged. Put simply *The Ambassadors* is an examination of what happens to a middle-aged gentleman, a pure New England type, when he is thrown into the most seductive humanist milieu of old Europe, situated in Paris. The two poles are Puritanism and aristocratic Humanism.

Europe is culture and civilization. It is courtesy and refinement. More concretely it is people who know how to live their lives as works of art, fashioning their movements with delicacy and charm and then subjecting them to analyses, so that they gain the additional pleasure of seeing the pattern of things, understanding. In the same year as Freud published his *Interpretation of Dreams* Henry James was giving his Europeans a rare capacity for psychoanalysis, one better integrated into their living, being a vital part of their social talk, rather than displaced onto the doctor's couch. The main representative of Europe is the beautiful Madame de Vionnet. She has immense reserves of style, from the skill with which she presents herself, the physical woman, the taste of her apartment and its objects, all old inherited accumulations, relics, to the virtuosity with which she speaks so as to touch the sensitive spots with a mixture of allusion and concealment. She is likened to Cleopatra. She has fifty different characters, in her magnificent opulence of interest. In Paris, language is used with a spare and directed precision, with a technical elegance reminiscent of a master violinist, so that each note is a strictly controlled hint. Such culture takes a lot of time to develop. Like the Europe with which both Henry James and his hero have fallen in love, Mme de Vionnet is not young. She is near the time when her physical graces will no longer draw men so irresistibly to her. But then, the charm of Europe is in its ruins, their mossy antiquity offering the depth and permanence that only great age can bestow. Nothing flashy, nothing vulgar; nothing clumsy, nothing naive. All is polish and the profound interior vaults illuminated once light penetrates the surface of a precious stone.

In Paris the ideals of freedom and romance find their highest aesthetic realization.

Lambert Strether is from Woollett, New England, in the vicinity of Boston. Woollett is undiluted Puritanism, without either aristocratic or humanist trace. Duty, piety and bourgeois rectitude rule. On the one hand it is innocent, lacking refinement and social grace. Its inhabitants live by principle. They are without understanding. On the other hand the failure of Woollett is to enjoy. There is so much propriety and control that pleasure is stifled. The main representative is Mrs Newsome, a wealthy widow, Strether's patron and fiancée, who has sent him to Europe as her ambassador to convince her son, Chad, to leave Paris and return to Woollett, to marry and take over the prosperous family business. Mrs Newsome is Queen of Woollett. In Kierkegaard's terms, Mme de Vionnet and Paris are pure aesthetic, indeed the aesthetic at its finest, more engagingly painted than by Kierkegaard himself. Mrs Newsome and Woollett are purely ethical.

Chad Newsome has been in Paris for years. In effect he has been educated there. What Strether meets is a young man whom he does not recognize, who has acquired the polished cultivation of Europe. His principal teacher, over the last three years, has been Mme de Vionnet, with whom he is having an affair, although Strether in his innocence does not realize this until late in the piece. Strether's first response to Chad, and his challenging question, 'Do I strike you as improved?' is that of the loyal ambassador: 'I haven't the least idea.' He can still stick to his New England principle. However, his own education is already well underway, with the help of the Europeanized American, the thirty-five-year-old Miss Gostrey, who has become devoted to him, and he somewhat to her. Strether has seen immediately that Chad is improved, in his later judgment, five times better, a man who has learned the art of living, of getting real pleasure out of life, a man who is always at his ease, with a happy blend of the cordial and the formal.

Strether's New England companion, Waymarsh, who is unimaginative, brash and awkward, does not see this improvement in Chad. He sticks to his Puritan virtue. He is likened to the impressive Indian chief, Sitting Bull, who was taken to Washington and shown around in a carriage, but who took no interest, remaining his own colossal self. Waymarsh does not understand a thing, and has no intention of trying. Strether is not like him, and will be eaten alive by Paris. As another Europeanized American puts it: 'I am now the bleached bones of a Christian.' That is what happens to Bostonian pilgrims in Paris.

Strether in his own undemonstrative way, hardly knowing it, falls under the spell of Mme de Vionnet. In love, he finds his mission as ambassador increasingly difficult to carry out. His love is generalized, from Mme de Vionnet to all she represents. He tries unsuccessfully to avoid her. He sees how she has transformed Chad, shows indirect signs of jealousy, protesting too much that her relationship to Chad is one of friendship. His advice to the "bleached bones" young American is 'Live all you can', do not be like me who has let it all pass by, until it is too late. 'If you haven't had that what *have* you had?' Freedom and romance have him in thrall.

The Ambassadors is tightly constructed, written in twelve books of similar length, with a series of symmetries that liken its structure to that of a classical temple. Technically it is without flaw. The architecture is, however, deceptive, as in a Poussin painting. The true lines of force, concealed, divide the story into five stages, all of them determined by Strether. The mild-mannered hero, hitherto dominated by the Queen of Woollett, a lamb as his Christian name intimates, a hesitant New Englander in awe of Paris, and bewildered, it is he who controls events. Stage One takes up the entire first half of the novel. Strether arrives and delivers his ambassadorial message to Chad, your mother wants you to return home, or else. Then he hesitates. He has come under the spell of aristocratic humanism, through its own ambassadors, Miss Gostrey, a Miss Barrace, and above all Mme de Vionnet and her daughter. The sheer poise has got to him, as it did to those Protestant middle-class boys once they entered the English Public Schools. He is also influenced by the young American disciples of this aesthetic religion. He likes what it has made of them. Because of his hesitation events stall. A motionlessness settles over things. Strether's pause is not simply because he has been seduced by new gods. He is also perplexed. Something is going on here which eludes him. There is some truth he has to discover before he can move. To continue as ambassador given his blind and uncertain state would be foolish. His inner voice says to him: 'Wait, you have more to learn.'

Stage Two: the second half of the novel opens with new ambassadors arriving from Woollett. Strether has been sacked. His immobility has rightly been interpreted as betrayal. The arrival of the new ambassadors changes nothing. It does, however, provoke Strether into action. He urges Chad not to go back to America yet, for he, Strether, is not ready to return. He needs more time. The pressure from Woollett is wrong. Strether has become the main opponent of the Queen of Woollett.

The third stage is the stay of the new ambassadors, led by Mrs Newsome's formidable daughter, Sarah. It gives Strether, with his newly formed consciousness, time to observe New England and what it stands for. He does not like what he sees. Sarah refuses to acknowledge Chad's improvement, sticking to her principle, calling his change "hideous". She judges Mme de Vionnet brutally: 'Do you consider her even an apology for a decent woman?' She then turns on Strether for having insulted 'the most distinguished woman we shall either of us have seen.' Strether is unmoved. Having reworked his ambassadorial role, now trying to represent the virtues of humanist Europe to Woollett, he has failed again. The new ambassadors will not be moved. His later conclusion is that Mrs Newsome is stubborn and ignorant, her method of reclaiming her son displaying a mean imagination. His vision is now clear towards Woollett. He rejects it.

The fourth stage is his turning the other way and finally gaining a clear sight of Europe. It is summer and he travels at random away from Paris to take a day in the country by himself. By sheer coincidence he bumps into Chad and a very embarrassed Mme de Vionnet. He realizes that the pair are spending a few days together. What he had taken to be a virtuous friendship between them is in fact a liaison. Mme de Vionnet's clumsy attempt to cover this up makes it plain. He now sees her for what she really is, beneath the sophisticated facade, a woman in love, tragically, for her partner is ten years younger and becoming restless. She is doomed. Strether is hurt. He has been used. She has played upon his devotion to her, having cunningly spun the web that caught him with the hidden promise of all sorts of vague possibilities. She was simply and ruthlessly fighting to preserve her love. She knows now she has lost Strether, her one ally with power. He feels cold and lonely. Miss Gostrey comments to him that Mme de Vionnet should have left town in shame after what she had done to him.

In the last meeting between de Vionnet and Strether she confesses in her own way. She is dressed in white. Strether's association is with Mme Roland on the scaffold. She admits that she has changed his life, separated him from Mrs Newsome, turning him against her, closing that door; she has upset his mind. She hates herself for this, for her selfishness. It has not even brought her happiness. She wishes they could have been friends, might be now, thus admitting that they were not friends before, that her duplicity denied that, whatever he may have imagined. She knew what she was doing with the full battery of her seductive powers. He leaves. There will be no friendship. She has deceived him. Humanism for all its cultivated allure is founded on the selfish pursuit of pleasure – all else is calculated appearance, that is deceit. He worked hard to delay Chad's leaving Paris, and succeeded, in part for her, and what has she given him in return, an obscure dream of happiness now exploded. He rejects Paris and Europe.

The fifth and final stage is with Maria Gostrey, the other woman with whom he has been half in love. She has become completely devoted to him: 'There's nothing I wouldn't do for you.' She has been a true and loyal friend throughout, the only one to whom he could talk openly, the only one who was honest. Moreover, she is like what he has become, a Europeanized American, enjoying the understanding and manners of Europe but having retained the conscience of America. They belong together, with their rare harmony of virtue and knowledge. He, however, says No. It would not be right. His only logic is to have got nothing out of the affair for himself. He has betrayed Woollett in not fulfilling his mission as ambassador. His honour requires that it cannot have been for selfish reasons, rewarded with the happiness of companionship with Maria. So he must return to Woollett although there is nothing and no one there for him. He does not believe in Woollett any more. He does not belong there. He does not belong anywhere now. At the end the three main characters are all left to the gloom of loneliness.

Once Strether's eyes are opened both ways, and he sees Paris and Woollett for what they are, he forsakes both, to save his honour. By what principle does he act? As a higher product of Puritan New England he has his Calvinist conscience, that which does not allow man to suppress within himself what he knows. The Calvinist God, however, is no more, and Strether has no perception of a higher order. So what drives his conscience? It is what Henry James calls "sacred rage", a term which originates with Plato. This force is bestowed on the least attractive character on stage, Waymarsh, the boorish, heavy-footed, narrow-minded New Englander who finds Europe an ordeal. 'The sombre glow just darkened in his comrade's eyes', and Waymarsh early in the piece commands Strether to 'Quit it!', his mission, for there is trouble brewing. In Waymarsh the rage is a rather crude cannon, with poor sights, tending just to blast away. He is the opposite of Mme de Vionnet, whose sights are set exactly where she wants them, but who has no sacred rage, no force. The rage is never directly attributed to Strether but it is there, simmering under the surface, while he is being trained, until by the end it has a perfect precision and accuracy of fire. What Europe does for Strether is train him, provide him with a context in which to apply his immense capacity for concentration on what is, so that he can get his response right.

Strether has his extraordinary intensity of concentration. He is taut, he is tense, he is stretched, as his name hints. When the male of the new ambassadorial party observes that Strether has come to Paris to have a good time, he is quite wrong, for it is not in Strether's nature to relax and enjoy himself. He is on a mission, a Captain Ahab in Europe, driven to find the truth however vile and monstrous it may turn out to be. The only one who is relaxed is Chad, for he has little at stake now he has taken all he can, plundered Paris so to speak, and he has too limited an imagination to be seriously troubled over his debts. Mme de Vionnet, the ambassador of aristocratic humanism, is no more at ease than Strether. Beneath the superbly constructed manners she is always anxious. She is helpless. She is powerless. Without the sacred rage she has nothing to save her.

The twice that Strether makes a decisive move it is in outrage. The first time it is the pressure from Woollett, New England stubborn insensitivity goading him, that stirs him into action, in effect ordering Chad to stay in Paris. The second time it is the violence of the revelation of Mme de Vionnet's deceit. On both occasions the signs of the depth of his anger are indirect. On the first, his iron resistance, the hate in his eyes, drives Sarah beyond all courtesy into her blind fury against Mme de Vionnet. On the second it is Strether himself confronting Chad with 'You will be a brute if you ever leave her.' This is untrue, a splash of displaced anger, spiked with jealousy, pity for Mme de Vionnet, and a protest that it is unjust that Chad, the one who has got everything, is also the one who will leave the scene unpunished, scot-free. There is more here too. Strether's earlier judgment that Chad had been improved wonderfully was an aesthetic one. He now overturns it, and ironically, without either knowing it or saying it, comes to agree with Woollett, that there is something hideous about what he has become. This is the ethical judgment, now taken up to a higher plane by Strether, beyond reflex moralism.

Only the innocents can act, in their moments of sacred rage. Without a raw and instinctive sense of honour, driven from within, the best alternative is humanist Europe, in which paralysis and emptiness are dressed up in stunning finery, interrupted by fitful passions and illuminated by moments of pleasure, softened by evenings of gilded understandings. There is some doubt about the pleasure, in spite of Strether's advice, 'Live all you can.' Mme de Vionnet is living all she can, but she finds herself trapped and anxious. She is gradually turning into another Hamlet. The message is close to that of Don Quixote, although his reincarnation here is as an uncomic pilgrim, a Puritan Brutus, left alone on the field of battle, corpses all round, with only his honour and his sacred rage. In his innocence he is outraged at reality. The difference from Don Quixote is that he is not dreaming, and *that* is due to his Protestant conscience. Chad also can act, but it is the action of a man strolling through life without serious engagement, and it becomes both arbitrary and uninteresting what he might or might not do. The state of his soul is not worthy of examination.

By the end humanism is finished. Mme de Vionnet is deflated, disgusted with herself, dishonoured, and not even happy. She will soon lose Chad. Humanism's fall is not, however, without some glory. Just as Strether has a new capacity for understanding, Henry James himself has developed a style of writing which in its exquisite precision, its subtle virtuosity, is his debt to civilized Europe. And after all, if the novel is a bourgeois form, then James is its greatest exponent. Against this is the deeper truth, that the Bostonian pilgrim in Paris had set out to unite Humanist and Puritan in one soul and thereby escape the clutches of nihilist modernity. This was not to be. Trying to move beyond, and failing, he ended up moving backwards, narrowing the options by reducing the bourgeois possibility to its Protestant core, eliminating the humanist extensions and refinements.

Henry James goes to Europe to encounter the humanist ideal, the high-point of the civilized, and he rejects it in favour of innocence, conscience and sacred rage. Luther would have been proud of him. However, he cannot tear himself away from the gracious drawing rooms with their honeyed conversations. In his great last three novels there is only one of the heroes he fills out to the full, developing him into a character in the round who can then dominate centre-stage. That is Lambert Strether. James turns him, through his suffering, into a fine man, then sends him back to Woollett, something James himself refused to do. A fine man, for what? That is the question. This is not a question one needs to ask of Achilles at the end of *The Iliad* or of Oedipus once he has put his eyes out and banished himself. The true tragedies were complete. *The Ambassadors*, by contrast, is unfinished. It is not free from the humanist epoch, therefore it cannot attain the rank of tragedy. Henry James has returned to the metaphysics of the Reformation, and before that Greek tragedy, but there are open issues still to be resolved. To what order does Strether now belong, once he has proved his honour?

The problem is not the traditional one, of the hero finding himself in bad times with his task to restore order. When Oedipus leaves Thebes balance returns, the lonely hero through his own suffering has sacrificed himself for the sake of the community. Antigone has her family, she sacrifices herself out of loyalty to kin. In *The Ambassadors* there is no community worth saving. Paris is there as a test for Strether, not in itself. In any case he rejects what it stands for. He also rejects the other community, Woollett. So where is the resolution, except in Strether himself. Here is James' stark Protestantism: the individual and his conscience is all. But as Kierkegaard warned, the theology and the faith have gone. While Strether is inwardly driven by sacred rage, what Kierkegaard called dread, the question remains, where and for what?

Strether is saved by his conscience. It tells him there is a law he must obey. He does not yet make it out, so he must persevere. It tells him that there is a truth to human behaviour. That too he does not yet know. Throughout, his natural desire is to find out what things "really" are. Paris, which lives off appearances, mocks this "really". Once Strether knows the truth he will know the law. Listening to his conscience he tiptoes along, cautiously, ever so cautiously, lest he take a false step. It is an art this listening, so as to hear in order to be able to act rightly. Woollett in the same position blocks its ears and stubbornly marches to its old principles, which leaves its inhabitants, as Strether puts it, playing at life, a parody of bourgeois rectitude. Humanist Europe does not have such a problem, for it obeys the pleasure principle, which has a clear logic. What Strether learns, aged fifty-five, is the old Calvinist lesson, wait until you hear your conscience, then act accordingly. This is his real education.

The Ambassadors is the great Kierkegaardian novel. It attempts to reverse the stages, starting with the aesthetic, moving into the ethical, and hoping to attain the religious. The categories are slightly revised. The religious is inborn, in the form of sacred rage. Waymarsh loses his sacred rage because it is not integrated into the ethical and the aesthetic. Once he starts to enjoy himself in Europe he becomes lost in the aesthetic, and is finished. For Strether all is one: all stages have to work together. He ends up an ethical hero, but alone, knowing he has done the right thing, he had no choice, sacrificing his pleasure for duty. He has to pay dearly, losing the possibility of happiness, not because he has sinned and is being punished, there is no theological calculus, there never is in genuine Protestantism. He has to pay simply because that is his condition. He is born the one who is stretched, just as Oedipus is born the one who will kill his father and marry his mother. Strether is not Abraham. He does not have faith. He is lost in his inwardness, an inwardness that drives him through life, enabling him to act, but not bringing faith. It does not project a canopy of belief. This is why Strether and his author are so tempted by humanism, for they have no explicit attachments, so why not 'Live all you can' for indeed 'If you haven't had that what *have* you had?' In practice they try out this humanism but their Puritan consciences stop them in their tracks. If Strether were to follow his 'Live all you can', a reworking of the 'We can become what we will', he would end the novel with Maria Gostrey. Why not? It is because of the sacred rage, shouting at him, 'Quit it!' He is not free. He has to say No.

The problem is pinpointed in the case of the great German sociologist, Max Weber. In his major work, *The Protestant Ethic and the Spirit of Capitalism* (1904/1920), Weber attempted to redeem the bourgeois from the Marxist caricature, showing that the success of capitalism depended on the new ethical integrity upon which the modern middle class was founded. That integrity was Protestant, a Calvinist derivative. Weber closed his book in extreme pessimism, perceiving that the ethic was weakening, leaving merely a degraded materialism. In a lecture delivered in 1918, late in his life, titled 'Knowledge as a Vocation', Weber went further. The subject was the contemporary university. Weber accepts Nietzsche's diagnosis of modern culture as nihilistic: having killed God it finds itself believing in nothing. He asks, how can the university function in such a disenchanted world? The university in its modern form has evolved from its Renaissance forefather, stipulated on the humanist ideals of a trained mind, culture, and the benefits to both individual and society of applied knowledge. But those ideals are dead. The main consequence is that students now come to university in search of answers to the great metaphysical questions, what to do and how to live. In other words they seek prophets. Weber's retort is that prophets do not belong in the university. The lectern is not a pulpit. He finds three functions left for the modern university, the advancement of knowledge, the teaching of methods of thinking, and the imposing on students of a clarity and consistency of thinking within the framework of already given ultimate values. Under the pall of Nietzsche's scepticism about the value of knowledge, Weber is only enthusiastic about his third function, but it depends on already given ultimate values, the lack of which is the problem that stimulated his enquiry in the first place. His argument thus collapses in absurdity. The one thing he can salvage is the virtue of "intellectual integrity", that the individual teacher should obey his conscience and fulfil his vocation. The hope is that the rigorously disciplined scholar, dedicated to his own branch of knowledge, will communicate enough moral authority to his students to fill the metaphysical void. This is a caricature of Calvinism, the university as a conglomerate of one-man sects each obeying his individual conscience, while all around the institution steadily decays into an aimless and moribund bureaucracy. Weber has described with devastating accuracy the post-humanist university of the twentieth century.

Weber's men of vocation, individuals with intellectual integrity, are Strethers. They are the descendants of Vermeer's geographer, astronomer and lace-maker, except the securing bourgeois milieu around them has faded away to nothing. Weber knew the game was over. He clung to the one root that still could hold him, if temporarily, the Calvinist one. So did Henry James, once he had tried the other one, the humanist one with aristocratic trappings, and found it to be rotten. The sociologist at the end of his tradition was no more than a gloomy diagnostician, as had been his own greatest teacher, Nietzsche. Henry James was more. Strether is not confined to the lecture hall, nor to the psychoanalyst's couch. He actually manages to live. Hence his Quixotic appeal. But in the end he has added nothing new to our story. America, the New World, is simply a purer form of Protestantism, quite familiar to us, failing to offer a way out, a new direction. We have not advanced from the predicament that Kierkegaard analysed with unmatched prescience. Some detail has been filled out, projecting from America a late Protestant salvo, one that misses the target for already familiar reasons. Kierkegaard had set the terms for the post-humanist interregnum. The one change is that dread is redrawn as sacred rage. Internal anguish may clothe a religious drive. James does not go further.

A society that is so fragmented that at best it contains a few individuals with intellectual integrity, and for the rest goes about profane routines, cannot survive. There has to be a unifying social conscience, an embracing and inspiring sense of community. There has, in addition, to be an over-arching higher conscience. Kierkegaard's categories fit Strether. His sacred rage in alliance with his new understanding drive him up out of the aesthetic into the plane of the ethical. They turn him into an ethical hero, rejecting his own 'Live all you can.' He has triumphed over nihilist humanism. He does not, however, attain the religious. His loneliness is not that of Abraham in the midst of the darkness of faith, it is that of the honourable man, the Puritan gentleman, who has lost his community. It is thus a partial victory with no future. Humanism has helped him, giving him understanding, but it is his Puritan conscience that has saved him, with its under-current of sacred rage. That is not enough. What Poussin did with his own sacred rage is again necessary. He used it to inspire a religious vision of the beyond, while tying that back to the here and now on earth, making human community sacred.

12

AMERICA'S LAST STAND

America represents what has to be built from scratch, out of nothing. That is how John Ford saw it. His life task was to create the myth that would give America a place to stand. Without the myth it would fail, and relapse into a condition worse than that of old Europe, which at least had its memories of a great past, and some surviving vestiges of tradition. America had to make its tradition. It was essential it be the right one. By the twentieth century all Western countries were in the same basic predicament, of having rickety foundations, the old ones having loosened theirs through their long affair with humanism. It was thus of far wider significance whether America succeeded. If America could do it, then the others might follow its path.

For Ford America is both the New World in itself, his country, and the place with a future where exiles from the decaying Old World flee in hope, to build anew. Ford knows that if America is to work it needs a foundation myth, a sacred story imprinted on its soul. He worked in practice to solve the problem for all modern societies, as Hannah Arendt theorized it in her book, *On Revolution* (1963), that of legitimacy. In what can I believe? Whom shall I obey? Arendt argued that America had secured its legitimacy in its political Constitution, which it had successfully turned into a sacred text, and embodied in a number of central institutions, especially the Supreme Court. We shall see that Ford considers the same answer, tests it and rejects it. His search was to take him over an immense stretch of territory. From *Stagecoach* of 1939 to *Seven Women* of 1966 he made thirty-three films of significance, with a prodigality of themes and images, all directed at finding a secure place to stand.

Axiomatic to the entire enterprise is the contrast between myth and history. Ford is in the tradition of Greek tragedy, as articulated by the young Nietzsche, that history, being the rational and dispassionate account of the past, is a sign of the death of culture. Culture is rooted in sacred sites, sanctuaries built out of myth, and it is merely a symptom of the weakening of the foundation myths when the humanist deification of Reason gets going, when logic replaces blood, and myth is deprecated as superstition. Forget history, disinter the myths, for it is from within their mystery that you may find out who you are, it is through them your ancestors speak. The rest is murk.

'I will plant companionship thick as trees along all the rivers of America.' So stated John Ford. Companionship is the key. It is at the heart of the ideal of community, being both what community makes possible, and what justifies it. Ford's vision is Catholic. But there is more to it. For companionship and community there has to be an ethic, independent of them. It is that of honour, which means individuals each taking an oath to which they are faithful above all else. Companionship, trust, loyalty, honour combine to form the magic circle. Where and under what circumstances is it to be found? That is the question. Ford gives different answers at different points of time, on his own journey wrestling with the angel with whom he could never completely settle accounts. They are represented respectively in his three great films, *Rio Grande* of 1950, *The Searchers* of 1956, and *The Man Who Shot Liberty Valance* of 1962. Fragments of them are to be found throughout his work, sometimes with different inflections.

Ford's first big attempt at a foundation myth is *Young Mr Lincoln* of 1939. The subject chose itself, the American Abraham, the father of the chosen people. Ford is interested in origins so he concentrates on the young Lincoln, before the start of his political career. The hero, like his country, has no past. He appears from nowhere, without father or mother, out of nothing. He finds his own anchoring point in the grave of his fiancée, Ann Rutledge, beside a river. At times of great decision he returns to the river to talk to the grave. It is the most authoritative image in the film. Ford's Lincoln is a man of the people, with a popular touch. He saves a helpless, fatherless family from evil bullies by making the legal system work. Rational justice championed by the gifted secular pilgrim will make America, securing its families and small communities. *Young Mr Lincoln*, however, does not succeed, at the high level of ambition at which it was pitched. It lacks the mythic force.

Ford takes another decade of varied experiments to find the community through which he can work his vision to the full. He finds it in the United States Cavalry. The third of the Cavalry trilogy of films, *Rio Grande*, is the masterpiece. The film opens with the return home, to the fort, of a regiment from a mission, bringing back cavalry wounded and captured Indians. The head is Colonel Kirby Yorke, played by John Wayne. The story moves on to the arrival of new recruits, including Yorke's own son, Jeff, who has failed at West Point, and in order to prove himself has immediately joined the army as an ordinary trooper. Father has not seen son for fifteen years, since he was a Captain in Sheridan's army during the Civil War, when in ransacking the Shenandoah Valley under orders he burned his wife's estate, Bridesdale. His estranged wife, Kathleen, is a Southern aristocrat. Jeff makes friends with two other recruits, Daniel "Sandy" Boone and Travis Tyree, both superb horsemen. Father tells son that things will be twice as hard for him, and that the Cavalry is not glamour and glory, but suffering, hardship and endurance. Jeff's initiation begins immediately. He shows his courage by imitating the brilli-ant riding of his friends, although he falls off. He is taunted into a fight by one of the tough old hands. His own slim boyish body, and soft fair face is badly bruised, but again he shows great courage, and the tough old hand becomes devoted to him. This is induction into the new community, and it is consummated by the new friends in a tent at night singing together, 'Aha, San Antone.' It is a cosy joyful scene. Ford is planting companionship.

Next mother arrives, humiliated by her son's failure, wanting

to buy him out of the cavalry and organize a soft passage back
to becoming an officer. As husband says to her: 'Still the same
old Kathleen, special privilege for the special born.' She is played
by Maureen O'Hara, making up Ford's most successful couple.
From the moment she arrives chaos ensues. Indians raid and
succeed in freeing their captured brethren. Later a mission to
send the women and children to a safer fort is ambushed and the
children captured. Marital discord begins to infect the community. The distracted Colonel has lost his usual military
instinct. In his tent with Kathleen after her arrival we see him
through a mirror awkwardly undoing his sabre – he is disarmed.
A fellow officer, who is French, his right eye appropriately
covered with a black patch, woos Kathleen.

Just as the younger generation is being initiated into the community, so too is wife, although the process is less smooth. She
has good reason to address her husband: 'Ramrod, wreckage and
ruin – still the same old Kirby' and soon after to say to her son,
'What makes soldiers great is hateful to me.' But she still loves
her husband. On her first night the Regimental Singers serenade
the tense pair with 'I'll take you home again, Kathleen.' She is
deeply touched. The community has its ways. Soon after, the
Sergeant-Major, whom she also hates for having set the match
to Bridesdale, sneaks up to escort her to see her son. She breaks
in on the recruit idyll. Standing at the door of the tent she is seen
by the boys as an image of the Madonna. Jeff introduces her with
a hushed tender voice. Companions leave. She kisses his bruised
face, the wounds that mark his initiation, which is a loss of innocence in the winning of manhood, and are also a sign of the curse
on his own family, because it is broken. Jeff too refuses to be
bought out of the army, telling his mother it would be quitting.

At this point the Indians raid, and Kathleen faints when one
is shot dead at her feet. She begins to accept that her feminine
assertion of the ethic of nurture, not to mention her snobbery, is
not altogether right, and the men's competing ethic of honour
has some value. Also she sees the army has a real job to do,
which includes protecting the women and children. In the next

scene with her husband she offers to do his laundry, and soon she is at the river with the other women. The proud Southern aristocrat has herself been ordained, accepting the most mundane side of the woman's role. She has her Necessity, as do the soldiers. She also accepts that she has lost the battle with Kirby over their son, and for good reason. Her concern with status, that Jeff should enjoy the privilege of being an officer, that he join the army for his own benefit and pleasure is self-centred. In true community the individual serves a higher end than himself. In doing humble penance washing dirty clothes at the river she begins to accept all this.

Then comes the pivotal scene in the film. At a formal officer's dinner, General Sheridan asks Mrs Yorke if she would like to propose a toast. She agrees: 'To my only rival, the United States Cavalry.' She watches her husband slowly drink the toast, then she is shocked to see him tilt his head back and dreamily luxuriate in his loving vision of the cavalry. She catches herself, smiles knowingly, then drinks. Her conversion is complete. Honour comes first, family second, the public ahead of the private, such is her husband, and such is life.

The US Cavalry has its own mother figure. That is Sgt-Major Quincannon, a dim-witted gentle Irish giant, with a heart as big as his thirst. He is a simple, devout Catholic. He inducts the recruits, telling them this is their home, ribs them, tells tall stories, and interferes in the fight to balance it. He does not teach a thing, he nurtures. Education here is not instruction, it is initiation, a test of character, in the same tradition as the English Public School. Furthermore it is Quincannon who makes sure Trooper Tyree is not arrested for manslaughter. The Cavalry protects its own: their individual pasts are superseded, by the ethos of the group, and its past becomes their past. The children tease Quincannon, for he himself is part child.

Is honour and its community enough? In the beginning the Colonel has told his son what is required: 'an uncompromising devotion to your oath and your duty.' The oath is to the army. Kathleen says what she thinks: 'All this danger to serve people as yet unborn – and probably not worth serving.' She has hit the target, although she unwittingly tramples on the justifying ethos of her own aristocratic class, that of noble service. The desolate and dangerous frontier is being tamed for the future, so that decent communities can settle and build. This is the making of America. The oath is to America, past, present and most importantly, to the unborn. Moreover, with oath and duty a higher community can be forged here and now, exemplary community, the cavalry itself. This is a good place for families; it is the best place for young men.

The children must be saved. In the film's opening scene the children run out of school to welcome home their fathers. The rescue requires an illegal mission into Mexico at night. The children are locked in a church and will be massacred at dawn. The three young companions sneak into the church and when the Indians approach start shooting while a girl peals the bell to signal to the rest of the cavalry to charge. Belltower and crucifix on the front of the church dominate the scene. During the rescue the Colonel is wounded by an arrow in his right breast. He has been punished, at last, for Bridesdale, for his broken family, and thirdly for crossing the Rio Grande illegally, although in a just cause. Mainly he is punished for Bridesdale, and for living, simply for having been born. Jeff leaps to his father's side, hat off, awed. The inviolable patriarch has been felled. This is a terrible moment. The father asks him to pull the arrow out; son braces himself at the horror. His companions intercede, Tyree urging him for the third time in the film, 'Get it done, Reb!', and Sandy echoing with the cavalry affirmative, 'Yo!' He does it. Then father addresses him intimately as 'Son' for the first time, asking him to help him to his horse. The film ends as it began, with the troops trudging into the fort after a successful campaign, the women anxiously searching for the wounded and dead. A fully ordained Maureen O'Hara runs through the dust searching for her husband. There is a final ceremony honouring the brave in which the wounded Colonel takes the salute, his right arm in a black sling. The fighting man has been checked. By his side

Kathleen smiles and moves in time to the music, relaxed and happy for the first time.

North and South have been united, the Civil War atoned. The vertical which is hierarchy is in harmony with the horizontal which is community. Indian scouts are decorated for bravery. The innocents are saved. Most importantly the right balances at the heart of community have been found. Yorke's wholehearted devotion to oath and duty was not fully right. He had sacrificed his family, what his wife calls the destruction of a beautiful thing. One of his punishments was a gruelling loneliness. By the end of the film cavalry and family are of equal importance, nurture and honour integrated. Similarly Kathleen had put the mother-son tie ahead of family, and the exaggeration of nurture had blinded her to the fact that the dishonourable life is not worth living. The second imbalance is corrected. In fact it takes a son with a very fine character, including the pride and stubbornness of both parents, to effect this restoration, with the help of companionship and the community.

It is rare almost to the point of uniqueness in the twentieth century to see a work that is without trace of decadence. *Rio Grande* is perfect, in its accuracy and economy of image, in its pacing, in its balances. The reward to those inducted into its community is twofold. First there is the experience that life is full. It has its cycle of birth, growth, decay and death, but over that cycle there is the duty of man, his oath that may not be broken, her oath that may not be broken, that the unborn enter a world worth joining. There is the redemptive experience of doing what has to be done. The code of honour and what it serves, the New World, are underpinned by a religious order intimated by a series of Christian icons. Second there is the spirit that follows. One of the greatest gifts to man is cheerfulness. The men, women and children of *Rio Grande* are buoyed up by a zest and humour, an enthusiasm and camaraderie. It is in the songs that accompany the action, full-blooded songs, the songs of the collectivity, the community. It is in the deep tones of the bugle that blows and in the ringing of bells, school bell at the start, church bell at the end. There are more songs in *Rio Grande* than any other John Ford film. Out of the cheerfulness comes gratitude. It is quite an achievement.

Ford could not rest with *Rio Grande*. It was as if in response to what might withstand the annihilating gale of modernity he knew he needed a stronger myth, a more deeply rooted and therefore tougher one. He turned to tragedy, and to a much harsher Protestant view of things than the more Catholic cavalry community had allowed. Significantly enough, between *Rio Grande* and *The Searchers* is the painting of the idyllic Catholic utopia in an Irish village, *The Quiet Man*, Ford's fantasy withdrawal from reality before he takes on his great epic. Now Kirby Yorke's 'uncompromising devotion to your oath and your duty' is put to violent test.

The background to *The Searchers* is also the Civil War, which Ford once referred to as his principal interest in life, ahead of movies. It is odd that he made only one full film on the Civil War, *The Horse Soldiers* of 1959, in which he fails to show much enthusiasm for the story-line. *The Searchers* is epic tragedy, a modern *Iliad*. The hero is Ethan Edwards, played by John Wayne, and for almost the entirety of the long film he journeys in fury seeking revenge. Like Achilles, he is a big man. He has not been seen since the end of the Civil War, three years ago, when he refused to surrender his Southern sword. He asserts that one oath in a lifetime is enough for any man, and he took his to the Confederacy. The film opens with his arrival at his brother's homestead, in remote country where community is new and fragile, and the struggle to survive in a harsh arid nature daunting. The backbone of the family is the mother, Martha, his brother's wife, who welcomes Ethan with a barely suppressed intimacy. Women love men, and he is the man.

Then comes the outrage. All that is intimate and precious is violated and killed. Ethan has ridden off with a posse after rampaging Comanches. It is a decoy. While they are away the Indians massacre his family and kidnap his two nieces. The search begins, an impatient Ethan storming off before the funeral service has ended. It is led by the Reverend Samuel Johnson Clayton, who

210

doubles as both spiritual and military leader of the community. After a punishing journey in pursuit the Whites are attacked, and just manage to survive. They decide to give up.

Ethan goes on. Nothing will stop him. Year after year, through the snows of northern winter to the scorching desert summer he rides. Seven years it takes. He is super-human. He is also a very violent man, at any point as likely to add to the moral havoc as restore order. He is utterly alone with his duty to his kin, and above all to Martha, in his avenging torment of will. There are rumours of crime in his past, he arrives with freshly-minted gold and wearing Union soldier's trousers. There is his intimacy with his brother's wife which might have wrecked the family if fate had not intervened. At the start of the search, in a blind fury, he shoots out the eyes of a dead Indian, so that according to Indian belief his soul will never rest. This violates the law of respect for the dead, an immediate allusion to Antigone, and the affinity of this story with the metaphysics of Greek tragedy. He massacres buffalo just to reduce the foodstock available to the Indians, a transgressive excess against Nature reminiscent of Achilles. Ethan Edwards is a berserk demonic man with little sense of limit. He is irritable and snappy. Even when he sits down with his family to dinner before the massacre he infects the domestic harmony with tension. However, in this situation, given what the Indians have done, to the limit of horror, only such a man will prevail.

Ethan is accompanied by the part-Indian adopted son of Martha, Martin Pawley – Martin is "poly" in blood and culture. Also there is Brad, the teenage boyfriend of captured Lucy. Brad's mother had pleaded with Ethan not to waste the lives of their boys in vengeance, a noble and entirely justified assertion of the female ethic of nurture against the male ethic of honour, the ethic of the hearth against that of politics. In the circumstances she is right but wrong. Politics is a necessary evil. The community will not survive unless the horribly violated order of things is restored. That requires retribution, and for retribution the logic of politics, power, is necessary. Brad loses his mind, being only human, when he realizes Ethan has found and buried the raped and scalped body of Lucy. He sees the horror in the contorted face of Ethan, who shouts at him never to ask him to describe what he found. Ethan is the only one who can take a direct look into the horror of existence. Part of his task is to hide the eyes of normal men from the terror they could not take. Brad is killed by the Comanches.

The Indian chief, Scar, is acting by the same code as Ethan. His sons have been killed by Whites, so he takes revenge. His own community has been violated and unless he can restore order it will fall apart. Restoring order requires vengeance, and on a large scale, until the ledger is balanced. Two cultures are at war through their two big men, each under oath, driven by honour. Only one can survive, and history determines it will be the Europeans. Ford is no relativist. Neither Ethan nor Scar have any choice. The obligation is to the culture into which you are born. There is no compromise, for inbetween is a cultural no-man's land. We are shown Whites captured by Indians then rescued. They have all lost their minds. Ethan knows this, spitting out that it were better they were dead.

Finally Ethan and Martin catch up. Debbie, the surviving niece, now a teenager, tells them she is an Indian, it is too late. Ethan wants to kill her, for in addition she is one of Scar's squaws, and therefore dishonoured – he knows her mother would have wanted it that way. Martin intercedes and Ethan is wounded by an Indian arrow. They retreat back to their community from where an expedition is mounted to wipe out Scar's tribe. Martin sneaks into the Indian camp the night before and Debbie changes her mind. After the dawn assault Ethan catches her as she flees from him. He grabs her, but on the point of carrying out her dead mother's wish he relents, takes her up in his arms and carries her back to the community. She is restored. Martin can marry at last, thereby rejoining the living chain, that the unborn may be born, and into a secure and worthy world. The film ends with its theme song, 'Ride Away', as Ethan leaves. No human community can incorporate him, he has transgressed far more than can ever be atoned. Like Achilles there is far too much blood on his hands. He has done what he had to do, under oath, but in the process cursed himself to endless wandering. His life is over. There is an old saying that he who seeks vengeance should dig two graves.

The paradox in the story is the change in Debbie, and even more the change in Ethan. Ford has supplied the answers. In the opening ten minutes the entire action is prefigured. A Calvinist predestination broods over the story. There is a special intimacy between Debbie, then a girl, and her uncle Ethan. He gives her a "gold locket" which is not the cursed gold (everyone in the film who takes and keeps gold dies), but silver, a war decoration in the form of a Maltese cross. The cross protects Debbie. She is unbaptised, which means culturally flexible. Also she has a strong character with sure instincts. When Clayton swears in his new deputies he is interrupted in the middle of the oath, at the words "faithfully discharge". Forgetting where he left off, Debbie pipes in with "faithfully fulfil", the stronger wording commanding a stricter obedience. She sets the terms of the oath, which will in practice include saving her. Ethan does not swear with the others, but it is he who accepts the obligation. Like the Ashdod boy, Debbie knows. Furthermore when her parents send her out of the house to escape the massacre she shelters next to her grandmother's grave, in the cemetery in which her family will soon be buried. She draws strength from the spirit of her ancestors. Ethan has seen or sensed all this. Debbie is fortified enough to survive the two cultures. Ethan's wounding at the key moment, as teenage Debbie stands on a bridge over a river, is an act from above, stopping him. Ford's favourite song, which repeats in *The Searchers*, is 'Shall we Gather at the River'. It is only Poussin's Matthew who himself does not need to cross over. Debbie does. So does Ethan.

The journey in retribution is gruelling beyond any normal human endurance. It is Homeric, and not pleasant to watch. There are two causes. The concrete one is in the rending of the moral order which is the massacre. For ten minutes the virtue which is family is painted with a foredoomed intensity, then it is

213

ripped to shreds. We see the truth indirectly, in the torment in Ethan's face and the mania with which he knocks out Martin, to stop him seeing the mutilated bodies. The other cause is the destiny of Ethan himself, who carries the mark of Cain, and is cursed never to settle. He is saved by his oath – Martha caresses his Confederate coat, sealing the unconscious bond. His "uncompromising devotion" is put to much severer test than in the benign world of *Rio Grande*. To avenge he must transgress, and at every turn the burden of his guilt increases. He is the true pilgrim in our story, the Kierkegaardian hero, making his life harder, guilt upon guilt, spitting out contempt at every comfort, every temptation of ease. He is inwardness and dread, but seizing hold of his own encaged lonely subjectivity in order to act, to do what he has to do. His character has tragic grandeur, and thereby so does his journey.

The gruelling length of the story is offset by comedy. The buffoon is an old fool, Mose Harper, who in the Shakespearean tradition mockingly mimics his masters, yet in his simple-mindedness sees the truth. Mose is battered by life, but he retains an impish vitality lacking in Rembrandt's old men. He has one remaining wish, a rocking chair by the fire. His old bones are cold. Here is Ford's leading symbol of restored community, a homeliness which can provide the rocking chair and the hearth. It is there at the end. Perhaps one day Ethan will return, in atonement, to his rocking chair by the fire. Indeed in an early scene in his brother's home it is he who is in the rocking chair. However, it will be a long time, if ever, before he is permitted to settle. That would require another story, an *Odyssey*, which by the way Ford tells in his next film, *Wings of Eagles*, and self-consciously, for a copy of Homer's second work appears on the screen. Ethan's own emblematic saying, contrasting with the fool's "rocking chair" and 'Thank you kindly.' is 'That'll be the day!' It is the assertion of indomitable power. No one and nothing will bring him down. Fate can throw everything at him but he will endure. At the same time he is so damned, so fallen, that nothing can hurt. Nothing can redeem him.

Ethan's Will is not that of the humanist 'We can become what we will.' It is not free, nor is it guided by reason. He is not interesting, not a personality, merely a big brute under oath cast in a predetermined world with a mission. We are back with hard-core Protestantism, and in a rougher vein than Henry James. Ethan carries out his mission. He is pilgrim warrior, another Cromwell. He is insensitive and inhuman, not likeable, except in his tenderness to the girl Debbie, and his forgiveness of the woman Debbie. Martin fears and hates him, although if the mission had been left to Martin, with his compassion, it would have failed. Ethan's motive is not his own salvation, but his obligation to kin. What he does is not for the state of his own soul but for the good of community, one to which he does not belong. He is demonic, but he is selfless. However, "holy sinner" is not the right category, not wild enough: Ethan Edwards is rather a mighty embodiment of "sacred rage", the last in a line in American culture whose great predecessors include Captain Ahab, Hester Prynne, Faulkner's Joe Christmas, not to mention the real-life figures like Stonewall Jackson.

What then is American? The challenge is founding a community in the wilderness, a decent place in which children can grow up. We are back with foundation. The task is much tougher than in *Rio Grande*. It requires tragic suffering, followed by a colossal enactment of vengeance. We start with a precarious order, no roots, the ground shifting. The New World is fresh born. This order is annihilated, then the test begins. What *The Searchers* establishes is a sacred site in the wilderness, around a burnt homestead, around the cemetery in which the mutilated bodies are buried, the site to which Martin can return after his long ordeal to marry the sister of the boy who went mad. There is plenty of blood in the soil. There will be singing and dancing at the wedding. Clayton will officiate, and Mose Harper will look on from his rocking chair. Debbie will be in the background, with her own indomitable will, Ethan's true child who will be there when she is needed. The threat has gone. The Indians are dead and the founding father, the agent of retribution, has ridden away

taking the pollution of all the blood-guilt with him. Companionship abounds. Americans who grow up in thrall of this myth
know that if they are boys they may one day have to occupy the
shoes of Ethan, if girls those of Debbie. They have been educated,
and know that it is the sacred rage that counts, but in the service
of community, in the service of America.

The American hero, in the towering bulk of John Wayne, is
wounded in the chest in *Rio Grande*, in the shoulder in *The
Searchers*. In *The Man Who Shot Liberty Valance* he dies. The last of
the masterpieces is a requiem to Ethan Edwards, made six years
later. In fact the film is dominated by his coffin. Now he is Tom
Doniphon. His time, that of the Old West, has passed, with the
arrival of railroad, irrigation, towns, law and education. The
America he struggled to found no longer needs him. He dies a
forgotten man, and lies without his boots in a pauper's coffin, in
his town of Shinbone. John Ford takes a direct look at the peaceful
and prosperous town for decent folk, the ideal that has directed
his earlier films, and turns against it with bitter satire. Tombstone
has become Shinbone, a prosaic farce of a place where the ancient
heroes die unknown, buried ignominiously.

What has gone wrong? Friends arrive in town for the funeral,
an old couple, Senator Ransom Stoddard and his wife Hallie.
They are besieged by the editor of the *Shinbone Star* demanding
to know why such an important man has come specially to a
small and remote town to bury a man: 'I have a right to the
story.' The editor is ignorant, brash and intrusive. The Senator,
with the approval of his wife, goes off to tell the story. Again it
is foundation, how they made America when they were young.

Stoddard had come to Shinbone straight from Law School in
New England. His coach is held up by Liberty Valance, an evil
figure of medieval proportions, without conscience and driven by
an explosive sadism. In one of his manic furies he whips Stoddard
half to death. The only man in town strong enough to stand up
to Valance is Tom Doniphon. Tom hopes to marry Hallie, and
is building an extension on to his house with that in mind. She
is the daughter of the family that runs the main eating place in

Shinbone, Peter's Place, a noisy, bustling heart of the community. Father and daughter are played by the same actors as in the main family in *The Searchers*. Stoddard's actual arrival is here, prostrate, carried in by Tom's loyal Negro servant, Pompey. Hallie cares for him.

Stoddard sets up in town as a lawyer, vehemently arguing that Liberty Valance must be arrested and tried according to principle of law. The theme music from *Young Mr Lincoln* accompanies him. Ford is reworking the same myth, guided by the same authority. The first problem is that the sheriff, Link Appleyard, is a sissy with only one large thing about him, his belly. There is no court. The one tenuous check on Valance is public opinion, led by the *Shinbone Star* and its founding editor, the town drunk, Dutton Peabody.

Stoddard starts a school. He teaches reading, writing and the principles of the American Constitution, above all the workings of democracy, government by the people. As Pompey recites the Declaration of Independence he unwittingly stands next to a portrait of Lincoln. He forgets the words 'all men are born equal'. The motto on the blackboard is 'Education is the basis of law and order'. In the same year Hannah Arendt was writing her version of American legitimacy Ford was testing it. Stoddard's most enthusiastic pupil is Hallie. The problem is that the gun rather than the lawbook rules Shinbone and Stoddard is both physically weak and inept with a gun. Nevertheless he refuses to be cowed by Valance or let anyone else do his fighting for him. Played by James Stewart he has a lanky, wiry, highly strung tenacity, resolute in his lofty principle and his faith in reason. Tom addresses him throughout as 'pilgrim'. The Constitution is a product of Eastern Puritanism. Valance calls Stoddard either 'dude' or 'dishwasher', the latter a reference to his dependency at Peter's Place, and how he pays off his board. His worst humiliation is when he appears dressed in an apron, the new 'waitress', and Liberty trips him up sending the food flying.

Hallie is fed up with the lawlessness of Shinbone and is swept away by the enlightened ideals championed by Stoddard.

Valance goads the lawyer into a gunfight, but it is Liberty who is shot. Tom realizes he has lost Hallie, gets drunk, then rides home and burns down the extension. Pompey saves him. Democracy is now possible. Tom forces Stoddard to enter politics by telling him that it was he, Tom, who shot Liberty Valance, from the side, 'cold-blooded murder, but I can live with it.' He tells Ranse that having taught Hallie to read and write he should now give her something to read and write about.

Before the telling of the story Hallie goes out to Tom's place with Link. He drives her there without even asking: 'I knew where you wanted to go.' She picks a cactus rose. The film ends with the old couple, Ransom and Hallie, leaving Shinbone on the train. He suggests that once his Irrigation Bill is through maybe they should leave Washington and return to live here. Her reply is immediate: 'Ranse, If you knew how often I dreamed of it. My roots are here. I guess my heart is here. Yes, let's come back.' She observes that what was once a wilderness is now a garden, and exclaims, 'Aren't you proud!' He asks whether it was she who put the cactus rose on the coffin. After her affirmation he is silent and meditative. An eager conductor arrives telling him they have rearranged the train schedules for him: 'Nothing's too good for the man who shot Liberty Valance.' Ransom is about to light his pipe. He puts out the match and sinks back. The train steams off through the garden.

Hallie's enthusiasm to return is genuine. Yet what she will return to is empty. She has observed at the beginning that everything has changed. We see no community in the new Shinbone. There is no equivalent to Peter's Place. In the Town Hall tower, which is similar to the church tower in *Rio Grande*, the bell is still. The ringing we hear is from the train, the bell of progress, and also from the telephone, and later in the school-room. The school has replaced the church as the institution for moral education: Ford acknowledges the victory of humanism. Peabody, the warm-hearted Irish drunk, with a love for the Press as the conscience of the people, a man who when he wrote could "tear their hearts out" with his eloquence, he has been replaced by a puffed-up vulture. The one thing still growing in Shinbone that Hallie loves is the cactus rose, a product of the wilderness. Her pilgrim from the East with his Irrigation Bill is about to replace them with real roses. Hallie knows and does not know. At Tom's place she observes to Link that he never built the extension that he talked about. She does not know that he built it then burned it down when he lost her. Yet she adds a wistful, 'Did he?', suggesting that she does know the real truth. Link remarks that of course she knows all about the past. Similarly she does not consciously know who shot Liberty Valance, but she does know. For the entire duration of the telling of the story she sits in vigil beside the coffin. On arrival her first move had been pilgrimage, to Tom's place, taking an empty hat-box. It is for the cactus rose. Link then carries it for her, reverently, as if it contains the holy relic. Grieving beside the coffin she sits on a simple wooden bench, Pompey on one side, Link on the other. Initially Stoddard paces about awkwardly. He does not belong. He leaves.

Hallie's story is a tragic one. In her young womanhood, working in the noisy heart of a bustling community, rough and uncivilized but vital, she was seduced by humanist dreams of education and democracy. The old community had worked in its own sort of way, although its law was that of the gun. Tom had kept Liberty in some sort of check; even Liberty took note of public opinion. Also Hallie is restless, a part of her called by the tune of civilization, as was Lambert Strether. She has some temperamental affinity with the pilgrim from the East who neither smokes nor drinks. She gives up the man she loves for her fantasy, and ruins her life. Her husband as agent for the inevitable march of progress, History as Necessity, destroys the place where her roots and her heart lie. What has she to return to? In fact there is now one root: Tom is buried there. She has something to tend. In fact she plants the cactus rose on top of the coffin in its bare soil, without a pot – its roots will feed directly off the body underneath. Apart from this extraordinary act Hallie is hardly more than a shade coming back to haunt a place from long long ago.

Yet Ford has put the case for progress in its most attractive light. Its champion is a hero, with his lawbook and his inviolable principle. Stoddard is a courageous man, more than Doniphon is, pitching himself into battles he cannot possibly win. He is a modern Quixote in his fearless idealism. Moreover he is a man of action, and he succeeds. He dedicates his life to a brilliant political career, to serving the nation, to planting and tending the mythology of Abraham Lincoln. His cause is shared by the earthy editor, Peabody, who quotes from *Henry V* and Horace Greely, who likens Valance to Achilles, and who when he does tear their hearts out does so with a hymn to development and democracy. It is Stoddard and Peabody, the two ambassadors of the humanist future, whom Valance takes to with his whip.

However, Stoddard's career and the entire mythology of progress is based on a lie. What Ranse has become is a man who is restless next to the coffin of the man who made him, at home only chatting pompously about politics with fatuous journalists – the only time he is, as he puts it himself, comfortable. The film ends with his recognition that his wife has always loved Tom and the thudding reminder that he is a fraud. The new editor gives him his own rationalization: 'When the legend becomes fact, print the legend.' The editor then tears up the true story. Stoddard can no longer do that. It has come back to haunt him. Death has done that, the death of Tom has shattered the life-long illusion. And the newspaper office is no Confessional.

Stoddard is courageous, but he has no weight, no gravity. His Irrigation Bill while it will let plants grow, will contribute to the uprooting of human community. All the gravity in the film is with Tom, in the shadows, in a back-street undertaker's room. One authority presides, his coffin. All the important action in the film takes place at night. In the fight scene Liberty orders Stoddard to get into the light. He does so for an instant. This is the light of reason. The school-room had been flooded with light, as were the political conventions. Valance belongs in the dark, as does Tom. Just before the fight Stoddard pulls down his lawyer's sign, for he has descended to the law of the gun, entered the dark.

The light he steps into is also the light of the lie, as Doniphon shoots out of the dark. The truth belongs in the dark. The editor tears up the truth. John Ford is back with Luther. More specifically, he proves that it is not courage, but gravity which is at the core of the male ethic, and it is tied to an authority based on power. Hallie is a modern woman, who in her foolishness falls for shiny fantasies, and pitches her life into the dark, a directionless dark in which there is no death of death.

Tom's story is tragic too. He has had enough of the old West. Like Kirby Yorke and Ethan he has done enough. He is ready to settle – farm, wife, children, and later rocking chair. History, however, is against him. His era is in its twilight and the ideals of New England, Protestant zeal injected into the American Constitution and the ideal of the pursuit of happiness, carry away his girl. She falls for the limelight and what is moving centre-stage. Tom is a background figure, acting from the shadows. At every turn he sees clearly and acts honourably, unlike Ranse who is blind to his influence on Hallie, his own motives, who does not understand that to fight to the death over a dropped piece of steak may not be absurd, and who has no idea who shot Liberty Valance. In shooting Valance Tom ruins his own life, saving Ranse for Hallie. Furthermore, in sending Ranse into politics he advances the very progress that is destroying his life. He is faithful to his code, in the same way Pompey is faithful to him. This is 'uncompromising devotion to your oath and your duty', this is Debbie's "faithfully fulfil", but this time family is not restored. Happiness is ruined. Tom also wrecks the lives of Ransom and Hallie, but for that he is not responsible, for he had no choice, responding to events initiated by them.

In spite of the ideals there is no liberty in the new order, just restlessness, either that of the new editor or that of Stoddard, who belongs nowhere. Ford has seen through the humanist fantasy. Hallie had one moment of a sort of freedom when she chose to ruin her life. The one free man in the film is Liberty Valance, who follows his instincts without hesitation. The valour implied in his name is in that he challenges all in his path to stand up and prove themselves, or else. Only one man can: he has valour. Doniphon, however, is the least free of all, with his oath and his duty, although when he gets drunk he goes on a binge of destruction reminiscent of Valance. As Poussin also knew, character depends on not too much repression of the demonic.

Hallie's fateful switch is not based simply on idealism, falling in love with progress, emancipation and the man of the future. Her first sight of Ransom is of him battered close to death. She nurses his helpless form. Again and again through the film he returns a bruised Quixote, and she cares for him. He needs her in a way Tom never will. There is something boyish about the physical weakness, the idealistic fervour, and the low sense of reality of Ransom. Hallie's deeper attraction is thus to a frail figure she can nurture. It is an old story, the Phaedra theme, but Ford is not a decadent like Euripides or Racine. He has the female erotic divided, between the boy and the man. She chooses enthusiasm over gravity, the one who in his youth rants, in his old age is rancid. Unlike Debbie she has not understood her own "faithfully fulfil", and as a result betrays her heart. She is not helped by her mother, who early on encourages the switch, much to the disapproval of her father. Here is another theme, pertinent to modernity. In Peter's Place the women rule. Father-husband is a comic figure in his own home, ordered by his wife to put on his trousers, not taken seriously. As a result the women are restless, seducible by humanist ideals. Already at the centre of the old community there is discontent, which begins the perversion of the female erotic. Ford underlines the theme by having Tom order Hallie out of the schoolroom – she refuses to go – and having him slam the doors shut at the political convention on a group of women who are looking on. He knows the full logic of his own world, which he futilely asserts against the mighty drift of liberalization. Only Pompey, the one independent witness to the true story, remains faithful. Pompey both has unerring instinct, being in the right place whenever Tom needs him, and understands. He is attracted by Stoddard's promise, to the point of standing next to Lincoln's portrait and trying to recite the

Declaration of Independence. He turns away, however, back to Tom's world. The old Hallie's one deep feeling for the living is in her embrace of Pompey, the one she should have followed.

Kirby Yorke's oath to the cavalry and America depended for its sense on the future, on the towns and gardens that might spring up in the tamed wilderness. Ethan Edwards is driven to avenge his kin, but his mission loses half its sense if there is no future, the obligation to ancestors always being linked to one to the unborn. *The Man Who Shot Liberty Valance* undermines the future. The new America, that of democracy and the Constitution, of education and development, depends on a different myth than that of the old West. It is the Lincoln myth. It is not enough; it lacks the gravity. Stoddard discovers this, that even he needs a legend from the old West on which to build his career. People want to be led by him because they have heard a story, not about how he used his lawbooks, but how he used his gun. The old West makes the new America possible, but the new does not work. All is clear and distinct but the streets are empty and the church-bells are silent. The Lincoln myth is superficial and the Liberty Valance myth a lie. There is one sacred site, the coffin of the Old West, but it is abandoned and forgotten. There was a man, indeed a far more admirable one than Brutus. After him there is nothing under the feet, the ground taken over by pompous chatterbox politicians and scavenger journalists.

Ford has come to agree with Kathleen Yorke: 'All this danger to serve people as yet unborn – and probably not worth serving.' His late pessimism runs through a trilogy of films, *Two Rode Together* (1961), *Liberty Valance* (1962) and *Donovan's Reef* (1963). The first is a dark story in which the community is not worth saving, worse it has so little sense it murders the innocent, and the hero, played by James Stewart, is a dandy egocentric marshal devoted to making money and living well. *Donovan's Reef* pictures a South Seas utopia, entirely split off from America. It is Ford's *Tempest*, with hope withdrawn into a fantasy world at a distance. America is lost. Ford is no kinder to himself. His life-work attempting to forge a binding myth has been no less quixotic

223

than Ransom Stoddard's Enlightenment. And like Don Quixote he renounces his vision at the end. In *Liberty Valance* he turns on his own legend and prints the truth. The truth is that the past, which was heroic, has gone: the legend is dead. The goal it fought for, the new America, proved false. The founding and the making was itself great, but what resulted was a whited sepulchre, the companionship fizzling out. History has won, determining that Tom Doniphon will be replaced by Ransom Stoddard, that the two are incompatible, unable to live side by side, and that a decent honest woman, the salt of the American earth, having to choose, will make the wrong choice. Unfortunately, the new America thinks it can do without a formidable foundation myth, its Lincolnian Ransom Stoddard being merely a twentieth-century copy of a Holbein ambassador.

The discipline of modern Sociology has produced two enduring theories. First, there is Max Weber's thesis about the formative role of the Protestant Ethic in the rise of the West and its own decline in the nineteenth century, leaving a disenchanted and nihilistic world. It is a theory examined in this book in its deeper and more encompassing form in Kierkegaard and Nietzsche. The second theory is that of Emile Durkheim, most extensively developed in his 1897 work, *Suicide*. Durkheim saw the determining feature of modern society as the decline of community, and the commensurate growth in the cult of the individual. The assumption is that the human individual gains his sense of purpose, direction and meaning in life from being integrated into a group, with which he shares a collective conscience, a common culture. Otherwise he will suffer from the characteristic modern pathologies of egoism and anomie, restlessness and rootlessness. John Ford makes similar assumptions in his work. *Rio Grande*, without knowing it, is a brilliant formulation of the sociological ideal of community, with an analytical precision and concreteness not to be found in the intellectual model. Similarly, *Liberty Valance* is an account of the decline of community in the particular modern manner, at the hands of noble humanist ideals. The reason Sociology has never gone beyond Weber and Durkheim is that the modern West has not taken a new turn since 1900. If anything it suffers progressively more from, on the one hand, weak community and a lack of companionship, and on the other, the disenchantment of a rationalized world without unifying sacred belief or attachment. Ford himself confirms this. His own final word is very close to that of Henry James. In his last film, *Seven Women* (1966), community is absurd and the hero is a nihilistic woman doctor. She is saved by her oath to her profession, the one thing in which she believes. She sacrifices her life for it. This is Weber's individual alone in the world with his "intellectual integrity". This is Lambert Strether's honour. For John Ford too, there is no escape from the confines of the humanist epoch.

Henry James tried to fit his pilgrim into the refinements of taste and feeling of humanist Europe, but had him flee in order to preserve his honour. John Ford tried to build and defend Catholic community through the pure sacred rage of the rugged Protestant hero of the Old West. Like Poussin, with whom he had much in common, he managed a plausible Counter-Reformation, but once he took a close look at what the New World had become he turned away in disappointment. The place he had created to stand in America would not hold, for History was too much on the side of a profaning humanism. He is reported as saying late in life: 'Our ancestors would be bloody ashamed if they could see us today.' However, it is also true that his own vision was too secular, no doubt forced by the place and the time. Its highest goal was a city of man on earth. No city of man is enough. Poussin had been wiser, insisting that sacred community predominate.

13

EPILOGUE

It is all a question of a place to stand. Nothing else really matters. Donatello found his in Padua, inside the cathedral. Poussin found his in Christian community with redemptive figures like the Ashdod boy, the Egyptian Madonna and Mary Magdalene. Luther found his in a vision of the darkness of faith and the death of death, for which it was necessary to find the monster and kill it. Shakespeare attempted it in a heroic portrait of the man of honour, shadowed the image and found himself left with Hamlet, skull in hand. Cervantes resorted to the fierce idealism of Don Quixote, a ludicrous solution. For a period the bourgeois managed to stake a humanist egoism to the Protestant rock, and find a reasonably gratifying way of life. Kierkegaard achieved at high personal cost a substitute, a certain stability in his own inward depth. It was not satisfactory, for faith eluded him. Henry James, buoyed up by his sacred rage, keeping afloat in the heaving fathomless ocean of modernity, tried to find a harbour and failed. John Ford just found his footing then abandoned it, in despair at his times.

Then there were the others, those who rather than take on the monster denied its existence and fled. No angel visited them, to whisper in the ear, no enchanted boy to point the way. So they set out to destroy everything that was solid. Their modern founding father was Velázquez, their most insightful prophet, Nietzsche. There was the naive utopianism of Descartes and the moral intelligence of Kant, an admirable man with the misfortune to be born into the wrong tribe in a bad time. There was the rancorous vandalism of Marx and the genteel but deceptively virulent nihilism of Darwin. Lastly there was the beguiling introspection of Freud, the drowning of self in its own unconscious, with its wretched precursor in Hamlet. I do not even mention all those who sought to believe that comfort is enough.

Humanism failed because man is not the centre of creation, in the sense of being creature and creator in one. The 'I am' is subordinate not pre-eminent, and honour on its own is not enough. There is no free-will in any important sense of the term, and human reason is powerful only on a narrow front within strict limits. What is of nearly infinite capacity in man is his imagination, his fancy. It was here that humanism flourished, with its fantasy of freedom and reason, that I can become what I will. It was this fantasy, represented as it was in the Gattamelata, Velázquez' self-portrait, Descartes' 'I think' and Nietzsche's Me versus Christ, that emasculated the existing real cultures – the ones that provided the Archimedean rock. This fantasy set the demonic free, in its modern form, which meant publicly the French Revolution and later the skyscraper bureaucracy, and privately Munch's Madonna and the rat-girl. At the same time the domain in which the humanist imagination became concrete, that of science and technology leading to the Industrial Revolution, produced an opulence of material power and comfort that allowed man to think, as long as he narrowed his consciousness down to his animal needs and repressed his conscience, that he *had* become what he wanted. Moreover, Darwin told him he was an animal. Thus while the humanist castle was tumbling down in the face of the psychological and spiritual reality, it was cemented together at the level of material comfort. Here was to be the modern context for Christ's 'It is easier for a camel to go through the eye of a needle, than for a rich man to enter into the kingdom of God.' The predominant thinking of the twentieth century has been that of an animal, that the good life is to consume, to procreate and to sleep, and in those terms there has been giant progress. Most Westerners *have* become rich.

Not only is man not creature and creator in one. He is not, as Darwin would have us believe, a highly evolved and supercharged fish. True, endow a fish with consciousness and what you get is modern man, material life lived under terror of the inevitable future, which is Death, an unconscious terror which poisons the pleasure. The creature is turned to stone. Under the humanist constellation, Death rules. But this metaphysics of man, a fish endowed with consciousness, sets him too low. It is the dregs of humanism. Consciousness is mind, it is intellect, it is reason – it is Descartes. It is not the fragment of divinity, the soul. The soul creates the guilt that ruins Brutus, that countermands his freedom to kill Caesar. In fact it makes him human, although Shakespeare does not realize this, so blurred has his consciousness become by the curse of humanism. Kant too was under the same curse, very close to a breakthrough, aware that it is the shamefulness of vice not its harmfulness that counts. He too had been so comprehensively seduced by the "Devil's whore" that he retreated into his sterile rationalist logic. Holbein's Christ Corpse and Ambassadors are fish endowed with consciousness, but Holbein, early in the day, was not yet so entranced that he could not be blunt about it.

What will come next we do not know. We are in a transition period. Whether we interpret it as the last century of the humanist half-millennium or the century of the post-humanist interregnum it is proving a long and slow transition. Whatever will be will be, is the most that can be said. There are, however, lessons from the past, things we have learned the new must include if it is to work. The restoration of Western culture will again have to draw on the great sources of authority in its own past. It will have to bring about a Second Reformation. There is no escape from the past, for its traces are deeply engraved in the characters of those who inhabit the present, locked in at conception, the bequest of the ancestors. There is no reason, in any case, why the West should seek to escape its past and start again, even if it could.

The story of the rise and fall of humanism tells us of two things which will be indispensable if the new culture is to succeed. One is the enthusiasm that the Renaissance attempted to enshrine, for man and his works. This is the 'I like him!' It has nothing to do with the rocket that launched the humanist Icarus, 'We can become what we will.' It is rather the simple zest for life, the buoyancy of existence that John Ford caught in his *Rio Grande*. It is the sublime balance of a man in form guided by his own concentrated mind – the Gattamelata. It is the beauty of the clarity and completeness of Euclidean geometry, that between Descartes and Darwin becomes cold and rank. Its defining emotions are cheerfulness and gratitude, as Nietzsche observed, but which he chose to identify with the ancient Greeks rather than the Renaissance. He thought they needed harsher soil in which to grow, one fed by suffering – most likely he was right. Ford believed they needed a certain robustness of community: they depended in good part on the morale of people living and working in close proximity to each other. They are absent, for instance, in Kierkegaard, and it is because of his own monolithic disconnected inwardness. The general point is that one of the central judgments about an individual or a group is whether they are cheerful, especially in adversity. As far as what men do is concerned, what they make and how they engage with each other, the key test of value is whether those who receive from them are grateful. Real work elicits gratitude. At a broader level one of the gifts of nature is the man who is grateful to be alive, cheerful because of and in spite of all. The right response to him is 'I like him!'

At the other pole, and of equal significance, is 'Alas, poor Yorick' and Luther's monster. There is Rembrandt and Kierkegaard's Abraham, the injunction of Luke 14:26:

If any man come to me, and hate not his father, and mother, and wife, and children, and brethren, and sisters, yea, and his own life also, he cannot be my disciple.

This is the pole of the dark night of the soul, of Luther's death of death. This is where whether there is a place to stand is decided, whether the response as the dread mounts will be that of being turned into stone, like Holbein's ambassadors and Hamlet, Munch's Madonna and the people of Ashdod, or alternatively that of Joseph the Carpenter and Poussin's Joseph of Arimathea, given what he sees. It is a question of the terrible angel. It has its roots in the demonic, close to the evil of which man is capable: remember Ethan Edwards with his 'That'll be the day!', a man who is more than a fish endowed with consciousness. Also it depends on shame, the repentance of transgression, the possibility of forgiveness, as with Mary Magdalene. It is, moreover, on this front that humanism floundered and proved that to celebrate the glory of man on its own is not enough, and worse, it nurtures unwittingly one of the nastiest of all monsters, rancour. It was on this front that modernity faced its greatest test, and even in the case of the one who understood the full momentousness of its challenge, and went out to meet it, it failed. The success of what-ever new culture emerges in the West will be decided by whether it can kill Luther's monster and achieve a death of death. This is why its decisive move will be a Second Reformation, one of extraordinary vigour, for it starts from a far weaker position than did Luther and Calvin.

However forbidding the task there is always reason for hope. There is a bountifulness in nature, and in man, that recurs eter-nally like the seasons. There is the sheer earthiness of life, the necessary cycle of birth, growth, decay and death, of labouring in order to eat, and eating and sleeping in order to labour, of sickness and recovery from sickness, of ambition and triumph and failure. There is the irrepressible rhythm of joy and despair. Above all there is the pitiless working of fate, where science has made no progress in understanding the important events in a person's life, where there is no enlightenment, why it was you who was conceived and born, and with that character, why those parents, why that chance meeting with that man who became your husband, and those obscure bends that guided you into that career, why such an illness then. About the important things we understand less than the ancient Greeks, and for that we can be thankful. A part of the picture is the great resilience of man, his hidden resources and his complexity of character. Both history and experience tell us that harsh times bring out the best in human beings, and some of the worst, and soft times bring their own ruin. This too is somehow part of the eternal cycle of things.

The second secure reason for hope is that there are eternal laws, and the human conscience, at its deepest level, is born understanding them, conscience in Calvin's sense of that which does not allow us to suppress within ourselves what we know. So, however much a particular period may distort and repress true conscience, it will not eliminate it. Moreover, the great articulations of that conscience endure, *The Iliad*, the Fourth Gospel, the works of Donatello and Poussin. The signposts of the central way of a culture, of our culture, survive, and are there for each new generation to read, if it will. That way is ever firm under foot.

Our story is told. Its purpose has been simple, to shout that humanism is dead, has been so since the late nineteenth century, and it is about time to quit it. Let us bury it with appropriate rites, which means honouring the little that was good, and understanding what went wrong and why. It was a seductive beast and we do not want to fall for its charms a second time. We are peculiarly vulnerable in that it has developed in us over many generations a sweet tooth for knowledge, an endemic weakness for its own narcotic, the exercise of intellect. Its rallying delusion that knowledge will make us better and happier, and that we are free, free to improve ourselves, is bred deeply into us by now. Here is the reason that its corpse has been in our midst for so long without the appropriate response. Our healthy instincts have been rationalized virtually out of existence. Where is our capacity for spontaneous and unselfconscious revulsion? This story has been to arouse the disgust, and for that it has been necessary to show just how good the alternative was, the one exemplified by Poussin, what a sublime reality was forsaken, one which could have firmly anchored the West. This story has also aimed at making a contribution to the funeral service. To say it once again, it is time to bury the dead, and to start the difficult business of restoring our capacity for life.

THE WORKS

Donatello: *Gattamelata* c.1447
Donatello: *Padua High Altar* c.1450
William Shakespeare: *Julius Caesar* c.1599
William Shakespeare: *Hamlet* c.1602
Miguel de Cervantes: *Don Quixote* 1604/1614
Hans Holbein: *The Ambassadors* 1533
Martin Luther: *On the Enslaved Will* 1525
John Calvin: *Institutes of the Christian Religion* 1536–59
Diego Velázquez: *Las Meninas* 1656
Rembrandt van Rijn: *The Sacrifice of Isaac* 1636
Rembrandt van Rijn: *Return of the Prodigal Son* c.1667
Nicolas Poussin: *The Plague of Ashdod* 1631
Nicolas Poussin: *Confirmation I* c.1638
Nicolas Poussin: *Matthew and the Angel* 1641
Nicolas Poussin: *The Annunciation* 1657
Nicolas Poussin: *Lamentation over the Dead Christ* c.1657
Georges de la Tour: *Joseph the Carpenter* c.1635
René Descartes: *Discourse on Method* 1637
Immanuel Kant: *Groundwork of the Metaphysics of Morals* 1785
Immanuel Kant: *The Critique of Practical Reason* 1788
Karl Marx: *The Communist Manifesto* 1848
Charles Darwin: *The Origin of Species* 1859
Søren Kierkegaard: *Fear and Trembling* 1843
Søren Kierkegaard: *Concluding Unscientific Postscript* 1846
Friedrich Nietzsche: *The Birth of Tragedy* 1872
Friedrich Nietzsche: *Genealogy of Morals* 1887
Sigmund Freud: *The Interpretation of Dreams* 1900
Henry James: *The Ambassadors* 1903
John Ford: *Rio Grande* 1950
John Ford: *The Searchers* 1956
John Ford: *The Man Who Shot Liberty Valance* 1962

INDEX

Index

Index

The Crooked Timber of Humanity

Chapters in the History of Ideas

Isaiah Berlin

'Reading Isaiah Berlin is always exhilarating.'

Anthony Storr, *Independent on Sunday*

'Berlin's preoccupations are constant. His commitment is to individual and collective liberty and to moral and political pluralism. His writing is an extended exploration of the conditions in which those ideals blossom and flourish or wither and perish. The eight essays collected here are all concerned with manifestations of anti-rationalism: utopianism, fascism, romanticism and nationalism are all passed in magisterial review. To read them is to sit at an unlit window and see the landscape of European thought illuminated by a spectacular display of fireworks.' Ian McIntyre, *Independent*

'To read Isaiah Berlin is above all to listen to a voice, effervescent, quizzical, often self-mocking, but always full of gaiety and amusement. These essays remind the reader on every page of the many thousands of listeners over the decades for whom that voice has brought the drama and passion and imaginative depth of the intellectual tradition to which they belong unforgettably alive.'

John Dunn, *Times Literary Supplement*

ISBN 0 00 686221 7

Joan Didion

Slouching Towards Bethlehem

'It was not a country in open revolution. It was not a country under enemy siege. It was the United States of America in the cold late spring of 1967, and the market was steady and the GNP high and a great many articulate people seemed to have a sense of high social purpose and it might have been a spring of brave hopes and national promise, but it was not.'

'So physically small, so temperamentally unobtrusive, and so neurotically inarticulate' that people tended to forget that her presence ran counter to their best interests, Joan Didion slipped herself into the heart of the Sixties Revolution, only to slip out again with this savage masterpiece, which, since first publication in 1968, has been acknowledged as an unparalleled report on the state of America during those curious days. Now that some of the posturing and pronouncements of those times are being recycled, Didion's sobering reflections are timely once again: 'the future always looks good in the golden land, because no one remembers the past.'

'One of the most devastating and distinctive portaits of modern America.'
New York Times

'Didion's essays of a world featuring barricades and bombings, mass murders and kidnapped heiresses make recent history as filtered through her seem a savage and passionate drama, something you can put a hand on and feel it beating, something you can put your ear to and hear its story.'
Village Voice

'Brilliant, troubling, indelible tales and reflections.' *San Diego Tribune*

'Reveals a wholly original analytic mind, a sensibility as expansive and idiosyncratic as a 19th-century novelist's.'
Mona Simpson

ISBN 0 00 654589 0

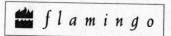 *flamingo*

Fontana Masterguides
Series Editor: Frank Kermode

Religion
Second Edition

Leszek Kolakowski

Does God exist? What do we mean by 'God'? How are we to speak of the sacred? If there is no God is everything permitted? How can we conceive of a God where evil abounds? These are the oldest questions, still regularly asked, still unconvincingly answered. In *Religion*, Leszek Kolakowski rehearses the arguments of the rationalists and the mystics, the agnostics and the faithful, reveals their suppositions, and denounces their false triumphs. He stresses the simple but little-stated truth that 'there is never a shortage of arguments to support any doctrine you want to believe in for whatever reasons'.

'Not an introduction to religions; not a canter round religious issues or practices . . . but a sustained argument about the existence of God and particularly about the conclusion that would follow "if there is no God" . . . His view is bleak – and yet his arguing of it is oddly exhilrating. What he does most impressively is to demolish the claims of unfaith to logical foundations, demonstrating that anti-religious positions are just as unfalsifiable as is belief.'
Gillian Wilce, *New Statesman*

'It is hard to do justice to this vivid but labile book . . . Kolakowski leads us a complicated dance among the angels: his God is evasive, but he pursues him with vigour and irony. His book is less concerned with the varieties of religious experience than the very possibility of religious belief.'
John Ryle, *New Society*

'It is hard to think of another book in this century that has exposed both sides of the debate on religion with so much learning and understanding.'
E. J. Oliver, *Tablet*

ISBN 0 00 686261 6

Luther

Man between God and the Devil

Heiko A. Oberman

'When Martin Luther challenged the ruling powers of his time, the movement he initiated changed the social, political, intellectual and religious structures of western history. But what did Luther intend, and what did he actually accomplish? Heiko Oberman, internationally recognized as one of the most distinguished historians of the Reformation, addresses these questions in this readable book. Presenting a vivid portrait of a man too often portrayed as a saint or a devil, Oberman shows how Luther – passionate, courageous and stubborn – simultaneously aroused fierce loyalty in his admirers and violent antagonism among his enemies.'   Elaine Pagels, *Newsday*

'Oberman rivets attention on Luther as he was. He prods the reader to set aside views mediated by tradition and prejudice, yet, paradoxically, by locking Luther in the past and showing us our distance from him, he unlocks a truer Luther for the present; Luther's passionate commitment and dynamism are freshly provocative. Oberman's hallmark is to combine rigorous historical scholarship with theological sensitivity. The book is a milestone in Reformation studies.'   Susan Moore, *Scotsman*

'Oberman makes such good sense of the man that all other attempts to explain him, as a maniac, or a martyr to constipation, or as a saint, seem trivial by comparison.'
                                  Eric Christiansen, *Spectator*

'This remarkable study, combining learning, realism, and literary adroitness, brings us close to Luther. Above all, it conveys Luther's power: the intensity of his faith, the coherence of his thought, the force of his personality.'   *New Yorker*

ISBN 0 00 686288 8

Protestants

The Birth of a Revolution

Steven Ozment

'Magisterial . . . a successful and rather timely piece of polemic that has plenty of documentary stuffing.'

John Bossy, author of *Giordano Bruno and the Embassy Affair*

Protestants tells the story of the birth of Protestantism in sixteenth-
century Germany – the revolutionary event to which all modern Protestant communities ultimately trace their origins. But Steven Ozment takes that oft-told history and strips it of the crust of myth and ideology which has been grafted onto it to lay bare the
tale of a people both bewildered and inspired by the inflammatory ideas loosed upon the world by Martin Luther.

'Steven Ozment is the leader of those Reformation historians who have lifted the religious history of the sixteenth century out of the closed and sealed realm of disputation among competing, hairsplitting theologians and set it down in the hurly-burly of city streets, brought it to the fireside of family life, and followed its influences into the hearts of lay people young and old, princes, nobles, and common folk. Here is the Reformation as it depended on Everyman – and Everywoman – defining popular opinion and in turn defined by it. Ozment has given us a scholarly book, gracefully written, raising from the dead the audience of ordinary and extraordinary people to whom Luther's reform was addressed and by whom it was shaped and made to endure. To read Steven Ozment is to believe that history is a living art.'

Richard Marius, Harvard University, author of *Thomas More*

ISBN 0 00 686258 6